Contents

Acknowledgements	iv
Foreword by Air Marshal Sir Geoffrey Dhenin	ix
Prologue	1
1 Going to War	7
2 Flashback to Schooldays in Germany	19
3 The Bomber Pilot	33
4 Malta, Medals and Meetings	49
5 The Business of War	61
6 Summer Visits and Sorties	67
7 Targets and Training, Love and Leadership	77
8 Off to the Continent	89
9 The Horror of War	105
10 Belsen	117
11 Peace	125
12 Germany and my German Friends	141
13 The Victors and the Vanquished	153
14 Demobbed: Matters of Intelligence	169
15 Star of Stage, Screen ... and Orchestra Pit	185
16 The Impresario	201
17 Stocks, Shares and Paying the Bill	215
18 Life Becomes Problematical	225
19 The Palmist	231
20 *Modus Vivendi*	247
Epilogue	265
Index	267

Acknowledgements

A considerable debt of gratitude is owed to those involved in the editorial work in preparing this volume. The late Evie Saunders, who had a particular interest in RAF memoirs, began work on this autobiography at the outset. Dennis Bardens – who has biographies of Churchill, Princess Margaret and Elizabeth Fry, among others, to his name – then took up the task. His copious notes were of use to Lettice Buxton, who then undertook the lion's share of the editorial work. We owe her an enormous debt. Letty had a wealth of material, often inchoate, to work with, diaries and press cuttings included, and it is largely due to her untiring efforts that this book finally took its present shape. Lilian Hécart contributed greatly with her keen and professional interest in this project and made several specific and extremely useful contributions. Mike Darton brought a fresh eye to bear at the finishing stage. His suggestions as to the final text bear the hallmark of his consummate ability and his track record both as an editor and a proof reader. Thanks are also owed to James McMullan, Catherine and Justin Glass of Chanadon Publications and to Maggie Macdougall for their advice. A common denominator for all concerned has been that each in his or her own way has grown increasingly enamoured of Richard Leven, both as an exceptional human being and as a war hero.

We also acknowledge with gratitude the kindness of Sir Geoffrey Dhenin in writing the foreword. Geoffrey – an author in his own right, whose career in some ways mirrors that of Richard – was the first man to fly through an atomic cloud and has gone on to a most distinguished career in humanitarian causes. He did not know Richard Leven personally but on reading the typescript he gladly took up his pen in the cause of appreciating a man of Richard Leven's stamp. Geoffrey stepped into the breach resulting from another death – that of Sir Ivor

Broom, who knew and valued Richard from their RAF days.

Anthony Newton, Richard's legal adviser and close friend, together with his wife Irene, above all made this whole project possible. Richard's friends were family to him, and many have lined up to give written tributes. It is invidious to select from their number, but particular thanks are owed to Eric Atkins DFC, Richard Lauren, Kenny McKay, Andrea Miles, Carrie Ray and Dr and Mrs Stenner. Andrea Miles, apart from making available for reproduction the painting of Richard in the guise of a clown left to her by Richard in his will, has shown the depth of her affection for Richard's memory by her many amusing stories about him and her interest in the progress of this book, which all those who were dear to Richard see in the light of a memorial to a memorable man.

Perhaps the last words in this Acknowledgements section should be by one of those closest to Richard Leven himself. Kenny McKay, an author and musician, can speak for all Richard's admirers when he writes:

Richard suffered many things, even more so because he was never convinced that violent confrontation is any answer to anything. His spirit was that of a man lacking the false swagger of egocentric pride. He was a more complex spirit altogether, yet somehow he overcame and dealt with his own doubts as many did, to put the future of his country's people first.

… It seemed as if at certain times in his life he was swept out of fatal danger by a kind of 'pathological innocence'… His inner cosmos seemed to keep his instincts sharp enough to sense the correct path for his integrity to follow, despite his understanding of his true realities, rather than Richard consciously creating the direction of his life…

Because he was seen as a potential 'loose cannon' – one who might be indignant enough to expose illicit dealings – he was

Acknowledgements

more or less overlooked and shunned by those who should have lauded and supported his bravery and humanity… I have seldom had the privilege to meet a more honest, modest, and genuinely generous-hearted man than he. I take my hat off to him. Richard's life was that of a desperate courage. I will never forget him, and those who died so that I can be here to write this today.

Richard Leven as a clown, painted by Barry Leighton-Jones.

[Reproduced by kind permission of Andrea Miles]

Foreword

*by Air Marshal Sir Geoffrey Dhenin
KBE, QHP, GM, AFC and bar, MA, MD*

I have been asked to contribute to the story of a remarkable man who lived a remarkable life in war and in peace. Why I should have been given this privilege, I do not know – except perhaps that he and I had two things in common: a love of flying and an acquaintance with moments of great danger. In my case they were infrequent; in his they were almost constant for many years.

Richard Leven's story begins with a childhood containing happy memories of visits to the theatre and, above all, the circus, with a benevolent grandfather. His early education included some time at a school in Germany where he learned to respect the efficiency and toughness of his fellow pupils, but also experienced some of their less admirable qualities, so that when he joined the RAF during the World War II he was not under any illusion that he was about to engage in a knightly contest with strict rules of chivalry.

He qualified as a sergeant pilot without being greatly extended and then began a remarkable operational career during which he flew daytime sorties on many types of aircraft, old and new – including my own favourite, the Mosquito – over land and sea for the whole of the War. He had great empathy with the crews that flew with him. They seem to have trusted him completely and became most efficient teams with a remarkable record of highly successful missions. He was soon commissioned and decorated with many orders, both British and Allied. I believe that he flew more daylight sorties than any other bomber pilot.

I have mentioned Richard Leven's empathy with his men. He was not in any way simply a 'gung-ho' warrior. I detect in his writings – particularly his poems – an element of the mystic,

Foreword

which I have noted in others who have led dangerous lives, particularly in circumstances when they are alone with none of the manifold sights and sounds of normal earthly existence. A relatively contemporary example is the solo ocean sailor and pilot Sir Francis Chichester, who encountered disorientation akin to mystical experiences during his long journeys.

After the war Richard Leven, like so many survivors, clearly found civilian life tedious, lacking the stimulus of that most dangerous drug fear, and he never really settled down. He returned to the excitements of his youth, the theatre and, especially, the circus.

Now he is gone, leaving me with feelings of melancholy – and pride in his achievements.

Prologue

When I think back over my life, I sometimes wonder how my chosen path has taken so many strange turnings. Can one ever know in advance what one is supposed to do? In a way, it's like a man being lost in a forest. He chooses a trail that he thinks will lead him through it and take him to a town or a village. Instead, he finds himself in a clearing where there are lovely trees and flowers and many birds singing. He likes it so much that he decides to stay there for a while. When he realises that it is time to move on, he follows the widest trail that he sees and suddenly he finds himself in a thicket full of briars and brambles that scratch him. Everything is dark and terrifying and the only thing that he knows is that he wants to get out as quickly as possible. So he follows another trail, and then another, visits many strange and wonderful places, some pleasant and some horrifying. One day he finds that he has reached the end of the road, and that the journey was not quite what he thought it would be.

I flew aircraft in World War II mainly because, of the options available, I had no wish to fight on land or at sea. Flying had never really appealed to me either, but at least in the skies I could feel to some extent in control of my own destiny. During the course of the War, I became a Squadron Leader and was decorated with the DFC, DFM and the Belgian Croix de Guerre Palme. In Blenheims, Mitchells and Mosquitoes, I flew 127 daylight operations – more, I believe, than any other World War II pilot. Three times I was the sole survivor of Blenheim operations I took part in. My being here to tell this tale was far from a foregone conclusion.

The Royal Air Force was for me the beginning of a long and, dare I say, unique career. Having fulfilled my duty to my country to the best of my abilities, I followed my own star with a devotion that may not have been appreciated by my bank manager as much as by my friends. I suppose that I have been a bit of a

Prologue

square peg in a round hole. Since leaving the RAF, I have worked in the City of London (briefly!), in a recording studio and the theatre, then reinvented myself in the roles that afforded me many of those thrills and spills that have been my lot in life: as an actor in rep, a circus ringmaster and, finally, a healer and palm reader. Only in the last role did I achieve a certain celebrity. A twisting path, indeed, but these various strands of my life ended up being more intertwined than anyone could have imagined. My path to becoming a palm reader was mapped out for me by a submarine commander at the height of the War, in an episode that, like so many at that time, ended in tragedy. However, that's not the verdict I would choose to apply to my life when looked at all in all, difficult though my last days have proved to be.

My childhood was a very happy one. From an early age I loved the arts and creative pursuits, especially painting and playing the piano. And I adored the circus, a magical world to which my beloved grandfather introduced me when I was seven or eight. He lived in Hampstead, in north London, in some style with servants who regarded him in much the same way I did: with a mixture of awe and affection.

My grandfather and I shared a secret life that blossomed in our outings to the circus. He was too large, or perhaps too important, a person to so much as bend down to tie his own shoelaces, a ceremony usually undertaken by his butler. On such occasions of high excitement, my grandfather would remind his butler that he was taking me to the CIRCUS. The word was spoken with some emphasis. He would fill his cigar-case, place his hand on my shoulder… and then propel me into a world of dizzying strangeness, dazzling allure! In the months separating these trips, my imagination would feast on them.

Once in the car we were off, fellow conspirators on a grand adventure. At Olympia we bustled past the magnificent gentlemen in pink tails who greeted all arrivals. The smell of sawdust in

Prologue

my nostrils and of animal life – a foetid, earthy, basic smell, somehow associated with thrills and danger – I clutched my grandfather's hand as he led me past the huge and magnificent elephants. The seats filled up, lights flooded the arena, the trumpets sounded, and then in came the Ringmaster. Resplendent in red, dripping with gold braid, carrying the shiniest of top hats, he would crack his whip and in a sonorous stentorian tone proclaim: "My lords, ladies and gentlemen".

I loved also to play by myself in our garden, imagining a world different from the everyday one tainted by bloodshed and horror. I did have a wonderful aunt and brother, and also a sister – though I intend to keep most of my family life out of these pages. Suffice it to say for the moment that a pall was cast over it in the early days because my mother was virulently anti-war. The spectre of warfare, and her attitude to it, was part of the air that we breathed. She would pray that after the horrors of World War I, peace would finally come to the Earth. I could see for myself why she felt like that. My father's life in the army included being gassed in the trenches and shelled in the leg. As an observer in the Royal Flying Corps, his plane – a Bristol fighter – crashed, nearly killing him. Those few words do not describe the revolting brutality of such an experience. My mother was the hospital nurse who had taken care of him. Little wonder that she was bent on instilling in me a horror of fighting, and that I absorbed the lessons.

I grew up none too keen on the military, to put it mildly. This did not change as war loomed. My education was also at least partly responsible for this. From 1934 to 1937 I was at Bryanston, the public school near Blandford Forum in Dorset. There was considerable political disillusionment among the Oxford-educated teachers. The boys, on the other hand, felt a keen anxiety about the economic situation of the country. Young as we were, we perceived the atmosphere of national depression that stemmed from widespread unemployment. There was a sense of impending social disaster. To balance this,

Prologue

the headmaster, T. F. Coade, was keen on the arts, particularly the theatre. I developed a taste for acting, and I played the viola in the school orchestra and the saxophone in the school's first dance band, which I helped to found. Many eminent poets and writers visited Bryanston: W. H. Auden, Christopher Isherwood and Cecil Day-Lewis chief among them. Auden was kind enough to compliment me upon my attempts at poetry. Such words from so great a man! I thought then, as frequently since, that I had found my *métier*.

This tale is not meant to be an autobiography in the sense of a full account of my life from the cradle onwards to as close a point to the grave as I can describe while my fingers are still up to pressing the keys of a manual typewriter. I will allow myself just one digression of any length about my formative years, and that only as it casts light on my attitude towards the War, the times in which I lived, and the mentality of those against whom I was to fight. I spent some time on an exchange visit to a school in Germany, Schule Schloss Salem in Bavaria, run by Kurt Hahn, who had become Headmaster of Gordonstoun in Scotland. It helps to explain why I joined up before many of my contemporaries.

But before going into that episode, I shall take a plunge into the earliest phase of my time in the RAF.

To my amazement, or perhaps that of my seniors, I was selected for training as a pilot and started my flying course at Babbacombe near Torquay in Devon. So began a new life in the RAF. Friendships would take on great importance in this new life – they could mean the difference between life and death. After I passed the course, I was sent to Burnaston aerodrome near Derby to be trained on Miles Magisters.

On my first solo flight, I took off and was turning to go round the aerodrome when low cloud, stretching almost down to the ground, enveloped me. I lost all sight of the ground while, at the same time, the aircraft began bumping up and down. I didn't recognise what I could see of the countryside. A violent storm

Prologue

blew up and I was hopelessly lost. The plane lurched violently. The compass was swinging. With considerable bravado, while controlling the stick with my knees, I pulled out the map stuck in my boot and tried to consult it. Each time I tried to unfold that map, the wind blew it out of shape. At length I thought I identified Derby, but then the surrounding country I was flying over bore no other relation to the map, by then almost blown out of my hand. Reading it was a lost cause. In rapidly fading light, the countryside took on a treacherous appearance. Mountains loomed; there was no sign of human habitation. I felt small and insignificant, but not frightened. I had this feeling that Derby aerodrome would suddenly appear and all would be well, though the rugged countryside and purple-and-red slopes argued against the notion. Odd chimneys now poked above rows of small, wretched cottages beside huge coal stacks. .

Daylight faded out totally. Just as blackness fell, the lights of a town showed up ahead. And a football pitch! I decided to make an emergency landing. After circling round and round, I approached with flaps fully down only to be buffeted back by violent gusts of wind. At the third attempt, again I was flung back by the ferocity of the gale. With the flaps fully down, I was unable to turn in time to keep the playing field in view. Mad as it seemed, something in me said, "Have a shot at landing." I pulled up over the far hedge and closed the throttle. To my amazement, the aircraft landed. I was not just on the outskirts of Sheffield but in the only possible field in the vicinity where it was possible to land, a mere hundred yards square. It was almost as if my aircraft had been removed from my control and put down in that small patch of land. Had some greater power guided and rescued me? It felt like it at the time. Anyway, I was alive and felt a huge sense of exhilaration simply to be walking on firm ground when just a few instants before it seemed unlikely that I would ever do so again.

What would it be like when I had also to face an enemy in the skies?

Richard Leven

1

Going to War

Flak
*Those sudden
unexpected bursts
of yellow flame,
and shrapnel smashing
round the plane,
sent dread feelings
down my spine.
Tension on my stick
increased
as every nerve
was strained to
resist the desire
to turn and flee
from the black balls of smoke
hovering where shells
had burst.
Oh Earth, in peace
beneath,
you never seemed more dear,
and yet so far away
that I despaired,
for you were no longer
of any aid.
The sky seems queer,
frightened, and alone,
without those bursts of flame
and black balls
around my plane.*

1 Going to War

I knew as well as we all did that we were to be engaged in a life-and-death struggle. Of course, there would be off-duty moments – I loved a drink with the boys, the company of pretty girls – but what mattered most was our final victory in the titanic struggle against Nazi Germany. Besides that, all talk of off-duty moments seem empty and prattling, and nothing I can report of that side of my life would differ in any significant way from thousands of other such accounts. I was flexing to face the music – in no light sense of that simile. I had to live on my nerves. That I could take to that way of life must have played a part in my salvation.

The weeks of learning to fly seemed to speed past. On 9 April 1941, I collected my wings and three stripes. I was a fully qualified Sergeant Pilot. I had generally been seen as a scruff, unreliable, and green around the gills so it was with great pride and a sense of importance that I sewed the stripes on. I felt that I had reached one summit of my career in the RAF.

I was not alone in not receiving a commission straight away. I had volunteered to operate on Blenheims and, a few days later, I arrived with all my kit at Bicester station. A taxi took me up to the aerodrome. Strolling into the Rose and Crown pub, I immediately recognised a sergeant there. It was none other than Mike Nolan who had been my friend in Torquay. He had failed in the elementary flying training so had volunteered to be trained as a navigator. We thought it was such a coincidence meeting like this that we at once decided to crew up together. Mike was from Dublin and had volunteered to join the British forces. He was a few years older than me, and sported a dark moustache and had a slight Irish accent. Somehow our destinies came together. Athough our natures were very different, we were to fly together as pilot and navigator on over 100 operations during the course of the War.

The next day our course began. I spent a week learning to fly a Blenheim while Mike was taught about the bombing apparatus and other navigational aids. Meantime we found a sergeant gunner who wanted to crew up with us.

1 Going to War

Mike and I flew together for the first time on 15 May 1941. During those early days we found it difficult working together. I was not used to having a navigator, always having flown solo before, and was always afraid of getting lost. I annoyed him continually by asking him to tell me our exact position. However, I soon discovered it was better to leave him in peace and only speak over the intercom when absolutely necessary.

I admired my friends. Most were sergeant pilots. I'll say this for them – they were characters, characters above all realised in action. It was on our course at Bicester that I met 'Poons', a sergeant observer. He was charm itself with a keen intellect and a sense of humour. I once asked him why, since his name was Ronald Parsons, he was known as Poons. He replied: "If Cholmondeley can call himself Chumley, why shouldn't Parsons call himself Poons?"

Poons would never board a plane without his red alarm clock that he clutched with quasi-religious zeal. It was timed to go off to remind him when he was flying over his target. A bit prone to having his head in the clouds in more ways than one, was Poons. He was tall and his head seemed to hang forward from his shoulders, sloping back from the top, as if someone had cut a slice off it with a carving knife. He had a mass of scruffy, sandy hair that matched his drooping and forlorn moustache. It might look like the moustache of a Mexican bandit foiled in his latest revolutionary coup but Poons had the air of a man who should have been lounging in some West End bar in London. An old, spotted green scarf completed the effect that he was wearing RAF blue through some mistake.

The uncertainties of war postings separated Mike and me for a short while, but then we were both posted to 107 Squadron based at Massingham in Norfolk. It was like going to a new school and daunting to be part of so famous a squadron. At the same time, it was unnerving to be hit with the facts. Losses had been very heavy. By the time I showed up, there were just eight

1 Going to War

crews left in 107 Squadron, including ourselves. So many had been killed that it was rare for anyone to finish a tour. But come what may, I had to carry on.

My active service did not start as it was to go on. All fighter trainers were grounded because of mud on the aerodrome runway. This resulted in my being taught to fly the twin-engined Oxford. When done with this, at Bicester, Mike Nolan and I volunteered to operate on Blenheims. After completing 70 hours in Blenheims, we were taught how to bomb up to a height of 11,000 feet. We were fit for operations – or so it was declared.

Soon we were given our first chance to show what we could do against the Hun. In spite of my excitement, I had misgivings. What would flak look like? Would I do the right thing when being chased by a fighter? Suppose my aircraft caught fire, how should I get out? Perhaps I would be killed. I had this vague feeling that if people were to shoot at me, it was up to me to get out of the way of the bullets. If I couldn't fly with sufficient cunning or my reactions were slow – well, then I deserved to be shot down. Death was a frightening possibility. It made me question the reason for my joining the fighting until I reminded myself that it was so that we might be free – free to be governed as we felt best. Such thoughts flowed through my head as the train rushed me towards my first operational squadron.

We were briefed for our first mission, a bombing run over Boulogne, on 22 June 1941. Wing Commander Petley was then commanding the squadron. Boulogne had to be attacked by 12 Blenheims flying at 14,000 feet as part of a flying circus – a massed operation with about 200 fighters flying at all heights providing a close, medium and high level escort. It was one of the first ever attempted. The purpose of the operation was to attract enemy fighters and draw German firepower away from Russia, where the Russian armies were being hurled back to Moscow. We, the bombers, were being used as decoys. It was

1 Going to War

very comforting, however, to know that we had this excellent cover.*

Wing Commander Petley finished the briefing. A terrible sinking feeling flooded my being, a sickness of heart; a sudden dread of what was going to happen. It was like standing on the springboard of a high diving platform trying to gather the courage to plunge in. But I was also keyed up with exhilaration. I collected my equipment, including my mascot, Annabella, a doll given to me by a very special girl called Joy Thornton whom I had met in Torquay. She told me the doll would be my lucky charm and never to fly without it. I boarded the bus to the runway, clutching Annabella. Everyone was chatting gaily, smoking cigarettes, laughing louder than usual. I didn't join in. I felt I must go over in my mind every possible foreseeable contingency. I had to concentrate on following my leader. I had to trust him.

As I left the bus, the awaiting Blenheim seemed to smile. But then some huge joke gripped its frame and it appeared to be mocking me. The impression faded. Someone helped me strap on my parachute. I struggled up on the wing of the aircraft and groped my way forward. The cockpit was a tight fit, smelly and rather dirty and I felt ill at ease. But no sooner had I slid into my seat and fastened the harness than I felt like a different person. It seemed as if the aircraft had become part of me. I felt at one with it. I was the brain-centre of this machine and it reacted to my

---

* On 'circus' operations, the Spitfires would come from Coltishall to provide escort for the Blenheims of 2 Group. As one Spitfire pilot, Laddie Lucas, later wrote in *Malta: The Thorn in Rommel's Side*: 'I escorted Blenheims on their low-level and almost suicidal missions against enemy naval vessels and heavily defended convoys moving stealthily round the Frisian Islands and close in along the Dutch and Belgian coastlines to Rotterdam or Antwerp. With well over 120 miles of turbulent North Sea to cross, these were just about the most lethal operations which Bomber Command asked the crews to tackle in wartime. If I hadn't seen them at first hand from the relative safety of a Spitfire, I would never have believed the carnage.'

1 Going to War

wishes. The wind flapping the rudder caused my feet on the pedals to move. Now that I was strapped in, it had grown more human while I had become more of a machine. Almost without thinking, I started the engines and taxied out along the grass runway, lining up behind the other Blenheims. This was my first operation, yet I hardly had the sensation of experiencing anything novel.

One by one, the Blenheims took off. It was my turn. Once clear of the ground, I pulled up the undercarriage, then the flaps, and at full speed raced after the others. We formed up in a line of six. I stuck my wing in close to the number four. It was a beautiful and hot summer's day with a clear blue sky. Concentrating on flying close to the leader, we rose rapidly to 14,000 feet. The thought kept returning to me: 'If you wander away, you'll be shot down.'

Quite mechanically, Mike said, "We're approaching the target now."

I had hardly realised that we had been so long in the air. I glanced at the comforting Spitfires, so close in. They would protect us, I felt sure.

Mike said in the same flat voice, "We're on our bombing run."

There seemed no flak in the sky. The bombs fell out of the aircraft ahead. I watched them falling, one after another, down, down, down to the world below and a feeling of relief passed through me. Now that our bombs had gone, there was less chance of being blown up. From the corner of my eye, I noticed our fighters weaving round. I wondered if there were any enemy snappers in the sky. England seemed so far away and I was so very tired of this formation flying. On and on we went. The sun was bothersome and as we descended my ears vibrated. Then the English coast appeared, a grey mass on the horizon. Despite seeing neither fighters nor flak, I suddenly felt that the operation had been an ordeal. It was a long and wearisome trip back to

1 Going to War

Norfolk. At last the formation split up as we reached base and I came in to land. The ground crews that met us were eager to know what had happened. I said that I'd seen nothing. The intelligence officer then told me that our fighters had shot down sixteen Jerries!

The next trip was in many ways like the first though not as eventful. Wing Commander Petley led us in a low-level daylight raid on Bremen but decided to return mainly because we encountered spotter ships near Heligoland.* The second attempt, on 4 July, was a very different kettle of fish. Wing Commander Hughie Edwards, of 105 Squadron, led it with nine crews who joined our six. He was an Australian who hadn't impressed me during a previous briefing. I flew behind him.

Mike sat in front of me carefully writing up his log. As we flew, the intercom was buzzing and crackling. The sky was grey and cheerless while, on my right, eight machines were skimming over the water. That's how low we were flying. The wing commander of our squadron was on my starboard. He was flying just above the sea. Every now and then his plane would rise as if it had bounced off one of the waves. The cloud was low, about 500 feet, and the sea in front of us was misty.

All of a sudden, a very large ship with four funnels appeared in front of us. I was alarmed. I couldn't pull over the top and so did a steep turn round its bows. We were in the midst of a large enemy convoy. How foolish not to bomb those ships! But no shots were exchanged and we flew on until land appeared. We were over German territory, the first time I had flown over German soil. It looked strangely like England.

We pulled up over the sandbanks and sped on. I dared not risk going too fast lest our petrol ran out, but no one seemed to be firing at us. All was well. Then things changed. There were

---

* Heligoland is 44 miles (70 kilometres) from the German coastline and is one of two islands on which there was a formidable Nazi naval base.

1 Going to War

heavy ack-ack guns in front. It was comical to see men rushing out from a hut in the corner of the field without their trousers. Up over the trees and down the other side, then down so that no one could get a shot at us. The cattle were stampeding – it was likely that the Jerries didn't fly as low as this. Chimneys appeared then row upon row of brick houses as a town emerged from the haze. Three barrage balloons were going up ahead of me. Wing Commander Edwards led his squadron around the north end of the town. Our own wing commander was turning into me. Had he gone crazy? I did a steep turn to port. Then I saw.

"Good God, Mike, Petley's on fire. On fire! Look!" The port engine was belching flames.

We had no time to give further thought to him, however. Tracer bullets were coming up on both sides of me. The gunner was targeting Mike.

"Bomb, man! Bomb, bomb, Mike, bomb!" I screamed at him.

Crack! We were hit. Another shot crashed between my leg and arm, and out above my head. I pulled the stick back. Up into the safety of the clouds. Good God, what was happening? The machine was out of control. I was diving faster and faster. The instruments were skewed and the gyro collapsed. My compass swung off. I couldn't fly in cloud like this.

"Which way do we go, Mike? Quick, tell me, man. Point with your hand, my compass has gone!"

That moment it struck me that the suction pipe was severed. A quick changeover to the reserve pump was needed. I did it and my instruments came back. The plane was diving at an appalling angle. As I heaved the stick back, we came out of the cloud and missed the roof of a house by inches.

I shouted to Mike, "It's all right, I can fly her. Give me a course home straight back across Germany and Holland. We're on our own."

As we gained height the cloud grew thinner. We had no protection now from Spitfires. Pray to God that the enemy leave us

1 Going to War

alone. There was a patch of water ahead. It was the Zuyder Zee. So we flew on, jumping from cloud to cloud until there was none left. We were flying alone in a blue sky at 7,000 feet. Because of the danger of fighter interception I pushed the aircraft nose down. As we sped faster and faster towards the water the sea sprang to life, the motionless mass of water heaving as we descended. I could see white horses chasing each other as I flew over the top of them. But the minutes passed slowly. I felt safe at last, but not jubilant. The sight of our wing commander going down in flames haunted me. Only a few minutes ago I had seen that sheet of fire on the ground. Yesterday the men in that aircraft had played cricket on the village pitch. I had watched them laugh together. I wanted to disbelieve my eyes, to imagine that I had been mistaken and that they would return, but it was no use. In my heart of hearts I knew those men would never be seen again.

As our aerodrome came in sight a surge of relief and joy went through me and for a brief moment I forgot about everyone else. We were alive when we should have been dead. As our wheels touched the ground, I actually sang to myself. The ground crews rushed to put out the wooden chocks under the wheels. The adjutant was waiting to greet us, his face anxious.

"Where are the others?"

"The Wing Commander was shot down in flames over the target. I lost sight of the others."

"You're the only one back so far."

The adjutant helped me out of my kit. I glanced at the gunner's turret. The air-gunner had chatted to me on the way back. I thought him unperturbed by the day's events, but he was sitting there, white as a ghost. He had been overcome by the ordeal and once we landed had become rooted to his seat. At last the adjutant persuaded him to get out and climb down. I thought he was going to faint, but then he seemed to recover.

He smiled a thin smile and said, "I can't ever face flying in a Blenheim again."

1 Going to War

When I reported on the Bremen raid to Air Vice Marshal D. F. Stephenson, I was met with little sympathy. Pilots used to call Stephenson 'Butcher' because he sent so many of them on suicidal raids. Indeed, our squadrons were losing more pilots than any other branch of the RAF. I believe that the low-flying raid over Bremen was a typical example of the misuse of aircrews.

I pointed out that cloud over the target had been a major cause of our failure. Stephenson didn't believe me. Wing Commander Edwards had said it was clear weather. What might just have happened is that he did have clear skies, but only after 105 Squadron veered away from my path to port. I reported that my plane had been badly shot up and that I had almost crashed when I swooped out of cloud after my instruments had collapsed. Mike Nolan backed me up in all points of my story. Afterwards, the entire 105 Squadron on that mission was decorated. Nolan and I, whose plane was the only one from 107 Squadron that got back, received nothing. It was a conspicuous omission. Edwards received a VC for the raid, the citation mentioning 'clear sky over target'. This raid established his reputation as a bomber pilot. Many years later, Squadron Leader Wellbourn – who was listed as missing but actually was being held as a POW (prisoner of war) – confirmed my story that there had been cloud.

At the present time, however, I had to tell Wellbourn's wife that he hadn't come back. How can I ever forget the look on her face? She had been married just the day before yesterday, and now her husband was missing. She had wanted me to give her news of him, good or bad, it didn't matter. I couldn't tell her anything as I hadn't seen him go down. What I didn't know was that he had been taken prisoner. She didn't burst into tears but instead smiled and thanked me.

After the Bremen raid, I went for a walk through the flat fields of Norfolk to clear my mind and calm my spirit. I needed to think. I needed to find my way back to myself much as a

1 Going to War

compass needle gravitates to true north. Corn swayed in the breeze and the cows moved sluggishly round their fields. All part of the common round of life, but after what I had been through, the scene was imbued with a sort of transcendent serenity. A farm labourer greeted me with a smile. The world was strangely peaceful. I leaned against a gate and held out some grass to an old horse. I saw him slowly step forward, almost afraid to trust me, and then I stood watching as he chewed the grass. It was a moment to reflect on where I stood in life and how I had got to this point.

When I had realised that Adolf Hitler might invade England and build concentration camps here, I felt that I must do something to stop him. It was nothing short of a personal crusade. Common humanity and hatred of vicious state authority no less than a love of my country had moved me to feel like that. What an irony it was that, whether by chance or fate, I had known so many boys who were now my adversaries. I wondered what they were doing at that moment and if we would ever meet again. Like my German friends, I was to fight with hope for a better world in my heart just as much out of patriotism, fear or fury. How life had changed from the halcyon period of my school days, and the time when I had begun to think like this.*

---

* Publisher's note: in the final souvenir edition of *The Mossie,* the magazine of the Mosquito Aircrew Association, issued in June 2005, Eric Atkins DFC KW wrote:

The late member, S/Ldr Dickie Leven said that he 'hated war', but went on to become a highly decorated pilot. He was not proud to be led into war, but he was proud to have done his duty. He was well-read and knew the reasons for WWII. He guessed at the weaknesses and dominances of Power and did his bit, like so many others, to reduce the evils of the day and preserve our safety. What Governments do is out of 'Necessity', what men do is out of 'Honour'.

2

Flashback to Schooldays in Germany

In January 1938, aged sixteen, I was on my way to faraway Germany. I was on this jaunt courtesy of Bryanston, my boarding school, which had an exchange system with Schloss Salem, a school in the province of Baden tucked away in the gentle sloping hills of southern Bavaria. When the chance presented itself to see how things were in Germany, I jumped at it. Anthony Eden, the British Foreign Secretary, was visiting that country at roughly the same time to establish friendly relations with Hitler. What a pity he did not have a chat with my fellow students! They could have told him a thing or two.

Prince Max of Baden, Imperial Chancellor and a negotiator of the Versailles Treaty, founded the school. He wanted to play his part in repairing the ravages of warfare to his country, and to do so looked to the sons and daughters of the German aristocracy and the cultured classes generally. Almost paradoxically, his idea was to provide the best liberal education. Through Prince Philip – Max's wife was Philip's aunt – the school had ties with the British Royal Family. These young German students in the main looked down on Hitler, regarding him as an upstart, and a man whom the British government was very foolish to trust.

After an inspection *en route* by *gauleiters* – their paranoid interest in what was in my trunk was of a piece with their hauteur and their Ruritanian uniforms – I finally got off the train at Salem village, weary and apprehensive. I trudged along the main street to the castle, the Schloss. It belonged to the Markgraf von Baden, son of its founder, who lived in one wing with his wife and mother. Like his father, he took a great interest in the life of the school. There was a stately old gateway at the entrance to the

2 Flashback to Schooldays in Germany

drive leading to the castle, its dull cream walls solid-looking, and, it seemed, sheltering. When I asked the way, some boys – few spoke English – gestured to me to follow them with every appearance of friendliness.

In the castle, I met the English master, Mr Smith, whose surname, given the circumstances, reassured me He was tall, very thin, and clad in grey flannel shorts and sports jacket. He appeared the archetypal Englishman abroad – until he started speaking. He lost no time in informing me that Salem had the same ideas about education as Bryanston. So far, so good. But there was this difference: the school curriculum had been altered by *fiat* of the German Government. Nevertheless, and despite interference from the state, there was 'liberty for the individual'. The cosy chat about cricket or tiffin that I might have expected was not going according to the script. What form precisely, I wondered, did this liberating freedom from the heavy hand of authority take?

Mr Smith was ahead of me.

"If a school rule is broken, guilty boys report the matter themselves."

My mouth fell open. My mentor continued: the boys voluntarily went on a punishment run!

I gasped. Did these exemplars of virtue decide off their own bat how far they had to run, serving themselves out a punitive ration of extra miles if they should judge their infractions the more serious?

What I said was merely, "Do boys really report their own sins?"

Mr Smith, in his turn, was taken aback.

"Of course. The system works extremely well. Now... you will have a boy in charge of your room. Every night you must tell him what you have done wrong; he will mark it up on a chart. When you have chalked up three black marks, you must go on a punishment run."

2 Flashback to Schooldays in Germany

Not 'if', but 'when'! I didn't like that. But how could these 'ideas about education' be billed as akin to those of Bryanston? Had Smith gone native? It was arguably the same code of honour but so much more *institutionalised* in the way it was implemented. There and then, I decided that unless caught red-handed in the act of breaking school rules, I certainly would not condemn myself to any unpleasant form of exercise. We British know when and how to be a superior race – and when not to run one!

Mr Smith took me off to my quarters and introduced me to my roommates: Lindemayer, Scharff (it was to be some while before I called them Paul and Peter, respectively) and 'der Mangel', the Crusher – a nickname used by all. He was the Head Boy of that study of four boys. If it is true that the first thing two Englishmen do on being cast away on a desert island is to form a club, their German counterparts no doubt would set up a positive hierarchy!

Der Mangel might well have seemed a man of 'blood and iron' to other pupils but to me he just looked a tall, clumsy, barrel-chested hearty. I soon learned that he could put the shot with unrivalled power; here, in person, stood the victor of the javelin event at the international Public Schools Athletics meeting at White City, London. Der Mangel could speak only a few faltering words in English. As I had no German, we mustered sheepish smiles; a kinship was on the brink of being formed. Mr Smith left us to get on with it. Peter Scharff suddenly became talkative, with his smattering of French and English. He told me that my bed, of all places, was where I was to put my scanty possessions. There were four beds, each folded into a wooden frame. When each bed was upright, as now, it doubled as a bookcase with curtains to cover the shelves. Clothes were to be stacked on the top ledge. No doubt a tidy system – during daytime! The ice, if not exactly broken, had started to thaw. It was not long before I found myself paddling the waters beneath, which I was relieved to find had some deep, warm currents.

2 Flashback to Schooldays in Germany

Lunch was in the dining hall, a fine old room with large windows and a stage at one end that served as the setting for school plays. These were designed to get across some philosophical message. The masters – in a fine display of *lèse majesté* – sat with the boys and girls at the long tables. Perhaps this was to keep a beady eye on them. Every boy wore a grey flannel shirt, shorts, and pullover; girls were kitted out in skirts of grey with matching jackets, but given a free rein of colours for blouses or jumpers. No girl, however extrovert, opted for the more garish end of the colour spectrum.

My neighbours laughed at the way I muddled up the German for plate, fork, and spoon. But one girl's smile spoke to me of more than goodnatured ribbing. Her name was Sigrid, and she sat opposite. I was in love straight away – or believed so. Sigrid was the most delightful girl in the place, no question about it, with fair hair, deep-set eyes of blue – and matching blue jumper. Her name, too, was quite the most fascinating name. Sigrid! It's that smile of hers – that open, pleasant, welcoming smile – that I so fondly remember.

Of such internal upheavals I said nothing. I was making friends. I was fitting in and I felt happy. This term in Germany turned out to be the most pleasant period of my life, and not just because of that smile of Sigrid's. There was a real comradeship among boys and girls, and a zest for living. It was striking how tremendous was their desire to put me at my ease. This was because I was a mad Englishman; that, or so they told me, was why I was popular. No doubt my curiosity value had much to do with it. My inability to sing in tune to their high standard confirmed them in their prejudice that there was something a bit odd about Englishmen.

Every student at Salem was allotted his or her daily task to perform. I was detailed to fill buckets with coal bricks and lug them up to the dining hall. Der Mangel, rather more appropriately, also had this task. Was this decided upon to point up a contrast

2 Flashback to Schooldays in Germany

between German and English manhood? Here was the strongest fellow in the school, and proud of it, whereas beside him I was a weedy specimen. He would often carry those buckets for me, boasting how feather-light they were. It annoyed him when I hit back by poking fun at his over-bulky body and ponderous gait. But he was a kind, sentimental, simple soul, like many of Herculean build. He was never more in his element than when, in the privacy of our study, he treated us to an unvarying repertoire of schmaltzy Austrian waltzes on his beloved accordion.

It felt far from home. Every morning, at six-thirty sharp, in all weathers, while girls did their skipping routine behind the sleeping quarters, boys went on a ten-minute run, wearing only shorts. I was not, like most, a super-healthy type and a cold, miserable thing I found it, puffing my way in the eerie dark through those woods, sometimes muffled in deep snow, behind the castle. Snowflakes swirled around – and onto – our half-naked flesh. I found it disturbing that our footprints scuffed that carpet of freshly fallen snow. It was my fancy that man was trampling underfoot the purity of nature. I was a serious young fellow, looking back on it.

Lindemayer was a quiet one and, it turned out, a highly sympathetic chap. He loved photography and reading poetry. He showed me pictures of his family's castle on the Rhine and of his favourite horse. I wasn't sure which he preferred. He was very conscious of the fact that the tragedy of Germany was to be ruled by men who were not gentlemen.

Peter Scharff was a very different type. He was always painting pictures in vivid colours filled with life and spirit. My efforts at art were as nothing compared to his. We would cycle the five miles odd to Lake Constance and there we lounged, gazing at Swiss mountains that were reflected in water nearly as blue as Sigrid's eyes.

On one excursion we had a conversation that has stayed clear in my mind, much as I tried to forget it at the time.

2 Flashback to Schooldays in Germany

"Do you intend to continue painting when you leave school?" I asked.

"I shall do nothing but paint. But Germany is no good for artists. I must try to find somewhere else to live."

"But why? You have such magnificent scenery here."

"You do not understand," he countered with a mirthless laugh. "Germany is ruled by strange people. Artists are not allowed to paint and express their own feelings."

"Why on earth not?"

"It is against the political regime."

"Oh, how stupid. Can't you protest?"

He looked sad.

"I am afraid it is difficult to explain… Now tell me, why have you only got a small army?"

"Ah! Well, because we are not a military society."

"You should have a larger army because otherwise you will not be able to fight us."

"Fight you? I don't understand – "

"Germany will go to war, and you will be beaten. It is foolish of you not to have a larger army."

"But tell me, please – why should Germany go to war?"

"We do not want to. We have to. For the same reason I cannot paint. I am not allowed to paint. Germans are not permitted to decide what they want to do. A pity that we are not allowed a royal family, like England. The last war was not all Germany's fault, but now we can do nothing. Absolutely nothing."

I could hardly take in all the implications. Was Germany a country run by dolts, monsters even, ones in whose mad calculations human happiness counted for less than a warped objective of war? Did we English live in a fool's paradise, poles apart from the Germans? There was such beauty there, in this lovely country. Below us was a shimmering, artistic palette of a lake. Its very calm now troubled me, as if it was somehow out of joint with the times. The physical world in front of my eyes seemed to be

2 Flashback to Schooldays in Germany

changing. But we were two young idealists typical of that time and place.

"Well, if you all think war is coming, why don't you do something about it? You know – start objecting and striking in the factories. Just throw out the present government."

"Huh! You can talk like that in Salem, but nowhere else in Germany. We would be sent to concentration camps."

"Concentration camps? But – ...Then perhaps you are right. You should leave this country as soon as you finish school."

"Impossible. It is very, very hard to get permission to travel unless on business trips. We are not allowed to take money out of the country. Dickie, England is the only country that can help us. She must be firm. She must not give in."

"No, of course not."

"I will have to fight, and you will fight me. Your country will lose, but I will come and rescue you."

"That is very kind of you – but perhaps it may be the other way round. England is quite good at warfare."

I was glad to get that in!

"She will have to be good! ...What have you been writing?" He glanced at my notepaper.

"Poetry."

"Can I see it?"

"No. You see, it's a love poem." A pause.

"... For Sigrid?"

My feelings were no secret, little as I discussed them.

Lindemayer later told me in his broken English that Sigrid's family were big landowners with a castle near his own family's. He invited me to visit him when term ended. I liked Lindemayer – a man at peace with himself. Although only eighteen years old, he might have been forty. He was a gentleman in the true sense of the word.

At the school, on Saturdays, there were dances; these were completely informal and great fun. The music was provided by

2 Flashback to Schooldays in Germany

radio, amplified by a loudspeaker. England was singled out for praise on account of having the best dance bands in the world. Salem boys were dance-band crazy; I gained kudos by telling them that I had actually founded one at Bryanston. They were keen on our well-known bandleaders and keener still on deploring the uninteresting German music. Was that political rather than musical taste? But der Mangel never struck up English tunes on his accordion. Music, to me, is the purest of the arts and the most satisfying, and knows no national barriers or political creed. My favourite record was a German version of *Gay Paris*.

At parades, the school branch of the Hitler Youth and Girls Contingent – that was what it was called – harnessed martial music to the cause. On such days everyone wore the regulation uniform with the Nazi Swastika, and some of the boys upped the machismo stakes with daggers, not always sheathed, inscribed with the words 'Blood and Honour'. The show as a whole was generally not much enjoyed. Salem tried to live up to the liberal traditions of its aristocratic founder and did its clandestine best not to encourage the National Socialist doctrine. I was told in so many words that the Hitler salute was ridiculous and that it was only necessary to half raise one's arm when greeting anybody in the street.

Although Germany had a secular government, the castle chapel was always crowded for morning service. On Sunday evening in the underground chapel, a string quartet, accompanying the organ in the candlelight, enhanced the spirituality of the service. Countess von Baden attended, and as she walked down the aisle she smiled at us, as if she saw us as her children and was happy to be there.

Towards the end of January, a ten-day skiing holiday was arranged for the school in the Austrian Tyrol. I was with a party of fifty who were going to stay in three small huts on the top of a mountain. Excitement was in the air. Peter Scharff and der Mangel were in my party. As the train sped towards the small

2 Flashback to Schooldays in Germany

village of Ritzendorf, my heart caught at the beauty of the sloping hills, the heavy clusters of fresh snow lying on the branches of trees and shrubs, their crystals, brilliant as cut diamonds, sparkling in the sunlight. The splendour of the scene, the vital, invigorating air, everyone joking and laughing and happy – it seemed the ideal life.

At Ritzendorf we had to climb the mountainside to reach our huts. We carried food for ten days. Girls gave their skis to the men. I had an extra pair of skis – it was preferable to humping one of the awkward tin food containers.

After two hours of hiking I began to feel really tired. We had spread out in a long file, weaker pupils dropping behind. With each step I sank over a foot down into the snow. It was a real slog. My rucksack contained the minimum necessary – a change of underwear and a washing bag – but it felt like an iron weight. The skis weighed me down. After four hours of climbing, my whole body ached. The light faded. I saw only the outline of the person a few yards ahead. The sharp wind sweeping over the mountain cut into my body, changing the beads of perspiration on my forehead to drops of ice. Pine trees were dark and foreboding shadows. After fully six hours of this climb, I sank almost to my knees in that cursed snow. If I stopped climbing, I would be lost. The alternative was exposure, freezing to death. I had to plod on. But I felt that there was no point. The mountain was far too high for me to reach the top.

Suddenly – just as reality was overtaking my turbid fancies – I saw lights twinkling, and dim figures at a hut door. I had made it! So comforting was the realisation that I decided to lie down in the snow for a short rest before attacking the final stage. I collapsed, closed my eyes and felt warm snow surround my body like a snug featherbed. A feeling of great happiness surged over me. I was drifting in a wonderful world of lights and music. I heard what sounded like a grunt and I was pulled to my feet. It was der Mangel.

2 Flashback to Schooldays in Germany

"Go on climbing, you fool. If you lie down in the snow, you will die. Now I'm going back to find other people that are missing."

I really doubt that I would ever have got up if der Mangel had not come. Consciousness had almost left my body. I felt a sort of petulance at having approached the threshold of death only to be dragged back to struggle on.

I staggered on up to the big hut where we were to stay. It was the very picture of an old rustic inn with gnarled wood benches, hurricane lamps soothingly swinging from two low beams and a great fire in the large, open fireplace. Steaming soup was ladled out and we all dug in with relish. A glowing welcome – though not yet for some of the party. It was fully two more hours before all were accounted for.

We boys had two old cowsheds at the back of the main building. They were very small with troughs of hay on each side. We slept eleven on each side, packed arm to arm so that it was almost impossible to turn without disturbing the whole room. There was one window consisting of a small pane of glass that could not be opened. However, chilling air came in blasts through cracks in the walls and from underneath the door. It was as well that my sleeping bag was warm.

In those mountains we were not taught Latin or maths or science but a more important lesson – how to live with each other. A lesson the world has not taken great care to learn. And we were taught skiing, which the world has on the contrary taken considerable care to learn. I experienced the thrill of speeding down an icy path to a small cafe with mouth-watering cakes, dancing in skiing boots under the soft, magical light of the hurricane lamps to lively Austrian music on accordions played by Amazon instructresses.

"Isn't this is a perfect way to live?" I was repeatedly asked. "Everyone helps everyone else and there is no such thing as a foreigner. We are all one happy party."

2 Flashback to Schooldays in Germany

There was a darker side to all this big-hearted living among friends. We were back at school. One night, seven boys – by common accord the most unpopular ones – were grabbed from their beds and tied up with ropes. They were then shoved, helpless, into mock coffins. The planning that must have gone into it! And each victim – selected no doubt from among the more sensitive and vulnerable types – must have required at least two or three stronger boys to pinion him. At daybreak, having been granted sufficient time to contemplate the mysteries of life and more particularly, death, their ordeal was rounded off with a more public humiliation. Each was hauled from his box to be paraded at breakfast, clad in a white shirt, with whitewash daubed on his face. Everyone thought these walking, shrouded corpses a great joke even if the ghosts themselves didn't seem to get it. They still were wrapped in their ropes.

It turned out that there was a 'secret' society at the school, the purpose being to play appalling japes on anyone disliked. In the summer term, boys were dragged to the river and dunked. Often. A sinister word in that context. The longer the 'dip', the more hilarious. Bryanston, this certainly wasn't.

One day, news came that the Germans were going to march into Austria. It amazed me. There were no English newspapers and I did not yet have enough German to read the state newspapers. An ardent Nazi, a Hitler Youth leader, put me wise in a cold-blooded, matter-of-fact way, ending up with the words, "...And if England fights us, we shall hang you up with a rope – outside the school."

It was starting to seem as if Salem's Garden of Eden had a goodly number of serpents. Unsurprisingly, thoughts of escape while there was still time kept floating into my mind.

News of the successful 'invasion' of Austria caused little enthusiasm among most of the pupils or even in the neighbouring villages. Flags were hung out from windows but people seemed oddly unexcited. People, reassuringly for me, had been told that

2 Flashback to Schooldays in Germany

the coming battle was to be against Russia, necessitating a friendly relationship with England. All this would help make sense of what I would hear much later on from the lips of the German Chief of Staff as well as the former German Ambassador to London.

One day, on the steamer crossing Lake Constance, a sailor clasped me by the hand and said in broken English, "I see you are English. Good. We are so pleased your Anthony Eden is over here. Now England and Germany will be so – " He slammed his left fist into his right hand to symbolise our two countries marching shoulder to shoulder.

My views by then were crystallising. I smiled more out of pity than the pleasure he assumed it to be. How could England offer friendship to a country that held power by the gun, sentencing opponents to a slow death in concentration camps? The average German seemed to me by now a slave to the state. He was told what to do, and it was his duty to obey.

The end of term came round and I was invited to a play in a small cellar in the castle – not just any play, but one banned by the Nazi government. I was to reveal absolutely nothing about it to anyone save trusted confederates. Invitations were secret. An extraordinary thing when one considers the risk, the detailed knowledge of who could be trusted, and the seriousness with which a mere piece of theatre was being taken. There were as many as sixty people present. The play was about the life and death of the soul of man, all very uplifting and excellently performed. The solace in the message was that here in Germany, though the forces of good were overwhelmed by the forces of evil, death would liberate the forces of good, which would soar up to the world of eternity. Not quite the comfort factor we might have looked for in England.

My time in Germany was nearing its end. No one could take from me the memories of the innocent, happy times Sigrid and I spent together. She, however, was now ill with yellow fever.

2 Flashback to Schooldays in Germany

I feared that we would never meet again. Before returning home, I stayed with Paul Lindemayer at his family castle on the edge of the Black Forest, seven miles from Baden-Baden. His mother and father could not do enough for me. Impressions remain of ancient, dark stone, towers, rich rugs, fine porcelain, old family portraits, heavy oak panelling – and the sadness of his parents at what they saw as the imminent collapse of their world.

One shining morning, Lindemayer and I saw across a river the white concrete forts that were part of the Maginot Line – that supposedly invincible rim of fortifications that was to shield France from invasion. In the pleasantly frosted air, it looked as if toy soldiers manned them. The hedges lining our side of the river had been recently planted.

The drift of Lindemayer's broken English was clear: "These hedges! We could move up an army behind them and no one would know. Even you have not noticed that the fields over which we walked have underground forts. The Maginot Line means nothing to us."

Paul and I parted, and when we met again it was under very different circumstances.

I will recount one more episode of those twilight days of peace.

I was aboard a train, and sitting with German working men. They were being sent, they said, to build a factory. They did not know what it was for, or where they were going to end up. Why they were going was quite another matter: their orders were to get on this train and await instructions. Did they like being ordered about, I asked? An expressive shrug said it all.

Having set out for Germany so short a time before in the simple hope of having an interesting and even an enjoyable time, I had grown up fast. Much as I did not want to fight my new friends, I saw that war was coming. What puzzled me was how they could have such a joy for living, given the circumstances.

It was terrifying to know that an efficient secret police force had been created to stamp out any trace of opposition and kill off

2 Flashback to Schooldays in Germany

such individual expression as still existed in a place like Salem. If such a system spread, civilisation itself would collapse. To play my part in preventing such a nightmare, I joined the RAF Voluntary Reserve on 19 June 1940 at the age of eighteen. I too became part of a military machine that I had always disliked.

3
The Bomber Pilot

My Friend
*He was my friend,
someone whose very laughter,
smile, and cheerful chatter
would bring happiness
to all who knew him.
I loved him more
because I knew,
although he seemed so gay,
within his heart there lay
great sadness.
I knew, and only I
guessed the reason why
there was great loneliness.
Yes, I was his friend,
and when he turned from me
the world was less bright
than before.
We took the path
that led from peace
to war.
We both knew that peace
could never bring
life as it was before.
We parted when we felt
all efforts had been
in vain,
and neither of us wished
to say
it seemed as if
hope
had passed away.*

3 The Bomber Pilot

The memory of the Bremen raid faded as other low-level missions succeeded it, albeit of equal danger, targeted on shipping and French ports. I continued in 107, the same squadron. We were now based in an old Norfolk rectory. There was great camaraderie.* 'Buster' Evans joined my crew. He was a large, beefy fellow who, before the war, had been involved professionally in building houses. He became an air gunner whose loyalty and enthusiasm for the cause was equalled only by the way he brought those qualities to bear on another goal: his insatiable quest for new girlfriends.

A low-level raid on the German seaplane base on the island of Sylt was planned. It was to be led by Squadron Leader Bill Edrich, who became well known as an England cricketer. Some people were nervous, if not downright fearful, at the prospect, though I was at a loss to see why. Our group captain tried to allay fears by making out that the raid was timed to coincide with lunchtime for the Germans. They were so keen on their meals that there would probably be no opposition. This blithe, if somewhat dubious, line of reasoning, even if seen as a humorous sally, was not quite the balm that he might have supposed. Little did this English squadron know how far he was from getting it right. The Germans lay in wait for us.

The sea was calm, but dark clouds at 2,000 feet cast a gloom over the scene. As we raced for the small island, the squadron leader's plane leapt ahead. I roared after him and as we flew over they gave us the works. Tracer bullets zipped past and heavy ack-

---

* Publisher's note: As cited in *Air Gunner*, by Mike Henry DFC:
 One of the squadron personalities during my term was Sergeant Dickie Leven. He was a pilot of outstanding quality and possessed a keen wit. He looked no older than 16 yet he was a very mentally alert 20. Before he flew on operations, he would drag up a stool to the battered upright piano in the mess and proceed to beat out a horrible dirge. It was the same piece on every occasion. The cries of derision from all present merely bounced off him. He was later awarded the DFM for his many cool-headed accomplishments.

3 The Bomber Pilot

ack exploded among us. From the leading plane, I could see the 'eggs' falling out as the bomb doors opened.

"Bomb, Mike, bomb!" I shouted.

Mike let ours go and we skimmed over the bay on the other side. We were racing flat out to get back over those islands to safety. The Jerries gave us hell. Spouts of water erupted in front of us and the machine on the far starboard side exploded into little pieces – there one minute, gone the next. We had to make another pass over the island. There was a sickening thud as the machine was hurled out of my hands. My starboard wing collapsed completely and wouldn't come up. My controls had locked and the waves were about to strike us. I closed the port engine and gave the starboard full throttle. The wing just cleared the water. I heaved the stick back with full opposite rudder. I couldn't hold her up much longer on my own. I shouted, "Help me fly her, Mike! Help me fly her!"

Mike looked at me with alarm and thinking me hit, stroked my wrist.

"Help, quick! Push her this way."

Mike stood up and pushed on the wheel as I tugged her over. The kite flew with one wing dipped.

Then Buster yelled over the intercom, "Snappers coming up!"

I looked up into the cloud, still at about 2,000 feet. I opened my port engine again and we staggered into that cloud before they got us. Mike was standing beside me, sweating like crazy. I tore my wireless bands from my helmet.

"Tie the stick up with this, Mike."

We hitched the control column up. I got my knee underneath it. Mike stood on the wheel. We were flying OK, but God I felt sick and faint. I must be wounded. But I couldn't pass out now. It was my duty to get us home. I got a grip of myself and the sickness passed.

Buster told me that the plane on my port wing had been shot up and had crashed into me. My port wing was consequently

3 The Bomber Pilot

buckled and the kite was very difficult to fly. We got back to England with no undercart and crash-landed on the aerodrome.

In a book written after the War by Bill Edrich and printed in the *Sunday Express*, the following passage appeared:

> *Twenty minutes later we members of the four planes that had come back were gathered together at the edge of the field, when a lone Blenheim, obviously in great difficulties, came into the circuit. It was one of the planes that we had reckoned to be lost over Sylt. The chances of its getting down safely seemed remote but, by superb airmanship, Pilot Officer Leven achieved a landing. Even now it gives me pleasure to record the details of Leven's feat. His plane had been struck by a falling Blenheim over Sylt and his ailerons and flaps on the port wing chewed up. When this happened, his aircraft was out of control at low level. Somehow he managed to gain height and by turning his lateral controls almost perpendicular set his aircraft on a straight course. He said afterwards that it was such a strain holding the controls in position that he called the navigator to help. He, in turn, took off his leather belt and between them they strapped the controls at the perpendicular. He made the necessary adjustments from there.*

Edrich might have been right about the improvised aeronautics, but he also stated, erroneously, that I had received an immediate decoration. Although I was informed that I had been recommended for the VC, I received no decoration at all.

The demands of war took their toll on us with little respite. I had some time off after the Sylt raid and went to Scarborough. I was free to wander round at leisure. But the seaside resort was dirty and deserted of holidaymakers. Barbed wire over the beaches prohibited bathing and the place provided little solace.

Another time, Gully Mason, my friend and co-pilot, invited me to stay over in Kensington. His father, Colonel Mason, MP, took us to dinner for a night out with Edmundo Ros, famous for

3 The Bomber Pilot

his big band, at the Lansdowne Club. This party at the former London residence of the Earls of Lansdowne in Berkeley Square where, as the song put it, the nightingales sang, looked more promising than the empty shores of Scarborough. I hit it off with Gully's sister, Anne. What fun it was – and might have been. Two weeks later, Gully was killed on Blenheims. Again I lost a great friend. Tragically, two years later, Anne died. The pain of recording all this!

The squadron was transferred to its Norfolk station in a Wellington (the 'Wimpy'). I felt distinctly nervous as a passenger rather than a pilot in the large, ungainly plane.

In the heat of battle the high-level fighter-escorted 'circus' became a regular operation. The worst mission I ever went on was the raid on 6/7 September 1941 on Mazingarbe.

Wing Commander 'Bunny' Harte, DFC, was a tall South African CO. It was a great comfort to know that someone so reliable was leading. I was flying on his port side. We quickly formed up and flew down south to pick up our fighter escort. The air suddenly filled with friendly Spitfires beneath and above us. It would be a brave Jerry who dared dive through that fighter protection.

As we climbed higher, I turned on the oxygen. It gave off a musty smell. The coast stretched out beneath us, flat and harmless in appearance. But I dreaded the approach. Boulogne was not far and the heavy guns were there in great concentrations. In the deathly calm, I knew instinctively that something was going to happen.

Bunny was taking evasive action as we neared the coastal fortifications and we were losing height, weaving from side to side. Then the first burst of ack-ack came – large black puffs of smoke all around us. My aircraft was hit; it bounced up, but I still had control of it. Another burst. We were hit again – nothing vulnerable yet. The stuff came up and burst with a yellow flame that disappeared leaving a floating ball of black smoke.

3 The Bomber Pilot

The others had turned back which meant only three of us were in the leading formation to carry on. Although the firing had stopped and we were past the range of the coastal defences, we took evasive action the whole way.

The stuff caught us to port and to starboard. We got another hit in front. My instruments went out of action. Bunny missed the target and was turning to bomb again. I thought he'd better bomb this time or I would crack under the strain. Stuff was still bursting amongst us as we flew towards the coast, but not so accurately. I was afraid they'd fire at us again, but they didn't. Fighters started to attack instead.

Buster yelled, "Snapper coming in – 500 yards, 300 yards."

"Shoot it down, man! Shoot it down," I ordered.

"OK, OK," he replied, "...Spits have got it."

It was a long trip back to base and strangely quiet up there in the fading light. The coast appeared red in the dying sunlight. The troubles of the world seemed insignificant and nothing mattered very much. When we arrived back over our aerodrome I tried to get my wheels down, but they wouldn't work. They were damaged by the ack-ack. I tried a second time with the same result: neither wheels nor flaps would come down...

I called up Control and reported on my situation.

"Hello, B for Beer calling. I am going to crash land. Stand by!"

"OK, B for Beer. Have you checked your undercart?"

"Yes, I've checked everything. Nothing darn well works, so I'm coming in now. Over to you. Over."

There were no runways on the all-grass aerodrome. I told my navigator to stand by to switch off the petrol and to be ready when I said the word. Then we passed over the wood on the aerodrome boundary.

I closed the throttles. As the grass grew closer I pulled back on the stick. Back, back, the aircraft was sinking. Crack! It was a hell of a jar. We roared along the ground before she skidded to port. The hooter was blowing and the perspex windows were all

3 The Bomber Pilot

cracked. At last it stopped. I turned off the switches and climbed out. A car drove up and Group Captain the Earl of Bandon, DSO, the station commander, jumped out.

"Jolly good show, Dickie. Are you OK?"

"Fine, thank you, sir," I replied. "Just ran into some flak."

"So I see!" He looked at the aircraft. "Damn good show. The Hun is still shooting straight, what!" He gave one of his short, hearty laughs. "Your crew have deserted you, I see."

Mike and Buster had been afraid the aircraft would blow up and had wisely retired to a safe distance.

He grinned again and added, "I'd have done exactly the same myself."

He climbed into his staff car and sped away. Looking back, I feel that it was his cheerful spirit and keen appreciation of our effort that inspired us all to fight on against heavy odds. We knew that the station commander would always be waiting for us to return and would sympathise when things went wrong.

There were ground crews, always anxiously waiting for us to climb out and tell them the news. They were good men, hard-working, dirty, not very disciplined, but the best fitters and riggers in the world. A few days later, one of the men told me that Flight Sergeant Smith had a present for me. I walked over to his office.

"Hello Chiefie, how's life?"

"We're OK. Had a good time, Dickie?"

"Not so bad, thanks. I'm told you've a present for me."

"Nothing much, Dickie, but I flannelled some armour plating and thought you'd like to fit it into position"

"You're marvellous. Thank you. It's just what I need. The Jerry is getting too damn accurate with his shooting."

"You needn't worry. Mark my words, you'll come back alive!"

It was with good reason, of course, that my rejoinder to that was: "I wish I could believe you. Nothing's certain in this world."

One doomed friend was Cullen, to whom I took from the start. His first words to me were "God, what a dump! Can you

3 The Bomber Pilot

tell me where I put these things and if there's a vacant bed? Is there anywhere I can play tennis around here?"

He stood at the entrance of our rectory carrying two large pigskin suitcases and a tennis racket under one arm. He turned out to be not only an excellent tennis player but our best formation flier. Mind you, he knew it too well, and annoyed everyone by constantly reminding them of it.

In those days the Blenheim squadrons took turns attacking shipping in the Channel from their base at Manston in Kent. I disliked shipping beats, having lost many crews from attacks on convoys. Cullen arrived in the squadron at the time it was slated to move down to Manston. One night when we were there, Cullen woke me up in the early hours of the morning.

"Dickie, I've just had a terrible nightmare. I was flying with my crew over a convoy and I knew I was shot down. I saw myself under the sea and I couldn't get out, although my navigator and air gunner managed to get out of the aircraft. I was left trapped in my seat. I feel that this is going to happen to me. If it does, will you please see my girlfriend and tell her how much I loved her?"

I tried to cheer Cullen up by explaining that we all had these nightmares, and that it did not mean we would die as we had seen it in our dreams. But Cullen insisted on giving me the address of his girlfriend and I promised I would visit her if anything should happen.

The next morning – it was 22 September 1942, I think – I was leading a raid on a convoy off the French coast. As I turned to attack and come out from the convoy, I saw one of my planes crashing into the sea. When we returned to Manston, I found out that my friend Cullen was the pilot who had disappeared under the waves. After the War I heard that his navigator and air gunner had escaped from the plane and become POWs. What Cullen experienced was exactly as he had described his dream to me. Then came my sad task of informing his girlfriend. The tragedy of war is to be parted from our loved ones.

3 The Bomber Pilot

After several more weeks in action my squadron was sent to Gibraltar. The news was put to us in a somewhat breezy way by the Commanding Officer:

"Now chaps, we are going tomorrow to fly down to Cornwall and from there to Gibraltar. Pack your kit for a three-week stay. Only take with you what is absolutely necessary."

Our Mediterranean cruise was about to begin.

Tropical planes in light blue camouflage (pale duck-egg blue Camotint paint) were arriving at Portreath for the 1,100-mile trip. I had to wait there four days with my crew, Buster included, as engine trouble delayed our flight to Gibraltar.

A new aircraft was sent down and after an exhausting flight during which the heat inside the cockpit became almost unbearable, Nolan pointed out the Rock. I knew by his confident tone that he was certain of our position, which was not always the case. As we flew down the Straits of Gibraltar, there was an amazing panorama of colour. On one side the Spanish mountains were rugged and barren, on the other the Algerian mountains were squat yet immense. Shades of purple, red and deep blue made them seem terrifying and so close that I was afraid that my aircraft would crash in their midst. I didn't much fancy the idea of being forced to pancake (land on the sea) either. There would be no hope of any sortof rescue there.

The heat and the bright lights of Gibraltar were delightful, so different from the blacked-out war world from which I had come. To my surprise and delight, as I was exploring the tempting local market, Poons, my Sergeant Observer friend, ran into me, still with his characteristic easy, carefree stride. He had crash landed in Portugal and had quite a tale to tell. The Portuguese authorities had confiscated his uniform and replaced it with a comical outfit. A pair of grey flannel trousers supported by a brown knotted belt was suspended about four inches above his ankles; his dirty cloth jacket was many sizes too small and could only be fastened by one large flat button.

3 The Bomber Pilot

We went to the Continental. It had been a dance hall, but now with no women allowed in Gibraltar after curfew there was only a forlorn band with a few sailors rolling about in a drunken stupor on the floor while soldiers idly tapped the rhythm with their hobnailed boots. Rankers like us were not welcome in the local hotels so we made the best of it, perspiring freely and without the solace of iced drinks.

Poons told me about his recent adventures before he eventually arrived in Gibraltar.

"I was asleep when Tommy, my pilot, suddenly woke me up with a kick in the back and said that we had only half an hour's petrol left. I pumped as hard as I could but the reserve tanks just would not work. So I suggested landing in Portugal, enemy territory, as we were only a few miles off the coast. We turned towards the shore. The whole place looked mountainous so Tommy came down very low to have a look. It was rather stony and we decided to crash-land on a small stretch of sand. A beautiful landing! In the distance somebody was approaching so I grabbed my little red alarm clock I always carry and hopped out. We had to set the plane on fire. Of course, none of us had any matches. I flung the dinghy out and used its flares. The plane blew up but – would you believe it, Dickie? – the IFF box (secret wireless installation) landed at my feet. That was where my scarf came in useful. I just picked up the box and wrapped it up, just as if it was some of my own kit. The coast-guard who found us was more than upset that we had blown the plane up; he would have been entitled to a percentage of the value of anything handed over intact to the government."

Poons eventually gave the IFF box to the British consul, undetected. He didn't tell me precisely how he had escaped, but apparently the officers of the 'reception committee' were thoroughly sporting. They laid on a party for him. They had a portrait of Churchill in their mess. Perhaps they took to this Englishman with his insouciant air, scruffy moustache and Oxford accent. We parted, picking our way through innumerable drunk sailors, some

3 The Bomber Pilot

lying incapable in the gutter, with Poons entirely indifferent to the scene save in so far as he took care to avoid the human obstacles to his path. He was due to go back to England soon after.

I was based in a hastily erected Nissen hut on one edge of Gibraltar's aerodrome. It had formerly been a racecourse of which the grandstand remained and was currently used for storing RAF supplies. A mattress laid over six petrol tins created an airman's bed, plus two dirty blankets. Sometimes the changes were rung and it was three wooden boards raised about four inches from the ground. All my belongings were tossed over a parachute bag by my side. Mike Nolan would carefully fold his blankets in correct military fashion. Sometimes we had beds of iron slabs. Often we rested our tired bodies on straw mattresses. If anyone had told me in peacetime that such would be my sleeping accommodation, I would have laughed.

In Gibraltar, I would stay in bed until midday if possible. I liked to be alone with my thoughts as the minutes passed slowly by. Every second, some memory could be recalled and the thrill of a moment recaptured. The voices of friends can seem to call out, so that a world more comforting, even more mysterious, drifts by in a dreamlike land. I could imagine Poons curled up in some armchair reading a crime story. Then again, with my eyes closed I could realise once more that feeling of loneliness and helplessness experienced when hurtling through space. I could shift back to a land of dreams where man is a slave to strange powers. I was gazing up at the sky when Mike showed up.

"Have you any saltwater soap, Dickie? I can't wash with mine."

I let him have a bar I had bought from the NAAFI (the army canteen). There was only one place to wash – a water trough behind a row of huts where the seawater trickled through, in the glare of the sun.

Later, Mike strolled into the hut and said: "Will you test our plane, now, Dickie? We are leaving tonight."

3 The Bomber Pilot

I was dumbfounded. Night flying did not appeal to me. Mike told me the plans. The job had to be done. Clamping my topi (pith sun hat favoured by British Empire officials) firmly on top of my flying helmet, I fastened my parachute straps and started the engine. Khaki-clad ground crews dragged the chocks away and I taxied up the runway. Clouds of sand enveloped pedestrians walking along the road. This was a very old plane. It was the devil to take off. We barely made it. I kept the kite flying low to gather speed. Up with the undercarriage, then the flaps.

"At this rate I'll crash on our take-off tonight."

I looked around. Visibility was about fifty miles. It was almost uncanny to gaze out to port and see the buildings of Tangiers at the foot of jagged mountains. They were vividly coloured in yellow, green and mauve, rising out of a deep blue sea, like some huge lake. It was glorious up here. At 10,000 feet the air was fresh and crisp. The world was ours. We were kings above the Earth as we gazed down on that magical panorama of colour.

Coming down, it was tricky flying as the air currents violently tossed the plane about. We got down safely. Mike and I strolled over to the beach for a bathe. The hot, sandy shore was idyllically peaceful. There was no sound other than ripplets breaking on the sandy shore. We shared one moment of freedom as we stood naked on the edge and gazed into the purple blue of the water. Then, almost ashamed at our carefree abandonment, we plunged in. The warm water flowed over my body, rocking it gently to and fro. I floated on my back and gazed at the sky through which we had just rushed madly. Life seemed purposeless.

"Oh hell! I've been bitten, Mike. Quick, get out! There are crowds of jellyfish here!"

Nature's sharp retort to idle philosophy!

Inland in Spain, thousands were dying of starvation. The prisons were full of Spaniards who had fought against Franco. Grim tales of misery were daily illustrated by a long procession of Spanish workers who could be seen returning home carrying bags

3 The Bomber Pilot

laden with loaves of bread and any other food they could get on the Rock. Gibraltar was crowded with sailors from the many Royal Navy ships stationed in the harbour. At night, the sailors crowded the main streets, lurching about in a drunken stupor. It was sad to see how appallingly Englishmen behaved abroad. Our sailors seemed to have no interest in life except to drink until they could hardly stand on their feet.

Since I was the most experienced Blenheim pilot available, I was involved an operation to protect the aircraft carriers *Ark Royal* and *Furious* on their way to Malta. These were to be loaded with Hurricanes to protect the island from Axis bombers based in Sicily. My brief was to fly out and meet the aircraft carriers halfway in the Mediterranean, then fly in a protective circle round *Furious* until the Hurricanes had taken off. Finally, I had to navigate to Malta with the fighters close behind. My wing commander was to take the fighters off *Ark Royal*, and then we were to receive further instructions. At this briefing the captain and other naval officers from both aircraft carriers spent a great deal of time discussing Morse code signals to be used should anything go wrong.

I could not read Morse, and I knew that Mike, my navigator, was as hopeless as I was at reading lamp signals. We decided not to mention this because the Navy would have been very upset to think that they could not communicate with us. A few days after *Ark Royal* and *Furious* left, Wing Commander Harte and I took off. I had only flown once before at night and was terrified of flying off in the dark without seeing where I was going. My plane had very sluggish engines and I was almost at the runway's end before I managed to get it into the air. Initially, I was alarmed at what seemed like jets of flame coming from the engines. However I got used to it and flew on until dawn broke. There were *Furious* and *Ark Royal*, surrounded by about ten warships. I flew down to low level and started circling *Furious* as planned. Thirteen Hurricanes took off.

3 The Bomber Pilot

Suddenly Aldis lamps started flashing at us. Of course neither Mike nor I could interpret the signals. Flying close round *Furious* I saw that one fighter had crashed on deck and that this would dangerously delay the flight of the last plane. Mike was worried because we were behind schedule and we might run out of petrol before reaching Malta. So I decided to fly off in the direction of the island. The thirteen Hurricanes now in the air lined up behind me and we set off for another three hours' flying across the water.

Warned that petrol might run short before we reached Malta, we had been equipped with extra fuel tanks only operable with a hand pump. As it happened, just half an hour before Malta, my main tank started running dry. Mike poured with sweat as he pulled the pump, a dreadful Heath Robinson contraption, up and down. It was with great delight that we suddenly saw the islands of Malta and Gozo. The fighters left us at Halfar aerodrome while we landed safely, if exhausted, at Luqa.

Although we were based at Luqa, we messed at Kalafrana Bay because of the continual bombing. Squadron Leader Barnes decided not to lead operations instead instructing me to lead every raid. He told me that Group Captain the Earl of Bandon had applied for me to be commissioned and was convinced that my commission papers would soon come through.

We flew on raids to Libya where the Eighth Army was retreating so rapidly. I led every low-level raid on roads and aerodromes so as to stop the advance of the German Army. Twice I was ordered to bomb Sicily, the base for Italian fighters bombing Malta. My first raid was to be Catania, on 15 April 1942. The railway turntable, where trucks held about forty engines, was the target. From the centre of that circle rails led like radii to the harbour and fighter aerodrome about five miles away. The enemy was patrolling the area.

Mike wanted his navigation to be accurate so I decided to fly up to Gozo and from there get a course at low level. I always find

3 The Bomber Pilot

waves! Naturally, I was concentrating on the water a few feet ahead. It was far from monotonous! One moment, dead ahead, was a submarine. It crash-dived on the instant though I had turned sharply to port. We sped on. From the haze ahead an outline of distant mountains appeared, crowned by the solitary grandeur of Mount Etna. Somewhere to the south was Catania.

After a typically heated argument with Mike about our whereabouts, we glimpsed Catania, visible at the foot of the mountain. Two dark specks, probably fighters, appeared above the target as we approached. The ground sloped up from the town. This suggested we should nip in round the back behind the hill. By keeping close to the ground, it looked possible to climb the hill unobserved before diving down the other side on to the target. I opened my throttles and we roared towards the coast, over the tree covered hillsides dotted with picturesque chalets. We actually flew beneath the balcony of one house and as we did so a signorina waved cheerily at us. Buster, always with an eye for beauty, took her photograph from the gun turret.

Planes that carry a full bomb load require a certain speed. This hill was deceptively steep which made it difficult to fly low and yet be at a steep climbing angle. As our speed rapidly decreased, I was terrified of stalling before we reached the top and there were anxious moments when I thought we wouldn't make it. Then, as I punched the stick forward, we glided over the hill and dashed down towards the town beneath us with the harbour looking quite empty – thank heavens we were not after any shipping. It was a grand sensation careering down that slope, the feeling of great speed heightened by the proximity of the ground. The plane felt like a skier hurtling down the mountain. I flung the kite about from side to side and up and down.

At that speed, all this was quite a physical effort but necessary, because one can never tell when the ack-ack will open up. I pretended to come down and bomb the port, but at the last minute pulled into a steep turn, doubling back to run straight over the

3 The Bomber Pilot

target. Tommy was close behind and we succeeded in putting it out of action. Suddenly there was a cry from over the radio. I looked up and to my horror saw the sky was black with planes flying at about 500 feet and passing in front of us. Their markings, clearly visible, identified them as Italian Caprioni bombers operating under German command. There was only one thing to do – dash beneath them and hope for the best. By that time the shore batteries were opening up, however, and not one of the planes fired at us or turned out of their formation. We passed under fourteen of them and had the pleasure of seeing that they were receiving the attention of the Italian gunners. We didn't wait around to see if any had been shot down.

On our return I thought everyone would be quite amused to hear our tale. Not at all. Instead the powers that be were most upset because the Navy had complained that one of their submarines had crash-dived leaving a man in the sea. He was picked up later so it wasn't really as bad as their reports sounded.

I was involved in the bombing of the aerodrome at Licata in Sicily, the base for Italian heavy bombers. On another occasion I was instructed to fly to Tripoli Harbour and bomb the ships storing weapons for the German Army. Wing Commander Harte and I did this by coming in from the town itself. As I arrived at one ship I was surrounded by flak from all over the harbour. Tracer bullets and heavy shells burst all around me and I thought at any moment I would be blown to bits. I attacked a big cargo vessel that according to my air gunner blew up a few moments after we passed over her. I prayed that there were no crew on board. I always loathed the thought of killing human beings. I hated this war which put me in a position where I might cause death or destroy a family, to say nothing of what it had done to people I knew.

Bunny Harte was killed on 9 October 1941.

Over a period of time, and during the many missions, the entire squadron that had come out with me from England had been killed.

4

Malta, Medals and Meetings

Fear in Flight
I have seen the cloud tops stretch
across the entire sky
when all the world was hidden
and none could see me fly.
I have cried within my heart
that earth and sky would meet,
for I have felt so lonely,
trapped within my seat.
I have felt the terror dread
of flying on my own,
knowing that the course was lost,
and none could guide me home.
I have flown through the night,
when flames shot out behind,
when all around was inky black
and I thought I was blind.
My plane seemed to be upside down,
I struggled on alone,
and oh, within my heart I wished
that I had never flown.

I was dispatched with two new crews to patrol the Gulf of Sirte off the Libyan coast. From there, the Germans were moving important convoys into Libya. The Eighth Army was retreating so quickly it was essential to sink the merchant ships involved.

The crews, a New Zealander and a Canadian, were sergeant pilots with no operational experience who had come out from England. Although I held the same rank, I had already led over

4 Malta, Medals and Meetings

thirty operations from England and Malta and had attacked targets off the French coast and in the Mediterranean. I had taken part in more daylight operations on Blenheims than any other pilot. For me this raid seemed to hold no particular difficulty. I was only worried about getting our aircraft off the runway. I remember that I had left the course to my navigator Mike and hardly took any notice of our instructions. This raid was just another target to be tackled in the madness of war.

I took off from Luqa without trouble and was pleased that the two new sergeant pilots were swiftly able to catch up and fly behind me in formation at low level. 'Low level' meant exactly what the words imply: we hugged the waves so that there were only about two feet between the props of our aircraft and the water. Although sparkling with brilliant sunlight, the sea was wintry and turbulent.

The moment we left, I felt strangely nervous. I sensed a curious atmosphere but neither Mike, who was as usual absorbed in his maps, nor Buster Evans, my air gunner, who was his normal cheerful self, seemed concerned. I knew they had no premonition of disaster and so I tried to persuade myself that all would be well.

After two hours of monotonous flying, I went into my habitual reflective trance. I woke up as Mike said, "Dickie, the convoy is over there to port." There was a merchant ship ahead. I knew at once it would be madness to attack a convoy that had such an escort; we could never get through it and come out alive. From my experience in past raids, my instinct told me to circle at a distance to discover how to attack with some degree of surprise. It was wiser by far to fly in with the glare of the Mediterranean sun behind me. That would prevent gunners on the ships from picking us out easily. So I turned straight ahead towards the sun. As I did so, the New Zealand pilot on my port side left me and flew towards the convoy. He never reached the ships, being shot straight into the sea from 200 yards away.

I circled out to try out a position with the glare of the sun behind me. The Canadian pilot on my starboard wing at once left

4 Malta, Medals and Meetings

me and also turned in to attack the convoy. He met the same fate as the New Zealander and crashed straight into the sea.

Alone and about 200 miles from Malta, I considered this raid suicidal; I could never succeed in attacking the convoy and still be able to return. So over the intercom I told Mike and Buster, "I think we'll go back to Malta. We've got no chance against this opposition."

Buster replied, "You've got to attack now Dickie."

"What do you say, Mike?" I asked.

"I think you can make it, Dickie."

"OK. Well, don't blame me if we buy it." (To 'buy it' was our way then of saying we'd be killed.)

I decided to take my time. Once again I circled the convoy and this time turned with the sun behind me. As I came within 300 yards of the convoy, two Macchi fighters broke out and flew towards me. One gunned my rear and the other pilot, who must have been mad, flew directly at me. As he tried to ram me, I raised my nose cone and saw the pilot's black helmet. He missed me by inches. He lost control of his aircraft and dived straight into the drink. About a hundred yards away, I saw the merchantman in a sea spattered with bullets and turned my aircraft from one side to the other to get out of the line of fire.

The art of attacking such a ship is to fly below deck level and then press the stick's bomb switch for the target, about 50 yards away. I did this and then pulled the stick up to get over the masts. While doing so, a bullet exploded through the front and half blinded me. Instinct told me that I was over the top of the masts and so I put the stick down. I regained my sight but one engine was out of action. The port engine was dead and the Blenheim wouldn't fly on one engine. Then I glanced at my navigator; Mike was hit in the cheek. Blood was oozing from him. Though I tried every emergency switch to get the port engine working, it was useless. One glance at the sea told me that the waves were far too rough to try to land on it.

4 Malta, Medals and Meetings

Suddenly, something suggested that I push the stick forward. I knew it was madness because it could mean forcing the nose of the aircraft into the sea and going straight to the bottom. But the feeling was so strong that I moved it forward only to find that the cage holding the magneto switches had been broken in half by the bullet that had exploded in front of me. I pushed the two magneto switches up and the engine came to life, missing the waves by inches. When I tried to push the throttle forward in line with the other engine it banged badly. The cylinders must have been damaged as she would only work at half pressure. But this was sufficient for me to fly at about 100 mph and I could gradually climb above the waves.

It was at about 5,000 feet that I realised that Mike, though alive, was unconscious, so I summoned Buster on the intercom to get me a course home. At first I couldn't get a reply from him, but when eventually he responded, he shouted that my wireless had been shot out of action. My position was terrifying: 200 miles from Malta with no navigator and no wireless. In front of me was a rough and turbulent sea and I had no idea what course to fly to get back to base. I had no alternative but to close my eyes and pray. O God, please show me the way back to Malta.

As soon as I had prayed, a course came into my mind and I took it. After keeping to the same course for over two hours, there was only five minutes' petrol left. Darkness was falling and the clouds ahead were almost red. I prayed again and, when I opened my eyes, some instinct told me to turn to port towards a cloud in the distance. I did this and found to my delight that Malta was under the cloud. As I turned in to land and approached the runway, both my engines stopped working.

The petrol had run dry. But it didn't matter. I was able to glide in and land safely. Mike was taken to hospital where they found that a small piece of shrapnel had lodged in his left cheek. Buster, in good spirits, had not realised just how worried I was about finding Malta without either navigator or wireless. I

4 Malta, Medals and Meetings

reckoned that the port engine could well have stopped functioning as it had only been working at half pressure. Ground staff found that a shell had penetrated one of the cylinders and were amazed that it had worked at all.

That evening I went down to Valletta, together with Poons – he had been sent back due to what he appeared to feel was a mix-up, and was to go to Egypt. We decided to forget about the war in The Gut. It was a ghastly place infested by scores of drunken seamen who stumbled along the narrow street packed with 'hostesses' and squalid drinking saloons, leering at young women. Not that Poons displayed undue interest in that sort of female company. Rather than give a blow-by-blow account of what happened that night, it is fairer to Poons' memory to say a little more about him personally. There are people who should not be forgotten, even if the war cut short what might have been their achievements.

In many ways, Poons was typical of the men who became RAF aircrew. He revived my faith in the English. He could have been an excellent writer. He had a theory that money should be abolished and replaced by a coupon system. He was a philosopher who didn't expect to be taken seriously. He felt that everyone had his own personal reasons for fighting. He was fighting for the right to think and write according to his own standards of what was just. I remember one of our conversations, prompted by my seeing him sit all day, book in hand.

"To be a successful writer, you must study your public. Give them what they want. If the public will pay good money for trash, I will write trash."

"Surely, Poons, you would not prostitute your art?"

"Yes, Dickie, I would write anything if it was the only way of living. After all, if an artist dies of poverty, no one will ever know how great his art was, unless it was recognised. Probably he will have died without creating his masterpiece. If, however, that artist had given the world what the world wanted, he would have made

4 Malta, Medals and Meetings

his name. Having made his name, the world would listen to what he had to say. They would respect his name even if they became confused at the expression of his art."

Poons had piercing eyes, sometimes mocking, sometimes with a faraway look. He hardly ever showed signs of emotion.

Another conversation went like this:

"By the way, Dickie, I bumped into Brian in Gibraltar. He said you knew him."

"Oh, yes I do. He was on our course at OTU (Operational Training Unit)."

"Well, he came down in the sea. Petrol ran short, or something, so they're going back to England. He told me that Bill had gone. Did you hear about it?"

"Good heavens! You don't mean old Bill Bullermont who used to throw such grand parties? Oh dear. How did it happen?"

"So far as I could gather," Poons drawled on, "Bill was on that Cologne raid. You remember?"

I certainly did. It was one of the biggest raids of the year and got front-page coverage in every newspaper. In fact, it was quite uneventful as some of the raids go. There was a little ack-ack over the target but only a few of the chaps were worried by fighters.

"Brian was chased by three fighters but was lucky in running into the escort of fighters sent out to meet the chaps coming back. Bill was on Brian's port wing. The fighters concentrated on them. They dropped behind and were shot down before crossing the coast. Apparently the plane burst into flames, so I don't expect we'll see Bill again. What are you drinking, Dickie?"

Poons' eyes seemed to say: "Let's change the conversation."

Poons rarely mentioned his past life. Yet every now and then he would tell a tale. I remember once when we had been drinking in a country pub back home and I casually mentioned that an oil painting of fishing smacks sailing out from a stone quay looked pleasing. He told me that the seemingly careless handling of the paint that gave such an unusual effect was typical of the

4 Malta, Medals and Meetings

modern school of Cornish artists. He happened to know it well, having spent part of most his summers down there and being something of a painter himself.

Our mess at Kalafrana Bay was sad and cold. Food was very scarce and with the bombing day and night, the lives of the Maltese were effectively ruined. I sensed that they blamed us for the War and would have liked the Italians to win as they considered us intruders on their island.

My being alive was due solely to the intervention of some strange force that seems to govern the world. My nerves were shattered and I just wanted to get back to England, and two weeks later my wish was fulfilled. Transporting supplies to the island by convoy had been abandoned as the convoys had been so badly attacked. Fuel and provisions were now transported by submarine. I was invited to go on HMS *Olympus*. Poons waved me off as I climbed down the conning-tower. As I caught a last glimpse of my friend's face, some instinct told me that we would never meet again: another great man would be destroyed by this ghastly war.

My friends and I in the air force had been fighting virtually alone. The Army had been destroyed at Dunkirk; the Navy was incapable of fighting back against the convoys off the Continent and in the Middle East. We poor pilots were the only attacking force and we were almost exhausted. All the strength of the Navy had been inadequate even for getting the fighters into Malta, a task that fell on our shoulders. The Eighth Army was on the run through Libya, unbelievably quickly. It seemed insane that a few Blenheims stationed in Malta should have to fly all the way to Libya to attack the German shipping bringing in supplies.

While I was under the sea in HMS *Olympus*, Japan bombed Pearl Harbor. Now the USA would come into the war. The tide would turn. We would no longer be on our own.

Captain Dymott, the submarine commander, was a most delightful man, with a love of English history and literature. As

4 Malta, Medals and Meetings

my commission as a pilot officer had been wired to Malta, he allowed me to sleep on a bench in the wardroom. I also received the news that, together with Mike Nolan and Buster Evans, I had been awarded the DFM.

The announcement made in the *London Gazette* of 19 December 1941 was:

> *Leven, Henry Richard 1166186 Sergeant, No 107 Squadron (Immediate) Distinguished Flying Medal*
>
> *This NCO is a pilot of a Blenheim in No 107 Squadron and has taken part in 34 operational sorties while stationed at Malta. The crew of which he was a member has set a very high example to the remaining crews in the squadron and they have at all times displayed a high disregard for their own safety in spite of having anti-aircraft fire from escorting ships of the convoys they have attacked. Their devotion to duty and their determination to destroy their target is deserving of the highest praise owing to the loss of officers in the squadron. Sergeant Leven, as pilot, has led numerous attacks against enemy shipping. The fact that all attacks have been conspicuously successful has been due in no small measure to the fine leadership of Sergeant Leven.*
>
> *Evans, Cecil Arthur 925183 Sergeant No 107 Squadron*
> *Leven, Henry Richard 1166186 Sergeant No 107 Squadron*
> *Nolan, Michael John 990776 Sergeant No 107 Squadron*
>
> *As pilot, air observer and wireless/air gunner operator respectively, Sergeants Leven, Nolan and Evans have participated in numerous sorties in which enemy shipping has been attacked. Undismayed by the defensive fire from armed escort ships, these airmen have shown great courage and determination to complete their allotted task. Sergeants Leven and Nolan have completed 34 and Sergeant Evans 27 operational missions.*

4 Malta, Medals and Meetings

At that time we had flown more Blenheim daylight operations than any other crew. Had we been officers we would have received at least two decorations – we noted that regular officers flew only a few sorties before they were decorated.

Smoking was forbidden when the submarine was beneath the surface. The atmosphere was suffocating. I felt like a trapped animal. When we surfaced at night, it was a great relief to struggle up the conning-tower and into the reviving spray shooting across the bridge. But I hated climbing up the tower with the air pressure rushing down almost dragging me off the vertical steps.

On 8 December 1941 we heard the news of Pearl Harbor. Captain Dymott and I went up on to the bridge. The sea was rough and waves crashed over us, splashing our faces and almost submerging us. Suddenly we spotted a ship ahead and the Captain ordered us to crash-dive. The Captain almost threw me to the opening and I scrambled down with the full force of the wind almost tearing me off the steps. We had been warned that men would be left on the bridge to drift off into the sea if they didn't scurry down the conning-tower ladder immediately. Once we were in the wardroom, the submarine plummeted down to the depths of the sea. We heard explosives bursting in the distance. They were coming nearer and nearer. I prayed that I wouldn't be blown up at the bottom of the sea. With the engines silent, we all sat round the wardroom table not speaking a word. One hour later we heard depth charges in the distance and knew the danger was over.

That evening, when the other officers left, Captain Dymott seemed curiously quiet. Then out of the blue he asked me, "Have you got any knowledge of astrology or palmistry?"

"None whatsoever…!" I replied. "I have never even considered the subject."

Then he looked at me and said, "From what you have told me about your flying experience I have the impression you must be psychic. Otherwise, I don't think you could have survived. Look at my hand and give me your impressions."

4 Malta, Medals and Meetings

I had never looked at anybody's hands before and I really didn't know what the Captain expected me to say. But because he was my CO, I had to do as he asked. Something came over me. I started talking without quite knowing what I was saying. Suddenly I stopped. A feeling came over me that the submarine I was sitting in would be blown up the next time it went to sea. I saw a whole episode take place. The submarine hit a mine and was blown to bits. The Captain looked at me very strangely.

"Remember my words," he said. "You have a gift which can help people. From the way that you looked at me, I know that you sense I will never return to England. You are right. I know it myself. You, from your experiences in the air, and I, from my experiences under the sea, have developed some gift that links us with powers beyond our comprehension. I knew when you came aboard this ship that flying had done something to you. I want you to remember my words and develop a gift I am sure you have discovered."

We docked at Gibraltar where I was the Navy's guest for Christmas on the battleship, HMS *Malaya*. Soon afterwards my crew and I returned to England on the Polish liner *Batory*, built originally as a cruiser for sailing round the world. It was greatly overcrowded for the crew and other non-commissioned men. However, the other officers and myself enjoyed first-class facilities. I had a luxury cabin to myself and was waited on in some style by my own steward and the Polish crew.

The submarine never returned to England.

After disembarking in Scotland I returned home for a fortnight's leave with my parents. They were delighted and much relieved to see me as they had received only one of my letters from Malta. I was still a child to them and they were unable to comprehend what I had experienced as an operational pilot.

It was at that time that the writer A. R. L. Gardiner asked me to join the Reform Club. I had mentioned that my family

4 Malta, Medals and Meetings

knew Sir George Beharell who was then the Chairman of the Dunlop Rubber Company and who I thought would second me. While I was at Malta, the Club had accepted me. It was a grandiose building in the heart of London's clubland, with a lofty, domed foyer, wood-panelling with murals and portraiture that echoed with history, and a potent atmosphere of sheltering respectability; it was a refuge for gentlemen of the old school. Most members were older than I and drawn from the law, civil service, diplomatic service and politics. There were few officers from the services and I cut a conspicuous figure, being the only pilot in uniform. Waiting for my sponsor to show me round, I felt isolated. A dominant looking man in an old Etonian tie came up to me. Incidentally, I never saw him wearing any other kind of tie.

"I understand you are the first RAF pilot to join this club. Let me get you a drink. By the way, my name is Guy Burgess. I work for the BBC and I would like to have a chat with you about your Air Force experiences."

He appeared to know everyone in the club and within moments was introducing me round. It was the first of many meetings I had with Guy Burgess. He was one of a very few members of the club who always wanted to have a drink with me. Soon after I joined the Reform Club, Guy introduced me to Anthony Blunt, Keeper of the King's Pictures. His dark suits were always immaculate. He was supercilious and difficult to talk to. His effect on Burgess was extraordinary: on his own Guy was entertaining and amusing; as soon as Blunt joined us he seemed to lose his confidence and adopted a servile attitude towards the other man.

In the rarefied circles of the Reform Club, there were opportunities to mix with the key figures of the day. Once, in conversation with the Under-Secretary of War, Sir Archibald Sinclair, I mentioned that No 2 Group, with which I operated, was the only command that used bombers in daylight for specific tactical attacks. Though these were successful, our death rate was higher

4 Malta, Medals and Meetings

than any other branch of the RAF. Had we had better-armed aircraft, I said, we could have been much more effective. I warmed to my theme. The RAF was concentrating on using heavy bombers to destroy towns at night. Why on earth was it incapable of attacking tactical targets? Surely it would be better for Bomber Harris to persuade Churchill to concentrate on making our heavy bombers destroy the German war industry? Apart from anything else, it would reduce the loss of men in the Army. And I did not approve at all of the bombing of innocent civilians. Sir Archibald left me in no doubt that he agreed with my sentiments. It was Harris, however, who convinced Churchill.

5

The Business of War

Flight Flight Flight
*I marvel there are scenes
beyond my wildest dreams
can only reach the eye
of those who sweep the sky.
The dying sun sends forth one flame
to lick the wing tip of my plane,
while clouds with golden linings make
weird fantastic snow-capped shapes.
Despite the beauty up on high
I feel so lonely when I fly,
I miss the very touch of ground,
and hate the same incessant sound.*

With leave over, Mike, Buster and I returned to our old station in Norfolk. New buildings and unrecognised sentries had transformed West Raynham almost out of recognition.

"By Jove, Mike – old Paddy is still here."

Our Group Captain, Lord Bandon, returned my salute. A smile of greeting, even of surprise, spread over his face.

"Well, well, Leven. Damn glad to see you back. Jolly good show. You chaps have done magnificently. Come along and see me."

We walked behind him into the office and stood to attention, feeling a bit at a loss.

"Now, Leven, what are you going to do?"

"I really don't know, sir."

"I'll fix something for you. You all need a rest. How did you get on in Malta?"

'Not too badly, sir, but we lost most of our crews."

5 The Business of War

"Yes, I know. Damn hard luck. Still it's a jolly good show on your part. I'm very glad to see you back. A damn good show."

Some instinct told me that my friend Poons Parsons might have died, although I prayed that that was not the case. I asked the adjutant if he could tell me if any Blenheim aircraft had survived after I left Malta. Though the squadron that came out with me had all bought it, other crews had been sent there and I feared Poons might have flown with them. After looking through the files, the adjutant told me in a subdued voice that Poons had been shot down somewhere over the desert three weeks after I left Malta. It was a great shock. It was Poons who had inspired me during those tragic and hectic days. Unable to cry, I felt deeply bewildered that such a delightful person could be killed when so many 'wingless wonders' remained alive. I felt that Poons had an eternal spirit. He believed in living while life was his. Though I would never laugh with him again, his spirit has remained with me. I have never forgotten his unique understanding of men.

My next posting was to an operational training unit as an instructor. My job was to teach pilots both to bomb and to fly air gunners around the sky.

The first few months at the OTU (Officers Training Unit) were not pleasant. It was February and bitterly cold, with snow on the ground. I found that most other people had been doing nothing but instructing for a long time, whereas I had not recovered from the strain of recent operations. I felt overcome by a mental sickness that made me hate aircraft and everything connected with them. I was truculent, unwilling to fly, and generally made a nuisance of myself. Gradually, I improved in health and other interests absorbed my mind. My responsibilities changed to flying observers round the sky in an Anson. Day after day, whatever the weather, I flew one, in the same tracks across England. I got to know the route by heart. However, when I flew the pupil observers at night, it was so upsetting for me that I had to summon up all my willpower to get into the aircraft and take off. A

5 The Business of War

dreadful fear of getting lost obsessed me. I didn't like looking out into the darkness, sometimes seeing nothing but the shadowy outline of the clouds. Occasionally, during searchlight practice, silver cones would stretch out around me like huge tentacles seeking me out. The stars were of no comfort. Only the warm, friendly red lights of flashing beacons gave me the courage to carry on. As each light flashed, I saw the Morse letters, and the observer could locate us. I was never at rest till I could see the aerodrome lights twinkling below and feel my aircraft wheels safely on the runway.

It was 1942. For a short time, I had lived in a fool's paradise, imagining that the fighting was nearing its end. It was time to rejoin the war effort in an active way. I decided to return to American Mitchells. I felt they were the best medium bombers, so I approached the wing commander who was forming a Mitchell squadron. I had already written to ask Mike, stationed elsewhere, if he wanted to operate with me again. He had trained as an astro-navigational instructor. He wrote back saying he would be delighted to come along with me. A week later we were posted to the squadron, ready to start another turn of operations together. We had two new air gunners, Buster having embarked on operations with another pilot.

We learned to fly the new aircraft and practised formation flying at high and low altitudes day after day. It was then that the Eighth Army started its magnificent advance through Libya and Tunisia. I pictured our magnificent Army struggling on the desert route along vast tracts of desolate land, fighting forward into the Algerian mountains. As they advanced, we trained, waiting for the day to operate again. As news broke of the fall of Tripoli, I remembered the ack-ack that greeted us when we dropped our bombs at break of dawn. All too quickly operations day arrived. I wondered if I could face the sound of ack-ack bursting around me again and if my nerves would stand the strain of waiting about for a target to be chosen. It was almost with relief when I went to the briefing room to be told of my first raid in those new aircraft.

5 The Business of War

As I sat in that room, the old atmosphere flooded back. There beside me sat the aircrews in dirty old battledress. As before, some wore coloured scarves and picturesque shirts, while others had removed ties. Everyone was waiting for the wing commander to speak. I puffed away at a cigarette. I felt just as nervous as before, but hoped no one would sense my fear. After all, they were new to the job and would follow the example of old hands. But it was difficult to appear calm when one's veins tingled with that unpleasant feeling which the expectation of battle always arouses. A cheerful smile can hide a faltering heart. I listened to the description of the target: a high level attack on the docks at Vlissingen (Flushing) in the Netherlands. It seemed cut and dried, and that there would be a good fighter escort …

I drew forward slowly in the aircraft, then gathered speed to shoot ahead. I called up my crew.

"Are you OK, Mike?"

"Yes, quite OK, Dickie."

"Everything all right behind?"

My new air gunner responded cheerfully.

"All right then, chaps, I'm taking off."

As we were all flying in close formation over the sea, I had time to consider the future and a time when the War would be over. Who would want the services of someone like me, whose only job had been flying bombers? I laughed inwardly, somewhat mirthlessly, I might add. Probably I'd end up selling matches in Piccadilly. Many fighting men had ended up unemployed after the last war. I called up my observer.

"What time do we start to climb, Mike?"

"Another two minutes, Dickie."

"Thanks, old boy."

The wing commander pulled his aircraft up and we climbed higher and higher up into the blue sky. Visibility was clear. I saw the Dutch coast and enemy territory again. Fear had vanished. I

5 The Business of War

watched the coastline approach. We started to take violent evasive action, which made keeping in formation hard work. There seemed to be no ack-ack as I looked around at our fighter escort milling around. It was on the cards that Jerry snappers were trying to get at us ... Then it all happened: a burst of flak on my port side, yellow flame and the aircraft shuddering as metal hit us. I called up the crew.

"It's OK, chaps. We're flying all right."

We let go our bombs. Almost at once there was a fearsome sound. The whole aircraft shuddered violently. It seemed as if it was being wrenched apart. As I struggled with the controls there was a terrific screaming noise. I'd never heard anything like it. One glance at my instruments told me that the port engine oil pressure was dropping. The port engine instruments were crazy: the plane must have been hit. I closed the throttle. It was still screaming. My observer was beside me.

"Are we OK, Dickie?"

"Yes, quite OK."

But I knew there was only one thing to do – to stop the engine by feathering it. There was a deathly silence. Oh God, had I stopped the wrong engine? We seemed to be gliding through the air. I looked at my instruments. No, I was mistaken, the starboard engine was working perfectly. By now we had dropped behind the main formation. The Spitfire escort didn't seem to have noticed that we had fallen out. I called them up.

"Hello, fighters, one of my engines is U/S. Will some of you stay with me?"

In the nick of time! Four Focke-Wulf 190s came up behind us. The Spitfire boys tackled them. My observer gave me a course for the nearest aerodrome. I struggled on across those 200 miles of sea. I felt sure we could get back though the minutes passed slowly and I had hard work flying the aircraft. I was amazed it flew so well on one engine. Seeing the English coast again was a great relief, and it was even better to feel the wheels touch down

5 The Business of War

on English soil. Half an hour later a fitter handed me a piece of shrapnel he had pulled out of the engine. The main oil pipe was smashed in half. A few seconds later and it would have burst into flames.

That night I sat on the lawn outside the officers' mess. A glorious, hot summer's day was waning. Now the sun was sinking and, as we were having coffee, a pleasant light breeze fanned our faces. During dinner, I had met an old friend who used to produce plays at the BBC. We discussed the theatre, new books, future politics and broadcasting. I forgot about those tense moments of a few hours previously. The world seemed very real, very solid as I sat there. Bees were making their last round before flying back to the hive; red roses exuded a delicate scent; a faint babble of voices floated from the anteroom. It hardly seemed possible that only a little time ago I had felt that life might come to an end. As we talked until the sun faded and the air grew colder, it now seemed endless.

Back in Norfolk the days and weeks of summer 1943 slipped past almost unnoticed. There were rumours of invasion and sometimes we wondered if we would find ourselves in central Europe before Christmas. About once a week I flew out on an operation. These were all flying circuses, some targeted on marshalling yards, some on aerodromes, others on ports and a few on factories. There were times when the Germans didn't fire at us – unnerving occasions. I liked to see the ack-ack bursting near me so that I knew how to avoid it. In a clear sky with the enemy coast stretching below, I felt that at any moment some unpleasant missile would hurtle through the air.

6
Summer Visitis and Sorties

Summer
When I have gazed at summer's shining day,
and watched the still quiet clouds, all alone,
gliding smoothly, slowly on their way,
I have paused, and felt so deeply on my own,
back within these solitary arches
churning out a rhyme,
watching for a glimpse of sunshine,
wandering sadly on my own.
It seems I drift forgotten
in a world of sound
which heeds no inner voice
crying all around

My Brother
It seems so short a while ago
I saw him climb away,
and fling his Spitfire through the sky
as though he were at play.

It seems but only yesterday
we played as other boys
and raced across the park
or broke each other's toys.

Those days we spent together
in search for nests and eggs,
and tramped the country side
with small and aching legs.

6 Summer Visits and Sorties

*No longer will he tramp
on life's long road with me,
for his Spitfire plunged beneath
a tossing, heaving sea.*

*Yet I seem to see his eyes
smile the same soft way,
and know that he is watching
each departing day.*

One afternoon, while I waited at the aerodrome for something to happen, the control office sent a message that my brother had arrived to see me. Don and I had spent all our childhood together. At Bryanston he was a success – a fine athlete and a most conscientious student, staying up late working to pass exams. He went to London University to study for his BSc. When I was a sergeant pilot during the Blitz, I visited him one afternoon in the City. He was fire-watching and had been blown off two buildings while trying to rescue people. I think that my visit had greatly influenced his decision to become a pilot. He had trained in America while I was in Malta, and now here he was, a fully-fledged sergeant pilot, waiting to see me. I felt a great glow of satisfaction that Don was here, yet I had a feeling of dread as well. I knew what perils the sky holds for those who fly and I didn't want him to see the sights I knew too well, to witness men with all the cheery spirit of youth become old in three months. Because he was now a pilot, I didn't want him to know that I was worried or afraid.

Don was pleased to see me. His eyes smiled in a strange kindly way. I was rather brisk, rather formal – hardly like a brother greeting his greatest friend. Somehow I seemed unable to bridge the gulf that separated us. Now that he was going into action I was afraid to tell him what to do, so I said nothing.

That evening he flew away, disappointed. He thought I hadn't enjoyed seeing him, that I was a changed and a different person.

6 Summer Visits and Sorties

He might have thought I was annoyed or standing on our difference in rank, he being a sergeant and I an officer. I couldn't expect him to realise not just that I myself was struggling to carry on flying but that I felt a great inner dread that something might happen to him.

Two weeks later I went home on leave. My father opened the door. I looked at his face and felt cold within. I went into the dining room where my mother, who had obviously been crying, was trying to look normal. My father handed me a telegram. It read 'REGRET TO INFORM YOU YOUR SON CRASHED AND WAS REPORTED MISSING THIS AFTERNOON. LETTER FOLLOWING.' I read that telegram over and over. I knew that this meant Don was dead. My parents hoped that there might be some chance of his being alive. I don't think my voice wavered at all as I told them not to hold out much hope for him. I had to stay calm.

That night I fell on my bed and burst into tears. I couldn't absorb the fact that Don was really dead. It was unbelievable. I had seen so many other people killed and had taken the news philosophically. The meaning of war now hit me with redoubled force, the splitting up of families and the loss of comradeship of those one loves the best.

Next day, I went to London and dined at my club with a friend. To the outside world I was just the same, chatting and laughing. I had to do it, just as I had to return calmly the following day to go out on an operation. How could I comfort my parents for the irreparable loss of a son, and for wounds that time alone can heal? What words could possible suffice? I would say what I could for the best and otherwise be aware that my words, gestures and tone of voice affected those around me. Why make a bad situation for others worse by adding to their burden the weight that lay heavy on my own heart?

In this life, the present moment was constantly eclipsing those that went before. When briefed, and with no advance warning,

6 Summer Visits and Sorties

that our squadron was to pack up and move to an aerodrome in the south of England, I got on with it. We thought it was probably the signal that an invasion was imminent.

The sudden rush of operations was followed by a lull – so, no invasion before Christmas. A new wing of Mosquito aircraft was set to conduct low-level operations. My Blenheim operations experience qualified me for Mosquitoes. I wanted to volunteer. Then I went to an RAF group headquarters party, a party like most RAF parties with good food, a dance band and plenty to drink. In one room couples shuffled round to the hot strains of the station band. The majority of people were crowded around the bar. Junior officers, senior officers and air officers were toasting the health of friends. Group Major Fulham, our group flak expert, introduced me to a tall group captain, with clear blue eyes and a mass of fair hair sweeping back over his head. This was Group Captain Percy Charles Pickard, DSO, DFC, Polish DPC, an impressive array of medals. As commander of the new wing, he needed someone with my experience and took me on.

I flew the Mosquito three times before setting out on my first operation – to attack a rocket-bombsite in the Pas-de-Calais area. We were warned that if our attacks failed, the Hun would be able to throw sufficient explosive on London to wipe out the city in two days or even less. We were all aware of the crucial importance of hitting our targets. Orders to attack these targets had come from the Cabinet itself. It was not without apprehension that I struggled up a frail ladder into the Mosquito, a difficult aircraft to enter. With Mike settled beside me, parachutes pushed into seats, we were packed like sardines. Pickard was flying his 'F' (for Freddy) Mosquito, I was number three in a formation of five of the many Mosquitoes taking part in that first raid on rocket-bomb targets. We could all see each other as we hugged the ground up to the English coastline and then flew down on the sea. I had seen so many Blenheim pilots hit the water and was ter-

6 Summer Visits and Sorties

rified of flying as low as these crews. The propeller blades of the plane ahead were almost licking the waves; I could have sworn I saw the spray leap up and catch the tips. As the morning sun shone into our faces, it was, however, very difficult to see.

The cliffs of France came into view for a terrifying few seconds. It seemed ages before we reached them and then pulled over the top. I felt quite naked in the air and couldn't understand why the defenders didn't blow me out of the sky. But we cleared the cliffs and then raced across land. As before, I saw men running to their guns in various stages of undress. People working in the fields stopped to wave. Cows stampeded and birds flew past in droves. One hit my windscreen with a thud that upset me, though no damage was done to the bullet-proof windscreen. When the leader pulled up, we passed over a large wood, the landmark to start climbing. I glanced round. Surely we were sitting targets for light ack-ack? Again I felt quite naked in the air. We climbed slowly up to 3,000 feet. Time to start searching for the target. I saw Mike anxiously perusing his map and then looking down at the ground. At last he pointed.

"There it is."

"Where?"

"Straight ahead – ahead."

I surveyed the landscape. Woods, rivers and trees as far as the eye could see. I shrugged and yelled, "Can't see the darn target."

Then I saw the other planes open their bomb doors, acting as a drag on the air speed. One after another, the planes swooped down to bomb. It was my turn. I pushed on the stick and noticed the air speed needle whisk past 300 mph. The buildings were straight ahead of me. I pressed the bomb-release button and quickly pulled up to avoid the blast of the bursting bombs. A steep turn to port and this time I dived right down on to the deck. Aircraft were speeding away at low level while behind me the target was a cauldron of flames and smoke. Hugging the ground, I rushed after the leading aircraft and at last we reached

6 Summer Visits and Sorties

the cliffs. There was an anxious moment as I swerved over the top and did violent side turns out to sea. How comforting the waves seemed now as I sped across them. My first low-level raid in a Mosquito was over – a great relief.

Our targets in France were the sites of the V-1s and V-2s, the weapons now supposed to be going to pulverise London in 1944. Heavy bombers were thought unsuitable for the purposes of knocking them out so the decision was taken that the only way to destroy them was by expert low-level bombing of their bases. Since I had flown on more low-level operations than anyone else, I was given a job that entailed the use of my Mosquito squadron. The net result was that we put the French bases out of action, arguably saving London from destruction. The story of what we did has been often told; what we experienced in the process can be readily imagined. Even in the context of the time, it was accepted that this mission was out of the norm and congratulations were the order of the day.

With the permission of the Air Ministry, I accepted an invitation from the BBC to record my views of these missions. I was not allowed to state that it had been our squadron alone that had immobilised the V-1 flying bombs. Although I could give details of the method of attack, I was forbidden to describe the appearance of the targets. At three o'clock in the afternoon, and feeling a very important young officer, I strolled into 200 Oxford Street, the HQ of the BBC's Overseas Service. After meeting my contact, George Brighton of *Radio Newsreel*, we decided a simple description of one of the raids would be of most interest. The secretary typed the details as I was speaking. The script had to pass through various departments to be censored. The next day, when it was ready, we entered a studio equipped with a jug of water, a cup, and a microphone suspended in the middle of the table. I was too terrified to drink anything. The scene reminded me of His Majesty the King broadcasting at Christmas. My instructions were to speak when the green light showed. Suddenly it flickered.

6 Summer Visits and Sorties

As I read the script, I tried to imagine myself taking part in an operation. Somehow I got to the end of the ordeal and a few minutes later I heard my voice played back to me. I listened in amazement, appalled at the ghastly sounds – it seemed as if a stranger was speaking, booming from the loudspeaker. Unfortunately, the censor decided to cut part of the script and so I had to record again. However, the whole thing was well worth it because a few days later the BBC sent me a cheque that paid for a good dinner in town.

On the whole, our raids in northern France were simple – the worst part was the initial climb up over the coast. One morning I was detailed to get up at 5.30 a.m., an unpleasant hour and a time when I most enjoy my bed. I got up most unwillingly, startled to find Mike already dressed.

After breakfast we were rushed by bus to the crew briefing room to learn the target and time of take-off, on that day to be done in pairs. To see two aircraft take off together with the possibility that one will swerve into the other always scares me. At last it was my turn to take off. I pushed open the throttles and away we went, the Mosquito gathering speed and the needle soon creeping steadily up past the 270 mark. The early morning sun had just risen as we sped over the English coast. People in the coastal town must have cursed us as we woke them from sleep by nearly removing their chimneypots. But over the sea everything was peaceful. The silver waves glistened in the sunlight, although I hated the incessant glare. Instead of a topi, I wore my service cap on top of my helmet firmly clamping it down while trying to guess my height in inches above the waves.

At long last, the dreaded enemy coast came into view. The leading aircraft pulled up over the cliffs and at once there were tracer bullets streaming out from the gun placements on my side of the cliff – a most unpleasant sight. They seemed determined to concentrate on me. Flaming onions skipped past my port wing and too late I swerved to starboard. A ghastly dull thud resounded

6 Summer Visits and Sorties

over the plane, then more tracers. I could see the gunners in their pits. "Right," I thought. "I'll give you b—s a taste of your own medicine." I pointed the nose of my aircraft at them and pressed the gun triggers. Nothing happened. I felt a complete idiot. Then I saw that I had forgotten to put the gun safety switch to the 'on' position. A glance at my instruments told me that both engines seemed to be working. Mike guessed my thoughts and asked if everything was OK. I told him yes, but at the same time wondered where that unpleasant-sounding shell had hit us. Whatever the answer, we seemed to be flying all right and caught up with the rest of the formation, then started the difficult climb up to the usual 3,000 feet. The target appeared. I dived on it and turned away.

Suddenly another gun opened up as we were diving towards the ground. Looking at the line of tracer bullets I said over the microphone to Mike, "You know, I think there's just room for us to get beneath these damn tracers and avoid hitting the trees."

"For Christ's sake, get down, Dickie – get down!"

"All right, old boy." I skimmed over the trees and had the satisfaction of seeing the tracers sail harmlessly over my head. We were still heading towards the French coast.

"My dear old boy, that was quite amusing. We completely foxed them."

Wisely, Mike did not respond to my humour at such a time. Keeping level with the ground, I climbed up and then roared over the top of the steep hill ahead, then across flat fields and ... there was the coast. This time nobody fired at us. But my troubles were not over. When we reached the aerodrome, my wretched port undercarriage wheel would not come down to its full extent. I flew round in circles while the control people kept encouraging me to get the thing down.

I flew low over the control tower for them to have a look at it, and heard a voice say, "You have only one undercart down."

The shell had damaged my plane and left me with only one wheel. I tried to pull the undercart that had gone down back up

6 Summer Visits and Sorties

because I knew from previous experience that it would be easier to land on the belly of the aircraft rather than on one wheel. Unfortunately, the one that was down would not come up again so I had to try to land on only one. I feared that if I landed like that, the machine would overturn, so I brought the Mosquito in as slowly as possible. Instead of landing on the runway, I chose the open grass. To my amazement, it landed perfectly on the one wheel. It gradually stopped and as it did, the wing on the starboard side dropped down and we came to a gentle halt, almost as smoothly as if we had landed on two wheels. Percy Pickard drove out to take us back to the mess and told me that he had thought, like myself, that the plane would simply overturn; he was amazed that it had come to a virtual halt and then just flopped over on to the port wing.

A few months after this operation, I was awarded the DFC. The announcement in the *London Gazette* dated 15 February 1944 read as follows:

Leven, Henry Richard, Distinguished Flying Cross (115287)

Since being awarded the DFM Flight Lieutenant Leven has completed very many sorties, involving attacks on airfields, railway junctions, military installations and other targets in enemy and occupied territory. On a recent occasion, in an operation against targets in northern France, his aircraft was badly damaged when hit by anti-aircraft fire on crossing the enemy coast. Nevertheless Flight Lieutenant Leven led his section on the target, which was heavily attacked. He afterwards flew back to base where he effected a successful crash-landing. His effort was typical of the determination he has shown throughout his tour.

7
Targets and Training, Love and Leadership

The Crewroom
*All was calm
and my mind
at ease,
until there sounded
the call for
action.
A thousand fears
beset me.
Standing in the
crewroom
I saw again
the ghastly sights
of planes
crashing in
flames.
The last
agonised screams
of crews
blown to pieces
haunted my mind.
This might
have been
my end.
I felt the fear
of going out
into the unknown.
Peace
can never fade
the memory
of those moments
before I sat
within
my plane.*

7 Targets and Training, Love and Leadership

Mike and I were posted to High Ercall in Shropshire where I was to train crews on Mosquitoes. In my spare time, between demonstrating various forms of Mosquito bombing, I read Plato's *Republic* and Tolstoy's *War and Peace*. Soon I wanted another more active job. When Mike was promoted to flight lieutenant and I was made a squadron leader, I was called back by Air Vice Marshal Basil Embry, DSO triple bar (as he later was). Embry had an impressive war history. Twice captured by the Germans, he had escaped, killing two men en route with his own hands, and had watched the Hun goose-stepping through Paris. Now he commanded the only medium bomber group in the RAF. Our kit packed aboard my dilapidated old Ford, bits and pieces tied on with string, we made our way to an aerodrome in Norfolk. There my new job was to organise a flight for the final training of aircrews flying Mitchell and Boston squadrons. I was in charge of a strange collection of aircraft: nine Mitchells, six Bostons, eight Martinets, three Oxfords and three Hurricanes.

A frantic week ensued. I was flight commander of No 2 Group Support Unit. An office, a crew room and a navigational office had to be set up. Instructors arrived. I drew up a suitable scheme for training crews. Finally, our first intakes appeared. I sorted out who should be trained on which type of aircraft, with one instructor per two crews. At last the squadrons were manned.

Our Air Officer Commanding (AOC), Basil Embry, summoned officers to a conference at group HQ at a country house near Oxford. We were invited to sit, and the AOC handed round cigarettes; then he returned to his desk. Small and vibrant, his dark eyes shone with a piercing light, and he spoke decisively, his words uttered in military-style staccato. He was a man who commanded attention by his every gesture.

"What I want, gentlemen, is to know how many men can be trained by the group support unit at one sitting, and how long it will take you to turn them out as fully operational."

7 Targets and Training, Love and Leadership

The telephone rang. The AOC listened impatiently, then barked, "Impossible? Don't tell *me* a thing is impossible! Why, if I had accepted the word of everybody who told me a thing was impossible, I'd have done nothing in this war."

He banged down the telephone and glanced round the room.

"Well, gentlemen, can anyone give me an answer as to how many men can be trained and when they will be ready?"

I leapt to my feet. "Sir, my flight can train ten crews and have them fully operational in six weeks."

"Right, Dickie, that's a good offer."

The details were discussed, and as the conference broke up Air Marshal Sir Arthur Tedder strolled in for a confidential chat with the AOC.

I returned to the group support unit with some vague ideas as to how to train ten crews in six weeks: ten pilots to be converted on to Mitchells, ten observers trained in bombing procedure, twenty air gunners taught to use the guns – and all of those brought together, trained for battle. My difficulties were compounded when, as preparation was under way for an invasion of the Continent, the group support unit went under canvas. My tent served as bedroom and office. It was midsummer and it was too hot during the day, too cold at night, and too damp in a rainstorm. In the evening swarms of earwigs crawled up the side of the canvas, no doubt a perfect jumping-off point for my camp bed, to set about infesting blankets and clothes, and generally disturbing my peace of mind. I instituted an evening earwig hunt to kill them all on sight, no quarter given.

Five days before the course started, I fell off my motorcycle, breaking my shoulder. Was that RAF hospital comfortable! Everybody was charming to the young squadron leader, but not very anxious to allow him back to work. On the fifth day of enforced inactivity, I persuaded the doctors to let me go, with my arm in a sling. Living in a tent with a broken shoulder, with poor

7 Targets and Training, Love and Leadership

washing facilities, and shaving with one hand, was the least of my worries; there was a job to do.

It was not all work and no play. Some chaps on the course had a free afternoon and we went out to sea with an RAF air-sea rescue launch. That day, at long last, news came of our invasion of Europe. On board there was an atmosphere of high excitement. Even the gurgling waves seemed to share our delight, if not necessarily the call to battle that we all shared. Neither Mike nor I liked training jobs. We felt out of it and wanted a crack at the enemy back on the front line. An expeditionary force had landed in Normandy, the RAF had a foothold on the Continent: we were sitting on our backsides.

Our senior air staff officer was Air Commodore David Atcherley, DSO, DFC. His charm masked a brilliance evidenced in his planning of night fighter missions and it belied his reputation for dashing adventures. He turned up to see how the group support unit was functioning. I asked him if he could get Mike and me assigned to a squadron, adding that we felt a bit on the old side for such fast machines as Mosquitoes; we wanted another tour of Mitchells. And we wanted leave. All was arranged, with no fuss.

I was bound, albeit temporarily, for a different planet.

After the practicalities of my makeshift life in the Air Force, I was vouchsafed anew a taste of life at the top. Lord Beveridge invited Sir Archibald Sinclair and me to luncheon at the Reform Club. Did they want to see how things were viewed from the perspective of an airman? Whatever the reason, the infinitely civilised atmosphere of the oblong dining-room overlooking the garden, on the opposite side of the club to the thoroughfare of Pall Mall – with the waiters respectfully intoning "My Lord" when enquiring as to our choice of dish – soon worked its charm.

Conversation soon ascended to the upper reaches of politics and economics; the clouds in which I was to battle for dear life were far beneath us. Beveridge expounded. Social and welfare

7 Targets and Training, Love and Leadership

services should be government controlled but yet, at the same time, he was one to reject nationalisation. Full employment, he maintained, was essential; social services, now – they were the first concern of the Government. This, I took leave to consider, was an inherent contradiction. Training my sights on twin targets, each larger even than Lord Beveridge, I added that both of the parties failed to understand that society cannot provide full social services for all in a free capitalist society. I had quite a joust with this champion of the free economy.

Lingering over the customary glass of port afterwards in the leather armchairs upstairs, Sinclair, who as before seemed disposed to think I was on to something, confided that I was the only person he had ever heard besting Beveridge in an argument. Even now, dare I say it, and despite the acceptance of the Beveridge Plan two years later, I believe that my arguments have been vindicated. My views on the importance of taking port at the Reform Club, however, have changed – as will be evident later in this tale. Certain principles come first.

Shortly afterwards, I was introduced to an enchantress. Patricia Hicks was a young actress playing the lead in the West End success *Arsenic and Old Lace*. Her first husband had been a pilot, killed in 1940. We were attracted to each other from the word go. She was the loveliest girl I had ever met. Her lustrous dark hair, her smoky brown eyes, and her baby face all filled me with a sense of the exquisite. She was sheer delight, made flesh. We shared a love of dancing. So it was off to the Savoy Hotel and a dance to Carol Gibbons, or to Kempinski's in Swallow Street, where George on the piano would make the very ivories dance, or to Edmundo Ros and his band at the Lansdowne Club; Pat and I danced the nights away as if there were no tomorrows.

But the War, always that War, came between us. Twice she suggested that we marry. Love was so precious but life itself so precarious. And then always the questions, always the considerations ... What if I died and left her isolated again? Could she sur-

7 Targets and Training, Love and Leadership

vive a second such shock? She might think so, she might implore, but I had then to think for the two of us. Even thinking about the possibilities of a life together seemed to cut across a snatched caress of romance. Every passing moment counted for so much. The whole future seemed unimportant in the balance, not a thing to be counted on, to be committed for. Her love, her fairie being, if fancy may be allowed free rein, were things of gossamer – no, not gossamer, they were too tangible; it was the passing moment itself that was feather-light – hardly of a piece with the weight of reality. Our lives did not seem to mix.

One of Pat's friends introduced me to the playwright Rodney Ackland, who was living in the Albany, that famous and highly prestigious block of flats near Piccadilly. He had written brilliant plays, including his best-known, *The Old Ladies*. Rodney, who had strong homosexual tendencies, wore immaculate suits and was a stimulating conversationalist. He insisted that I read his hand. I told him that in ten years' time he would marry the daughter of a playwright. He laughed out loud and insisted that I had to be wrong because he never had, or would have, an affair with any woman. Years later when I left the RAF and was directing a play of his called *A Multitude of Sins* at the King's Theatre, Glasgow, he married Mabs Lonsdale, the daughter of the famous playwright Freddie Lonsdale.

Terence Rattigan and J. B. Priestley, whom I met during the War, also had flats in the Albany. One evening, during a heavy bombing raid, I volunteered to fire-watch with J. B. Priestley. His nose was out of joint because his housekeeper could not get back to her home and so he felt obliged to put her up in his flat. He offered her only a chair in the hall. I felt it both arrogant and selfish of him not to have given her a bed, especially as he had no other guests at the time. Extraordinary that a playwright whose work featured so many socialist themes should behave like an insensitive and autocratic businessman. A gentleman would not have adopted so snobbish an attitude as this rich socialist; a

7 Targets and Training, Love and Leadership

gentleman would certainly have given his poor housekeeper a suitable bed. Were all socialist writers such hypocrites? Did they enjoy raking in the money while preaching social concepts and living in a more elevated style than the aristocrats they pretended to ridicule?

My adjutant at the group support unit telephoned to say that the posting notice had arrived. I was to go to No 98 Squadron as flight commander of A Flight. The news, already anticipated, gave me a feeling of elation coupled with a chill realisation that I should once again have to leave friends. It meant returning to activity and to the carefree atmosphere of operational aircrews who know that the order to fly may come at any moment. I feared that I would never be able to escape this atmosphere and at the same time yearned for it. It was a fear of fate holding surprises up its sleeve; perhaps also a death-wish. I have never been afraid of dying, but the thought of a sudden discontinuation of a life that I had enjoyed filled me with apprehension. These thoughts haunted me for only a moment, and then I cast them aside. This was the course I had decided on. Life or death remained in the hands of whatever powers control man's destiny.

At the end of our leave on 25 August on a drizzling day, Mike and I arrived back at our Mitchell aerodrome in Dunsfold in the south of England. No one was interested in our arrival or seemed to have any idea of where we should sleep. Eventually, an airman who knew the whereabouts of 98 Squadron directed us. I forced my old Ford up the steep hill and down a muddy, tree-lined path. One dismal, dripping tent out of a sorry line of tents was empty – it was cold and damp with neither lighting nor a stove. I threw my baggage in and unpacked my camp bed, which I then made up with all my six blankets carefully tucked in. I found Mike still struggling in his tent and told him I felt much too miserable to stay around. We agreed both that it was ghastly still having to live in a tent, let alone one even worse than the

7 Targets and Training, Love and Leadership

group support unit's, and that the only thing to do was to drive over to the mess for a drink. It turned out that the officers' mess was ill-lit and had only beer and whisky on offer. Apart from a couple of officers mooching disconsolately around, it was dead – not at all the atmosphere to be expected in the company of operational crews. In the end we drove to a pub the better to reflect on this return. It was difficult to settle down in the new squadron. But by emptying some of the wooden huts – one occupied by armourers and two others by old bicycles – I at least organised the office, the crewroom and other rooms.

Picking up the information available on our arrival, it emerged that I was flying Number Two position to Calais, the target where small pockets of resistance needed bombing. We, the only RAF bombers, were to do the job – just knock out a few Germans who were foolish enough to carry on fighting. Calais, however, had always been a tough nut to crack, with a whole lot of guns, and I wondered about there being hardly any opposition. But it was useless to worry about what sort of evasive action I should take because this time I was not leading but simply following someone whose skill I would have to trust.

Everyone crowded into a tent on the airfield for a briefing. I stood on the outside making a few notes on starting up, taxiing and take-off times and the order of aircraft. Blue Leader was the name of the leader of my box. Each box was identified by its colour, which was useful when transmitting information. The briefing was as much a part of the operation as the actual flying, and probably the most apprehensive time for all aircrews. At that moment it was driven home that at any given time we might have to take to the air, fly over enemy territory and invite all the attention the Hun had to dish out. It was not pleasant to listen in the briefing tent with so many vivid memories of past action to remind me of what to expect.

At the squadron HQ I issued everyone with rations and waited for the observers to come back with all their navigational

7 Targets and Training, Love and Leadership

gen. It was a miserable wet day with an overcast sky. When they returned I saw Mike struggle out with his navigational bag and equipment.

"Everything OK?" I asked him in a matter-of-fact tone.

"Yes – should be quite an easy trip," he replied in the same sort of voice.

We understood each other so well by now that we didn't have to say anything. We were used to each other's habits and knew each other's fears.

There were two new flight sergeants whom I liked and who seemed to know their gunnery. They smiled at me and said, "OK Skipper," when told to climb aboard. I dragged myself into the aircraft. My doll, Annabella, attractive as ever in my eyes although slightly faded from long service, hung in her usual place, bobbing away as, once again, I found myself behind two engines throbbing with barely contained power.

The Mitchells rolled off their dispersals and formed a long line heading towards the runway. Already aircraft from other squadrons were taking off and the air was alive with engines. Then it was my turn. Down the runway and we were in the air. I opened my throttles wide to catch up with the leading aircraft. Cloud was down to 500 feet when the aircraft suddenly pulled up and disappeared. I was flying above a thick grey blanket of cloud and wisps of it were making it difficult to see. I pulled up. It was grey all round and impossible to see anything – even my wings were invisible. I gazed hard at the instruments. The artificial horizon which records the movements of the wings started to topple over and my gyro-driven compass started to spin in the opposite direction. I pushed the stick to port. The elevators became more central but the compass was still whirling round in a terrifyingly mad circle: the aircraft was out of control.

Mike called up, "What course are you steering?"

It was all I could do to fly the aircraft, let alone steer the thing, so I muttered, "Just a minute and I'll tell you."

7 Targets and Training, Love and Leadership

I pushed harder on my stick. Surely that wretched compass would stop turning. I glanced at the air speed indicator. To my horror, the needle had fallen back below 150 mph. We were apparently climbing at an alarming rate: 6,000 feet and still in cloud. I wondered how on earth I would ever find my leader. Speed was dropping. It would be terrible to get into a spin and have to right an aircraft inside a cloud. I pulled the throttles wide open. Golden rays of sun penetrated the thick grey above. As blue sky appeared, I pulled back. The wings were visible, though one was right down and we were only just above the cloud. Thank God for that. I breathed again.

All around, aircraft were bobbing in and out of the thick white mass below. Flying along the cloud tops gave a frightening feeling of speed and brought to mind the awful thought that to hit that white sparkling surface would mean a certain crash. Mitchells were circling all around in a vain attempt to find their leader and the air was full of people calling up. I picked out one clear voice.

"Hello, Yellow formation, Yellow leader calling. I am angels eight [at 8,000 feet] and firing red red [double Red Star cartridges]."

There was no sign of any red cartridges being fired.

"This is Blue Six, calling Blue Leader. Where are you?"

There were 42 Mitchells milling around trying to find their correct positions. I told my crew to keep their eyes peeled for anything looking like Red Leader.

Then, as if by magic, the various aircraft started to collect in groups and circle round in twos and threes. Red Leader called up, "Hello, Red formation, Red Leader firing green green now."

The aircraft ahead fired two green cartridges.

"Thank God! Found the formation at last," I yelled triumphantly to my crew.

Within a few minutes everyone had found his position in a box. It seemed a miracle that the crews had managed to fall back in formation.

7 Targets and Training, Love and Leadership

As we set off across the sea for Calais and reached France, the clouds started to break up. Between the gaps I could see grey patches of water. At 11,000 feet we turned into attack. I thought: 'This is terrible. Any moment now flak will appear and our damn fool of a leader is making no alterations in height!' The nearer the target, the more anxious I became. We were still at 11,000 feet when the leading box started bombing. Our turn next.

"Bomb doors open ... Bombs gone!"

I saw the 'pills' fall from the leading aircraft before my observer spoke the welcome words. When we were out to sea and away, I chuckled to myself. Calais was bombed and not a shot fired. Once again formidable cloud barriers threatened us. Our leader dived steeply – much too steeply, I thought. I had to keep squeezing my nose and blowing hard to clear my ears. Down we went, 8,000, 7,000, 5,000, 4,000, 3,000 – and at 2,000 feet the cloud barrier still faced us. At 800 feet above the water we were just under the clouds with the waves dangerously close. I had a sneaking feeling it would be difficult getting back to base.

The cloud was even lower over the English coast. The box split up. The weather was treacherous with rain sweeping down and a sort of fog and drizzle lowering the cloud right to the ground. All the other aircraft had dispersed out of sight, doubtless trying to find an aerodrome as best they could. The hills of southern England seemed to have attracted even more low cloud. Hugging the ground as I climbed a hill, the top of which was in cloud, my vision was completely obscured by rain. I had a nasty feeling we were about to crash – a sudden unpleasant end. With a violent turn to starboard I opened up my throttles and pulled the stick back. As we soared into the clouds I watched the altitude needle flick up 2,000 feet. We were not scattered in little pieces on some Surrey hill!

After half an hour's flying around I managed to get a homing [a course to steer] to an emergency strip. This was an especially large runway built to accept aircraft caught out by sudden bad

Targets and Training, Love and Leadership

weather. Although we were descending rapidly, once again I had to fly through cloud and I suffered again that awful fear of crashing into land before we were clear of it. However, all was well and at 700 feet I could just see the fields beneath. Five minutes later and there was the landing strip. It appeared almost as wide as it was long and the numerous lights enabled me to make an easy landing. I then waited for the weather to clear before returning to base. The operation had been easy – that was true – but the weather had caused me so much mental strain that I felt exhausted.

8

Off to the Continent

Meanwhile the British and American armies were sweeping forward. Paris and Brussels were liberated. Our daily missions varied between attacking mere pockets of resistance to bombing important targets such as those in support of the men of Arnhem. I flew there twice and was amazed to see the ground beneath seething with parachutes. Once again I was faced with the ordeal of flying through heavy flak barrage and then completing the long journey back over Belgium, France and the North Sea. To continue attacking such targets it was clearly vital to have a base on the Continent, so it was hardly a surprise to hear that we were going to an aerodrome near Brussels. Here was a chance to see the Continent again. Furthermore, I should be one of the first to see a liberated people and to discover the realities of the German occupation. The idea delighted us, and later it was confirmed that we would be the first medium bombers to land on the Continent.

During a few days' leave I broke the news to my parents as gently as I could. With my brother's death and my time in Malta always in mind, I knew that they worried about me. I was able to reassure them that now operations would be far easier. Even if the aircraft was shot, there was far more chance of landing on Allied territory than before. There would be no question of struggling for miles over the sea knowing that one engine was out of action and the other liable to pack up at any moment.

We eventually received orders to fly to Belgium. On a bright September morning I clambered aboard my Mitchell and tied Annabella firmly in her place. When the two air gunners and Mike were also in position I started up the engines. It was a difficult trip. The clouds swept low over the sea and I had difficulty

8 Off to the Continent

in keeping the formation together. Over France we had to dodge rainstorms, but as we approached Belgium the weather cleared. Mike echoed my thoughts when he said how strange it seemed to be flying over France at that height without being shot at. It was only two weeks ago that the last Hun had fled and I was subconsciously prepared for signs of opposition, half expecting the flak to open up. But the villages beneath us were peaceful; the clouds of war seemed to have been completely swept aside and there at last lay Brussels. From the air it looked a delightful town, large though compact, as if its arms had opened to welcome us. With some excitement I called up my formation and told them to keep in tight as we flew low over the city. The RAF bombers were going in to their first continental base.

When we landed at Melsbach a dispatch rider waved me to follow him round the perimeter track to my parking-place. On both sides we saw awful evidence of our very accurate bombing. This was an aerodrome of death. It looked as if nothing living could have survived. All the buildings had been hit. The hangars were a mass of crumpled steel. Smashed German aircraft were everywhere. Apart from the perimeter track, the whole field was pitted with bomb craters that the RAF aerodrome construction unit had worked hard to fill in. This was the most complete proof of the effectiveness of Allied bombing. In one way it was satisfying, but it was also appalling to see the comprehensive damage that bombs could inflict.

The officers' mess was in the only building not completely destroyed. A convent about three miles away housed the NCOs and airmen. It took three days to establish ourselves, boarding up rooms without doors or windows and removing German debris: gas masks and pictures of ruffians such as Hitler and Himmler. On the third day we started operations to support the Army, then struggling in Holland. This was easy with good weather and little flak opposition – but still, as we returned we felt that we had begun to justify our expedition to the Continent.

8 Off to the Continent

On my first evening in Brussels I wandered into a café where a three-piece band was playing. The old waiter who brought me a drink beamed at me, "You are English Air Force? Very good Air Force."

I smiled, gave him a good tip and we were both happy. Later, a singer sang a haunting waltz – *Fascination*, I think it was. I closed my eyes, feeling the appeal of it wash over me. The notes lingering in my mind, I asked the waiter to invite over the singer for a drink with me. She was about forty years old, with a rabbit-fur coat that had suffered several years' wear draped over her shoulders above the dark blue close-fitting dress that she had brightened up with cheap jewellery. She was full of fun. I told her how her waltz had uplifted me and asked if there was something about the way she sang the top notes that suggested it held memories for her too.

"You are right," she replied. "My husband and I have starved and have had to live a very hard life under the Germans. We refused to play or sing for their troops so we couldn't get any engagements. Many a day I had to dig for potatoes in the fields. My husband was shot through the chest. Now we are working again and that waltz brings back memories of better days."

I was surprised to hear that the artists who had performed for the Germans were not doing so for the Allies. She was disappointed that we were not giving more encouragement to those who had opposed the Germans. Soon she had to hurry away to sing at another café. I stayed at my table and watched people drinking and enjoying themselves.

A girl with a basket of flowers in her hand was wandering from table to table. As nobody seemed to want any, I bought a bunch and gave it to a little girl who was helping customers with their coats. A few minutes later, the waiter told me that I could take her to a room upstairs. He seemed surprised that I didn't want to take up his offer and had only bought the flowers out of pity.

Returning to the aerodrome, I asked a man at the crowded tram stop where to change for Melsbach. Replying in English, he

8 Off to the Continent

insisted on accompanying me, although it was obviously out of his way and would result in his having to walk back home in the rain. He typified the genuine welcome that the Belgians gave us.

After a time I gave up café night life, where it seemed less and less likely that I should meet anyone of interest, and decided instead to visit the RAF club, then based in a house lent by Baron Lombard and organised by Lady Cunningham. I walked up the red-carpeted stairs, through delightfully furnished rooms with a band at the far end of a ballroom glittering with chandeliers. Lady Cunningham introduced me to some charming girls and at once I began to receive invitations to dinner.

It was in that social whirl that I met Quentin Hogg, later Lord Hailsham, who upset me by refusing to meet Belgian friends who wanted to form a united Europe. He said that England was going to tie itself to the US dollar, so there was no need for a united Europe. Not to put too fine a point on it, I found him quite brusque and was to remember this years later when we met on the terrace of the House of Commons.

Amidst the spacious luxury of the club, I took tea with a girl called Annique. In excellent English – I didn't dare speak my imperfect French – she recounted thrilling stories of the underground movement against the Germans. When I asked her what she thought we should do with the Germans when Germany was finally defeated, her reply was unhesitating.

"Be hard and ruthless and treat them as criminals. They have caused us so much misery that they must never be allowed to live decent lives again."

I wondered if that was the best thing. She smiled with a touch of sarcasm and, shrugging her shoulders, said, "If you had lived under the Germans, you would think the same."

"Is that a Christian way of thinking?" I asked, with memories of Salem and old friends still cradled affectionately at the back of my mind.

She was silent for a moment.

8 Off to the Continent

"You cannot treat Germans as human beings."

Though I had often heard this sort of thing said, I thought that years of oppression and of cruelty had affected her judgement and that her opinion might change over time. In the evening, we dined together at the club where the atmosphere was intoxicating and I was happy to forget that the seeds of peace had to be sown after the wine of victory had been quaffed.

As time passed I made friends in Belgium, among them Count François de Castelanne. He was a cheerful and sympathetic companion and had an extensive knowledge of good wines and good food. François represented the height of European culture. He was polite to everyone and always listened to what was being said, no matter how absurd the topic. He was more liberal in his approach to the problem of Germany than most people. After telling me that his brother was in a concentration camp, he remarked "You must remember that there are both good and bad Germans. It was such a pity that some of the old families could not retain power after the last war. During the occupation there were officers who did their best to help us, and openly admitted that they disliked the regime."

Another acquaintance who proved to be a good friend was Viscount Werner de Spoelberg, a charming and amusing aristocrat who believed that he lived the life of a 'Grand Seigneur'. He gave me an open invitation to his chateau at Wespelaar and spoiled me by giving me many luxuries. We did not discuss the problem of Europe because I felt that he would only be diplomatic and noncommittal – but then again, I doubt if he would have been sufficiently interested in considering the problem. A Grand Seigneur understands how to live his own life. The problem of Germany was solved for him the moment Belgium was liberated.

One of the pastimes I most enjoyed was touring the art galleries searching for artists able to express the spirit of liberated Europe. During one of these sojourns I was fortunate enough to find and buy two paintings, one of which moved me greatly. My favourite was the first I discovered, *Cork Trees Near Paris* by Eric

8 Off to the Continent

Wansart, son of Adolphe Wansart, the famous French sculptor. Behind the twisted forms and weird shapes with ground obscured in deep shadow, a few rays of light gleamed through the branches. It was a message of faith and hope. Mankind had been tortured and blinded by the terrifying arm of the invader, but through the confusion and the misery, light shone as if it to penetrate that screen of despair and to brighten up the whole world. For the few pounds spent, I felt that I had acquired a priceless gem.

As a result of my purchase and our talk, Wansart invited me to his large studio, and there I admired his watercolours. His pleasure in life, he told me, came from working only at what interested him. Nothing gave him greater delight than painting from inspiration and working on it all day. During the occupation he had not exhibited and had got by, ignored by the Germans, who did not appreciate his work – or, I felt, understand the subtle message behind it. The moral of the tale to me was that there was one simple remedy for Europe: man must be taught to feel beauty and live for the search for truth; only then would ugliness, poverty, misery and war cease.

My second purchase was also emotionally stirring: a painting of a church in Brussels as seen from a side street. This was a simple yet evocative canvas with the only patch of light in the picture, otherwise painted in dark shades, being on the church steps. A focal point of hope in what appears a dark and oppressive scene. It was painted in 1941 when the artist must have felt that his world was closing in on him and his country. These feelings I could relate to very closely, following hours of cramped cockpit conditions, and it was the reason for my purchase.

Overjoyed as everyone was to see the back of the Germans, the Government came in for widespread criticism. There was discontent and distrust of the leaders. Prices rose while people died of starvation. Food was scarce, bread hard to obtain, butter virtually non-existent. The black market flourished open-

8 Off to the Continent

ly. Women came round the cafés selling small pieces of bread at 40 francs each at a time when a tram driver was only paid 45 francs a day. The miners were on strike and industry at a standstill. It was an alarming political situation, fraught with danger.

The climate conspired to accentuate the gloom. Winter was harsh, with frost, rain and overcast skies. Yet we seized every opportunity to fly. I well recall those terrible climbs through clouds with ice gathering on the wings while the aircraft became increasingly sluggish. It felt as though it was falling from the sky. We would struggle on, hoping to chance across a clear patch, praying that the ice wouldn't thicken.

On one raid, clouds forced me up to 16,000 feet. My heater wasn't working and as we were putting on oxygen masks my breath started to form small particles of ice. Lack of oxygen made me feel weak. If I fainted, I wouldn't be able to go on with the flight. Just when my spirits were at their lowest, the flak started. Those customary black puffs appeared, but this time we saw the eruptions of yellow flame as the shells burst all around. I pulled up and up.

With miraculous precision, the gunners followed us while again and again the sharp retort of bursting shells resounded through the plane. As always those minutes seemed endless. Then there was the difficult journey back with the added problem of finding large enough gaps in the clouds to bring down a whole formation. As the evening grew darker, we found our base. We had to contend with bad visibility as well as numerous other aircraft milling around, but we did land eventually – and my goodness, we were very glad to struggle into that large three-ton lorry that ferried us back.

The Army wanted the Mitchells to blow up the bridges at Venlo, on the German-Dutch border, Roermond on the River Maas (east of Düsseldorf and inside the Dutch border) and Denmer, north of Brussels. This we undertook and completely smashed the bridges – no mean feat from 12,000 feet. Such were the bare facts as given to the press and the BBC. I led one of the

8 Off to the Continent

boxes of six aircraft chosen to attack Venlo Bridge, a target of considerable tactical importance in that it was a key German supply line carrying the main rail link from The Hague in Holland through to Düsseldorf and Mönchen-Gladbach in Germany. I had to taxi all round the aerodrome to reach the runway in use. The Junkers 88 intact on the field were evidence of the recent German occupation of the airfield. Behind me lay the familiar sight of a long line of Mitchells, purring with power and anxious to be off.

With my eye on the end of the runway, I opened up the throttle and the aircraft rose into the air. The other aircraft of my formation rapidly caught up and took up their stations. It was satisfactory to see Numbers Two and Three flying in close on either side. The pilots grinned back at me. I wondered whether they still felt afraid, or if keeping in formation took their minds off the difficulties ahead. Beneath us Brussels lay quiet, disinterested, as though the War had already ended while we, poor fools, were still fighting.

We set course over the aerodrome at 10,000 feet. In the bitter cold, my heater refused to work and a continual draught of frozen air crept down my back. My fingers hurt and stiffened from the cold. I had to keep banging them against my side. Inside my flying boots, my feet were numb. What an idiot I was to go on flying! I thought of the people below in their snug offices who would never have any idea what it was like up here in the intense raw cold where the whole time you felt that fighters would suddenly swoop down on you. If there were no snappers, then there was bound to be flak. No experienced pilot ever underestimated the enemy who always did his uttermost to prevent us from hitting our target. I climbed higher and higher leaving layers of cloud beneath. Ahead were patches of cumulus cloud that had to be avoided.

"Are we over enemy territory yet?" I called up to Mike.

"Coming up."

"Should I take evasive action?"

"Yes, you might as well start now."

8 Off to the Continent

Six boxes of aircraft, each box acting as one, flew ahead of me. It was as if their leader controlled the other five aircraft. I watched them weaving over the sky, climbing and diving. It was hard work keeping my box out of their slipstream. Then, without warning, the boxes ahead were smothered with flak and surrounded by black balls of smoke.

Though so far unaffected, I didn't enjoy seeing what was likely to come my way in a minute or two. I was now heading for sky filled with drifting smoke. Bursts had shot up in a barrage that filled about 2,000 feet. Instinctively, I turned away to port and tried to circle that ominous web. The guns were obviously waiting for me to enter that part of the sky and then they would give me the works. I was just turning back, having avoided those guns, when a battery opened up on my starboard side.

"Turn 20 degrees starboard," Mike said.

"That's where all the flak is!" I yelled.

"If you don't turn, I can't get a sight on the target," he shouted back.

I turned to starboard and pulled up 1,000 feet. Those gunners were crack marksmen and the stuff came all round us.

"Steady! Steady!" Mike warned.

I kept glimpsing flashes of exploding shells flying through balls of soot. The other pilots must have been straining every nerve to keep in formation, but at last Mike announced, "Bombs gone!" I needed no better tonic. With my wing tip dipped over to port, down I went 2,000 feet in a steep dive. The chaps behind were still in good formation. Then I pulled up again, 500 feet, 1,500 feet higher. The flak, deadly accurate, started again. I was shaken to find the sky ahead filled with it, the black puffs of smoke a formidable barrier to fly back through. But I had to run the gauntlet and so turned to port and dived down, the flak still chasing me. Then, turning to starboard, I pulled up several thousand feet. The guns opened up again. The minutes passed so slowly that I thought we would never be out of range. The whole area seemed

8 Off to the Continent

to be saturated with guns. Down I dived again. The stuff still burst near me. Again I pulled up, up into the sky above when ugly bursts of flak made me go down again, faster than before.

It was unbelievable: there was no flak and we were left alone. Surely it was a mistake and the guns would be aligned on us again any second.

"Have we crossed the line?" I asked Mike.

"Yes, we should be clear now."

"Thank God for that!"

I breathed again. The Germans had put up a formidable barrage to try to stop us bombing the bridge at Venlo. They had been guarding this crossing to keep the supply lines open.

After tackling several similar targets, I felt exhausted and badly in need of a rest. Despite the excitement of successfully completed missions, the stress of survival was taking its toll on both my crew and myself. A charming Belgian family I had met invited me to spend the week with them, and so I packed my bags and, with a week's rations, set off in a borrowed car to stay with them. Their hospitality was overwhelming. They produced the best wine to accompany the meals and each morning I lay in bed until eleven o'clock, then spent the day playing the piano and revising some of my poems. Mike was also enjoying his leave staying with another family who looked after him just as royally.

During those few relaxing days, I gained an insight into what life had been like in this country under German domination. The tortures perpetrated by the Gestapo were well known. Among many gruesome tales was one that concerned a cousin of the family I stayed with. He had been placed with a small pump in a hole into which water flowed. The poor fellow had to pump to keep out the water. The Germans starved him so he eventually became too weak to pump and drowned.

Generally, it seemed that the population had been reasonably well fed under the Germans and the country quite well administered. But it was now obvious that the food situation had deteri-

8 Off to the Continent

orated. Although the country had been liberated, real starvation had set in, hence the flourishing black market. Rations were insufficient. People would pay any price for food. Those unable to pay simply starved. There was control over neither prices nor food distribution, a combustible state of affairs that saw the unpopularity of the Government increase daily.

As if all this was not enough, news came through on the radio of a surprise attack by the Germans, and a major one at that, penetrating 30 miles into Belgium. They were back in the Ardennes. My good hostess wept tears of grief, such was her terror that Nazis would again lord it on the streets of Brussels, letting the Gestapo loose to slaughter everyone. Scared strangers would buttonhole me to ask the latest. One needed but eyes or ears to understand just how the Germans were hated.

It was not, however, all bad news ...

A reporter from the *Sunday Pictorial*, Rex North, having discovered that there were more daylight operations notched up to my name than that of any other pilot, sought me out for an interview when I was on leave. The result was a full-page spread about my exploits and those of Mike Nolan, the sensationalised headline giving rise to the pious hope that perhaps the Hun at last would realise what he had coming at him! Then again, I am not entirely sure that British news was daily reading material in Hitler's bunker – no doubt one more mistake chalked up to Adolf's record.

Sunday Pictorial, 10 December 1944

THEY'VE JUGGLED WITH DEATH EIGHTY TIMES

It's Today's Greatest Air Partnership
says Rex North

They were leaning on the bar at the Thoughwood in Torquay. Dickie was a veteran. He had been in the RAF a whole week and his hat was beginning to look as if it belonged to him. Dickie had called in for his last drink as a civilian.

8 Off to the Continent

"Have another beer," said Dickie to Mike at a frontline aerodrome yesterday – "Remember the first one we had together five years ago?"

And the greatest surviving partnership of the air – they have flown on eighty missions together – clinked glasses, and said, "Here's to us," just as they had done on that first, nervously boisterous evening five years ago.

I talked to these two men who by the laws of chance should be dead, looked through the diary that Squadron Leader Dickie Leven has kept, and intends to publish one day, of the flights they have made.

Eighty of them: think of it. Eighty times they have juggled with death together.

Eighty times they have been scared – very scared – and are big enough to admit it.

And they are more scared now than when they started. Of course, if you strip operational flying of its thrills and glamour, you will realise that this must be so.

They feel they are too young to die. Dickie, an old man in experience, is twenty-three. Flight-Lieutenant Mike Nolan is thirty. They want to get married and settle down.

Yet they are determined to complete a hundred operations together.

It seems so long ago now, but they remember that first night when Dickie, the kid who had not so long before been playing saxophone in a dance band and selling odd bits and pieces in a department store, had been awake most of the night listening to the rain dripping off the roof.

8 Off to the Continent

He was afraid. Like all flyers at one time or another he had a persistent and horrible intuition that he would not return from the following day's raid.

The target was the German seaplane base on the island of Sylt – but let us see what Leven's diary has to say on the matter.

> We saw the island and raced for it. The squadron leader's plane left ahead of us. I roared after him. They gave us the works. Tracer bullets flew past. Heavy ack-ack explored among us. I watched the leading plane. The bomb doors opened and the eggs fell out.
>
> "Bomb, Mike, bomb!" I said.
>
> The Jerries gave us hell. The machine on the far starboard side blew up into little pieces. It was there one minute, gone the next… We had to go over the island again. A sickening thud. The machine was hurled out of my hands.
>
> My starboard wing collapsed right over. It would not come up. The controls had locked. The waves were about to strike us. I closed the port engine and gave the other full throttle. The wing just cleared the water.
>
> "Help me fly her, Mike! Help me fly her," I remember saying.
>
> He looked at me with alarm and stroked my wrist. He thought I was wounded. Mike stood up and pushed on the wheel as I tugged her over. The kite flew with one wing dipped. We staggered into a cloud before the fighters got us.

You see what I mean. Flying is not just a question of roaring into the clouds, dropping bombs, and landing back at drome to say, "Wizard prang, old man. Absolute piece of cake." No, there

8 Off to the Continent

are hopes, fears, and dreads. And to go on doing it eighty times and live.

Gibraltar, Malta, Tripoli, so it went on. Two men, always together, shooting up troops and shipping, and being shot up themselves.

Then it happened. They both knew that one day it was bound to.

They attacked a convoy off Benghazi. A destroyer, an armed merchantman, four fighters and a bomber gave them a rough time. Mike cried out, and fell back clutching his face. Yes, it had happened – one of them was hurt at last.

The machine was out of control, hurtling towards the water. By a miracle Dickie righted it, but in his diary you will find this note:

> I have faced death before, but those few minutes were like hell. Death laughed at me as I saw our graves in the water ahead. Only a miracle saved us.

They said to Dickie that evening, "What are you going to do – fly with another observer now that Mike is hurt?" and he answered, "I feel as if I never want to fly again."

With the CO he went to the hospital to see Mike. His face was swollen and bruised from a splinter, his fingers were bandaged, and there was shrapnel in his leg.

I got told that there was a rather awkward silence, as there always is when visitors arrive at a hospital bedside. Mike broke it with a nervous cough, and said to the CO, "I don't feel I can carry on, sir."

So Dickie had a rest while Mike got better. One thing was certain; at least he would not fly with anyone else. They went back to England, travelling part of the way in a submarine, and it was while on board that they heard they had been commissioned. They were sergeants no more.

8 Off to the Continent

"What are you going to do?" they were asked back in England. "What about the new American Mitchells?"

It started all over again. The briefing room, with its carefree laughs that hide suspense and, let us be frank, fear, the thrill of a new plane, the relief at finding yourself alive after another raid.

From Mitchells to Mosquitoes. The diary of this great air partnership was still being written.

Again let us turn the pages in admiration:

> Suddenly another gun opened up. I looked at the line of tracer bullets and said to Mike, "You know, I think there is just enough room for us to get underneath these damn tracers and avoid hitting the trees. For heaven's sake get down."

In the front line they are still flying today. Flying towards the hundredth operation, and toasting themselves with a glass of beer after every one. What, I wonder, would have happened to them if they had not met over a glass of beer in Torquay?

And all the time they fly think of the day when Dickie Leven will go home to Hall Place Gardens, St Albans ("What's it like at the Red Lion these days?"), and Mike Nolan to Sandy Cove, Dublin.

But whatever they do, whether or not their ambition to work together in peace as they have done in war is successful, they will leave something behind.

And that something is one of the greatest partnerships and feats of mental and physical strength and endurance the skies have ever known.

9

The Horror of War

After what had been, on balance, a delightful leave, I made my way back to Melsbach aerodrome. The urgency of the task ahead for us all was plain to see. The fog lying over the whole arena of battle lifted. In the early hours we went up to bomb the enemy's lines of communication and his supply dumps. Day and night it went on – even on Christmas Day the squadron was out.

We bombers may not have seen bombs explode on the ground from close to, but that is not to say that the human dimension of what was happening was far from our thoughts. One day, some of the boys ran into a packet of flak. I rushed out to an aircraft that had overshot the runway and landed on one engine. As that crew was unhurt, I hared off to another aircraft that had crash-landed. One look in the observer's cockpit and I felt sick. The observer was lying slumped over his bombsight. Flak had hit him in the back. His grey face showed straight away that he was dead; it had been his first operation. Poor fellow, he looked so young, so completely innocent of the world – a boy so far removed from the causes of war. How it would grieve his parents to know that death had come so suddenly. The rest of the crew, horror-struck, just stared at their dead friend. I quickly set them to work to remove equipment from the plane to help take their minds off that pale, lifeless face. They were soon whisked away to the briefing room and to the companionship of other friends.

How can anyone glorify war when it means the senseless slaughter of innocent people? Going to the aerodrome in France, I passed through Mons. It was badly smashed about. Homes lay in ruins; streets were littered with debris, and with old German tanks pushed on one side. One hardly dared look closely at all the signs of misery – young children with old faces and legs like

9 The Horror of War

matchsticks begging for food, and the men with hollow, drawn faces. These people were not being killed directly by bullets but were dying of starvation. War was killing them just as surely as if their fate had been sealed by the clash of arms. My whole being revolted at this utter outrage to our common humanity; victory or defeat, the population had to bear the suffering. Much as we might want to shut our eyes to this misery, the stark truth, undeniable and dire, was there for any witness to see.

My next posting was to Eindhoven in Holland. We were to move forward with the army, bringing in supplies by air. It was to be the last time I would fly against an enemy. My spirit had been sapped of its vitality and I felt like a small child who has wandered far from home. Six months' worth of such bright lights as Brussels had to show exerted their pull; also, continual fighting in the air had weakened my willpower. I did not look forward to commanding my new unit, keen as I was to see with my own eyes what was happening on the ground.

Eindhoven was not seen by my own eyes to advantage, thanks partly to the bone-shaking, open jeep in which I made my initial tour – whatever possessed the Americans of all people to design so uncomfortable a vehicle? – and at the mercy of driving snow. It was a drab industrial town, surrounded by flat, dull countryside that seemed to have affected the spirits and certainly the designs of the architects who had constructed it. It was built for workers of the Phillips Radio factory. People now were starving, ill-clothed and nursed a loathing of all things German. At the door of the Hun was laid the ruination of the country and, over and above that, many individuals had been personally humiliated. I was surprised that the inhabitants did not gaze at me with hatred. Their eyes were dull and lifeless. The victims of mass bombing seemed to be completely apathetic. They had nearly all become 'bomb crazy'.

There was much talk of unspeakable crimes inflicted by the occupying power.

9 The Horror of War

A young Dutch officer told me quite casually: "When I set foot in Germany I shall have no hesitation in robbing and killing as many men, women, and children as I please."

"You will run the risk of being shot as a murderer."

"Then I shall not let myself be discovered."

It seemed as natural for him to plan how to vent his hatred as it was for him to drink whisky. It was useless to argue. The poison of hatred had blinded him.

91 Staging Post, which I commanded, was a mobile unit that worked from tents on the airfield during the day, at night being transported to town billets. As the Army planned the move forward into the German heartland, my job changed from that of bomber pilot to an overseer for supplies reaching the Army. In addition I was responsible in my designated area for the transit of air passengers. The officers' mess, sergeants' mess and the hotel for air passengers were sited in different parts of Eindhoven, so it was as well that my stay there was short.

Before leaving Eindhoven I received a signal instructing me to report to my Group HQ in London. My main memory of that fleeting visit home was a dinner at the Renaissance club in Kensington with my friend, the playwright Rodney Ackland, who was then working on his adaptation of *Crime and Punishment*. My experiences on the Continent sounded only too fantastic when recounted in a London that had remained comparatively sane. The walls were covered in paintings by local artists, the candles on the tables glowed softly and the pianist's melodies were dreamy; the effect combined to bring home to me how only those who had seen the feverish gaiety of Brussels, the sadness of Paris and the misery in the Ruhr, could truly understand liberated Europe. Rodney wanted to know about the life of artists during the War. What to tell him, beyond the fact that Picasso and Matisse had spent their war years painting more incredible pictures? In theatres the same productions that had been a success under the German occupation might be playing, but orchestras were not performing

9 The Horror of War

works by new composers, poetry too often lacked any depth of feeling. Europe seemed to have stagnated. Now it had been given the chance to live again – but would it take it?

I think I made Rodney depressed. I always found him sensitive to other people's problems. He had the soul of a true artist and distress always saddened him. He told me that he considered that love, in its true sense, could provide the only solution for Europe. It took us all of thirty minutes to solve the world's problems. Men were too materialist and now must understand their relationship with God. Man's self-made world would collapse again unless this was recognised. It was interesting in the light of Rodney's subsequent fame as a dramatist to hear how he felt about what he was doing. In his later years he was wont to say that he cared not so much for posterity – what he wanted was fortune and recognition during his lifetime.

"I feel I have been an escapist. I ran away from the War and have done nothing to aid this great fight for freedom."

"Nonsense. You have been writing. That is worth more than all the bullets and bombs we have delivered. Any fool can destroy, but there are few people who can prop up our crumbling civilisation. That is your job. Teach the world more of truth and our fight will not have been in vain."

"I still feel I have been an escapist. The most I can do is to promise to write what I feel is the truth. You cannot persuade me I have not been an escapist. So many of us have been, you know."

"Most of us who were fighters were also escapists. We have not got the guts to continue our fight when the battle is all over. We shall merely return to our negative existence, and dream of the days when we were heroes. If you are an escapist today, we shall be escapists tomorrow."

Rodney smiled. Perhaps he agreed, but probably he thought I was being maudlin or melodramatic.

I flew back to Eindhoven the next morning. It took me half an hour to make my plans for the unit's move. I summoned all

9 The Horror of War

my officers and gave them instructions. We would have to send an advance party to erect the tents and attend to any transport aircraft that might arrive. Thirty lorries could travel with the advance party. We would need ninety for the main party. The transport loading of all stores and equipment was to be handled by the MT (Military Transport) officer. The rations and field cookers were to be organised by the catering officer. The adjutant would prepare a list of the personnel of both parties. The senior traffic officer was to be in charge of the advance party. The signals officer would go with him to establish communications, and the intelligence officer must prepare for our security.

I gained my best results in the RAF by simply telling my officers what had to be done. It was up to them and the senior NCOs to see that the details were sorted out and that everything went according to plan. This policy proved to be so successful that I could not help but think that the Government should realise what a wonderful gift for improvisation an Englishman displays when left to himself. The Government should not attempt to carry out the minutiae of its own plans. They should merely concern themselves with telling the country what is the true position, and suggest what needs to be done. Then, if they were sensible, they could sit back and do no more work. The job would be done, and the Englishman would be happy because he had not been watched over, and harangued about every minor detail. It seemed to me that after the war the Conservative Party would collapse because it had no plan for the future; the Labour Party would gain power but then collapse because it needed an army of civil servants to carry out its plans. The Liberals were the only people who might be able to govern England with a plan, but had insufficient numbers of officials to enforce it.

Perhaps I was wasting my time thinking such thoughts. If men wanted to be enslaved, they would be enslaved. If there were a desire for freedom, freedom would remain. Politicians at that time were behaving like film stars who appealed to the gutter for

9 The Horror of War

applause. It was folly to believe that any political system would help the world until such time as men accepted a true and untarnished philosophy and understood more of the art of living.

The Army swept forward and I had orders to move the unit to the Rhine aerodrome in the Ruhr district.

I inspected the new aerodrome in a two-seater Auster passenger plane. Flying over Germany at low speed, a few hundred feet above ground level, the effects of war could be seen at first hand. It was what would become a familiar sight – the total destruction of a whole town. Over Goch, on the Rhine, not a single house was undamaged. In the sunlight, brick rubble, bare walls, bomb craters filled with water – all could be picked out with cruel clarity. There was no visible sign of life; it seemed hardly possible that human beings could exist amid such devastation. It was all too obvious that men, women and children had been killed by the thousand in the crushing of the Ruhr to a pulp.

One could hardly play the victor gloating over the vanquished at such a moment. I knew then that I would have to retire from the RAF. The idealism with which I had begun my military career had undergone a reorientation. I looked forward to the day when I could disassociate myself from an armed force that could not be relied on to protect civilisation. It had been brought home to me that only the force of ideas and the spirit of goodwill among men could armour man against armies.

At the Rhine aerodrome, with the Army in occupation of the town, the overall picture was filled out. The fighter wing had only just moved in. All the aerodrome buildings were smashed. The men were in tents beside their machines where a casualty evacuation unit was being established. It was strange to find attractive young girls helping out, so close to the front line. The gaily-coloured scarves that they wore over RAF battledress were good on the eyes, reminding me of the home I increasingly longed to see. But on the other side of the field were old German men and

9 The Horror of War

women, taken there in lorries. Neither fed nor paid for their work, they looked utterly apathetic, their eyes lacklustre. As I drove into town in a borrowed jeep, the road was potted with holes and larger craters, and on both sides were the remains of houses, all destroyed.

Fighting was taking place a few miles beyond the town. There was widespread looting, out of sight of Germans, and without doubt by some of our troops. Thinking such thoughts, I wandered about a ransacked large house that had escaped excessive damage, aside from smashed doors and windows and gaping holes. In one room, women's clothing lay strewn all over the floor, and pictures there were slashed by bayonets – which argued for an invading hand at work – and books torn up. In a girl's room, love letters lay on a bed in a scattered heap. Everything of value had gone. I glimpsed two soldiers carrying a vacuum cleaner and an umbrella. As they passed, a ragged little boy, possibly one of the many orphans, hands clasped behind his back, defiantly whistled the song *Lili Marlene*. Suddenly he spat at the soldiers and ran away. Stopping at the street corner, he began whistling the song again. One could not help but admire his spirit.

When I returned to the aerodrome I asked a senior officer what was being done about the looting. He laughed and said, "I'm telling my men to take all the cars and equipment they can find. The Hun is getting what he deserves."

I was horrified by what I saw: whole units were returning from the 'front line', gold watches strapped on their arms, rings on their fingers. Perhaps we behaved like all victorious armies, but it was hard to believe that high-ranking officers apparently put no stop to this conduct.

Thousands of displaced persons had crowded into the Rhine aerodrome from labour camps, concentration camps and POW camps, wretched men, women and children, with drawn and haggard faces, sometimes standing for hours in the pouring rain, clinging to packages containing their worldly possessions.

9 The Horror of War

With two marquees, there was just no room to house thousands, so army movement control officers helped me send over 2,000 a day to Brussels.

As the Army moved forward, roads were congested with wandering Dutch people, as well as Germans, drifting from town to town. Houses were looted at random, women raped and men stabbed or shot. No one could expect mercy. Only the cunning and the strong would survive, it seemed; the sick and the weak were left to die by the roadside.

These millions now on the move would be expected to maintain our civilisation in the years ahead!

A few days after I arrived at Rhine aerodrome, the Germans had been pushed back to the aerodrome of Celle. Although fighting continued on the fringe of the aerodrome, I was asked to fly over and assess it for the possibilities of operating my unit from there.

I set off in an Auster aircraft towards Celle. Just as I was thinking about the peace, and Germany's future, I detected an unpleasant note in the engine. I had always flown in a twin-engined aircraft; if one engine failed the other could usually be relied on to keep the aircraft in the air. From the discordant, throbbing jerk of this single-engine aircraft, it was clear that in a few short moments the engine would seize up. The oil pressure was rapidly rising. Something was very wrong. Beneath me were woods that might hide SS troops who would no doubt be delighted to shoot me out of hand.

My engine gave a final bang and stopped completely. A small field was in view so I put the stick down, performed one gliding turn, then floated above some trees. A ploughed field rushed underneath my plane. I feared the aircraft might overturn on landing. I held it off the ground for as long as I could and then stalled it tail first onto the ground. In about ten yards, the plane stopped with no damage done. Naturally, I was greatly relieved. Pistol firmly grasped in my hand, I jumped out. Some children

9 The Horror of War

came running across the field towards me. When they reached me, they stood there gawping. Speaking in German, I asked if they knew where I could contact the nearest English troops. A little boy of about eight answered proudly in German.

"The English are in the village. They had a wonderful battle on this field." He pointed. "The English artillery are there. The Germans were no good – no good. The English were good."

It did not sound as if he was simply giving a due credit for the best martial score. He had no fear of me, or at least showed none, and he seemed glad that the Wehrmacht had lost.

A man appeared at the far end of the field. The boy clutched me, obviously frightened.

"That Russki is a bad man. He comes at night and beats us. Then he takes Mummy and makes her scream."

The man was a Russian ex-POW. He – and no doubt many others like him – were roving the countryside seeking vengeance for ill-treatment meted out by the Germans. He came right up, thickset and sullen, eyed me, and more specifically my pistol, then scowled and stomped off. I told the children that it would now be all right and asked them where I could contact the nearest English officer. The boy volunteered to run to the village so as to alert the English about me. They all scampered off. After a nail-biting half hour, a jeep drove up, the occupants being three British soldiers and a captain, the latter making amused observations for my benefit on the subject of crashed planes out of the line of enemy fire. He kindly gave me a lift back to Celle and also undertook to have the vagrant rounded up for despatch to a transit camp. Leaving a soldier to guard the aeroplane, we rattled our way past cottages outside which stood little children, on whose minds the effect of war could be gauged by their holding hands above their heads as if expecting that we would shoot at them. It was hard to conclude that anything else than a plague on both our houses, Allied and German, was the wish of the impressionable young.

9 The Horror of War

I arrived at the airfield late in the evening. The battle seemed to be taking place north of the town, about three miles from the airfield. There was a good deal of gunfire and the woods were covered with a pall of smoke. I wandered over the aerodrome buildings. They had escaped serious damage. Furniture and personal belongings had been left in every room. The Hun had fled in haste. At the end of one building there was a foul stench. A woman had obviously occupied rooms in this block; her scent, powder and make-up were still on the dressing table. I pushed open a door. The floor was wet with red liquid. Then I looked at the bed. A young girl had been bayoneted. She was lying there, her blood dripping on the floor. I rushed over to her but she was dead. Her body was not yet cold. I felt sick and revolted.

I remembered a Major explaining to me: "When the troops go into battle, they get the blood lust. Nothing will stop them. They plunge ahead and shoot anything in their path. That's the medicine to give the Hun."

What right had I to be revolted? I, who had dropped hundreds of bombs on targets that might, or must, have killed women and children in an even more gruesome way. Perhaps I was responsible for causing untold pain and misery to innocent people. I tried to comfort myself with the thought that my bombs had not been deliberately aimed at civilians. If they had missed the target, it was because of enemy action or the hand of fate. My observer had always done his best to hit a military objective. My reasoning did not comfort me. The soldier who had bayoneted this woman must have been blind with fear, and thought a Hun was going to shoot him. He too would attempt to clear his conscience with the excuse that in order to remain alive it was his first duty to act first and think afterwards. And that was the kindest explanation. I knew at that moment with certainty that I hated militarists and those who attempted to glorify war. It gave me no comfort at that point to remember that my own decorations had been awarded because I was determined to

9 The Horror of War

commit deeds that might have terrifying consequences. It was to the sick and distressed that medals should be given in an ideal world. No, the world of tomorrow, a new world order, must be built on a foundation of love and compassion; surely everyone must see that it was in the best interests of all?

But of horror, there are degrees. This I was shortly to discover.

At Celle, it seemed that the populace did not share the same intensity of hatred as in so many places that I saw. The town was largely undamaged, the people shielded from the worst of direct experience of war. Before I made what was going to be, for myself and many others, one of the most chilling discoveries about man's inhumanity to man, I found out something about my own intrepidity.

Captain Aldershaw was typical of British army officers who had served in Poona, in India. He was a thoroughly cheerful soul. He was a small man with a thick moustache, red cheeks, small twinkling eyes, and bandy legs. His large cap came well down over his forehead making only his moustache and red cheeks visible but which gave him an aggressive appearance. All his other features disappeared into the shadow cast by his peak. He was an old cavalry officer of the previous war and walked about in riding breeches as if he had spent his life on horseback. He needed only tabs to come across as the very pattern of a general. Aldershaw suggested to me that we ought to go riding.

"With luck we shall find the stables which house the German state stud. Of course you don't mind riding blood stallions?"

I was scared stiff, having only the guts to say so!

"Leave it to me. I can pick a quiet horse for you. We should have some fun."

"My dear Captain, surely you do not really intend to make me ride a blood stallion!"

He laughed.

"Leave it to me. I know my horses. These German geegees are as quiet and well-mannered as you will ever want to find 'em!"

9 The Horror of War

Once we found the courtyard where they were stabled, I had a good look at the first ten out of the forty or so horses that were in the care of stable boys. My heart sank to the soles of my boots. I was at pains to mask this from the Germans. The Captain beamed at me and arranged for a grey to be saddled for me. This one would give me a very good ride, so I was assured. I was glad to hear this expert advice because the animal was energetically resisting all efforts to make him so much as stand still. With great determination, I slung myself in the saddle and immediately my worst fears were realised. I can well recall the Captain calling out: "Speak to him and he will be as quiet as a lamb!"

That horse was not going to be bothered with merely walking. When the first car passed, the wretched animal whipped round in a circle and snorted to show its marked disapproval. Then he bolted. Tugs on the rein were of no avail. It was only a matter of time after one of my feet had slipped from the stirrup that I slid off his back. Someone fired a rifle and the grey then stopped … for a moment. By the time I picked myself up, that horse had gone.

When I returned to the stable, the Germans were most apologetic about the behaviour of that beast. I suspected that they were not being wholly sincere. Only later I discovered that the Captain himself had been thrown from this very horse, which was reserved for enthusiastic Englishmen! I do not believe that it was the German horse that was determined to make fools of my fellow countrymen.

10
Belsen

Madness
*War seems to be
some strange,
incomprehensible
clash of powers.
Man fighting man
with fierce endeavour,
and no greater desire
than to throw down arms,
and rush headlong
back to his home
where, in complacency,
he retires and watches
the same great powers
striving to bring about
a final disaster.
Can it be that man
is the image of madness,
and Christianity become
the religion of
despair?*

"You've no idea; you just can't imagine what a frightful place it is."

"What *are* you talking about, Tony?" I asked.

Tony Bartley, my second in command, a squadron leader, ace fighter pilot, with film star looks, who sported a spotted silk scarf, suede shoes and corduroy trousers, was going to marry a real film star, Deborah Kerr. Tony, I, and a couple of the others, were

10 Belsen

having tea and a chat when he made an exclamation not in keeping with such an off-duty moment of relaxation.

"My dear fellow, d'you mean to say you haven't heard about Belsen? The most frightful place I've ever seen. I had no idea anything could be like it. It was just too awful. The Doc drugged himself and still couldn't sleep. If I told you what I saw, you wouldn't believe me."

This was the verbal picture that Tony Bartley painted of Belsen.

Captain Aldershaw and I, and two officer friends, decided that we had to see this hell for ourselves.

I suggested that we wear rubber boots; it sounded as if we might have to walk over dead bodies.

We set out in a captured enemy car. Through the forest, huge pine trees cast shadows on tramping, weary, displaced people as we motored along the road to Belsen, past old women dragging carts piled with bits and bobs, past ragged members of the Wehrmacht, past a stumbling, bent, old man with shoes in pieces. Increasingly inured to the misery about us, we went on through neat villages with clean cottages and past red brick farm buildings dotting the countryside, and then again through forest. It was early May and the sun shone in a clear blue sky, bringing everything in the countryside to life. I drove slowly to admire the scene.

A large red sign proclaimed: DANGER, TYPHUS.

Aldershaw folded up his map. "We're arriving at the camp. Trust the Army to get you there."

We laughed, needing till the last moment to hang on to our cheery mood. We fell silent. We were approaching a concentration camp, behind a tall hedge in a clearing in the forest. It was surrounded by barbed wire and made up of squalid, grey huts. We found the main entrance that led to the solid red brick buildings where the staff lived.

We parked by the HQ building. A squad of slovenly, thickset, hard-faced men marched by, two of them carrying whips. They

10 Belsen

were Hungarian guards coming off duty. They were the same guards who had been there before but, because of a shortage of troops, we were unable to replace them. The corporal in charge saluted, an insolent apology of a salute. The sense of irony that those men must have been feeling!

The atmosphere of the camp was dreadful. A captain officiously refused us permission to tour it, impervious to the explanation that our AOC requested us to see the place so we could describe the conditions to our men. Absolutely forbidden, he said, to visit the concentration camp area. So we drove to another gate in the enclosure. As we approached, a priest emerged from a wooden hut and took pity on us, as if one could use those words in such a context.

"Come along and get dusted", he said, as he took us inside.

He made a bit of a charade of it what with pouring powder down our trousers, inside our shirts and on our hair, to prevent our catching any of the skin diseases prevalent in the camp – but even Captain Aldershaw was in no frame of mind for his customary joshing.

The priest then admitted, "I'm sorry, I can't make it. I've been round once today and simply can't face going round again."

A young captain offered to act as guide, suggesting we go in his car as the smell was so appalling.

There was no road, only a muddy track filled with water. We were glad of our rubber boots. We drove past rows of grey broken-down army-type huts. Men and women in tattered clothes wandered around. Dead bodies were propped up outside huts and a heap of them lay in front of every hut. On both sides of the track dead bodies lay shrivelled and twisted.

The captain remarked, "Things are getting better now. At least they've begun to bring out their dead."

We drove on. Six men were struggling to carry a sheet containing four loaves of bread. Men and women were dressed in filthy black-and-white-striped trousers and coats, which looked

10 Belsen

like pyjamas save that the white had turned to grey and the cloth seemed to be a mass of insects. The captain asked if we would like to see the women's enclosure. He pointed to some tall pine trees, the ground beyond which was ash grey. Emaciated children played there on a heap of dead bodies. All the camp inmates had sunken cheekbones, pale yellow complexions and staring eyes – the eyes of the dead. We saw women pulling up their skirts and squatting like animals between the trees, and in their drawn haggard faces there was no detectable hint of feminine charm. Yet these people were alive and human.

We drove on, then stopped and got out. That awful stench of decaying human bodies! It was a sickly, dry, penetrating, almost suffocating smell. A large pit was filled with thousands of twisted, mangled bodies. A cart, filled with more bodies, was waiting to be emptied into the pit. SS guards had to do this work but were now locked up after having worked all day.

The captain told me that five days previously when the camp had been liberated, there had been 60,000 people alive and 20,000 dead and that they were dying at the rate of about 500 a day.

He said we should look inside one of the huts. When I peered through the door, I saw a dead man lying on a wooden rack next to a second man. This man blinked, and I realised that he was alive. He was clutching a dead body. I saw where he had torn the skin away from it and had tried to eat part of his companion. As we left the hut, a man tottered to the door then fell. I went to pick him up. It was useless. He was a dead man. When we drove to the main entrance, amongst all the horror, a young couple were fornicating.

Some people seemed to be more human in appearance; they were apparently the latest admissions to the camp.

A French intelligence officer was interrogating one of the SS guards and our Captain suggested that we go and see how it was done. In a small room, a thin little Frenchman sat on a table. We

10 Belsen

filed in behind. A tall, black-haired man stood rigidly to attention, his face to the wall, flanked by two British officers armed with Sten guns.

Seated at the far end of the room were a haggard, young, French girl and a man. The French officer announced that he was about to start his questioning. He shouted at the SS man to turn around and face him. The SS guard obeyed, clicking his heels with strict military movements. He looked ordinary and was wearing an open-necked shirt, black SS trousers and jackboots. Wavy hair hung over his forehead and he stared straight ahead. The Frenchman dangled his legs under the table and stared at the man. Suddenly he shouted with such force that I almost jumped. He wanted to know how many people had died every day in the camp. The guard replied that it was about 200. This was because the Germans had been unable to find enough food to give them. After many such questions were shouted at him, all of which he answered in a firm voice, he was ordered to face the wall again.

The Frenchman then told us softly "That man spoke nothing but lies. This time he will begin to speak the truth. I know how many people died here and why."

Once again the SS guard was ordered to 'about turn' and face his interrogator. Again the Frenchman shouted his question and the guard repeated his reply. No sooner had he stopped speaking than the Frenchman slid off the table, ran towards the man and dealt him a terrible blow in the face. I was thunderstruck. It was so unexpected and delivered with such force. The room was charged with electricity. The guard still stood at attention but reeled slightly at the blow. The Frenchman jumped back on the table and questioned him again. The answer was not satisfactory. This time he gave the guard two punches in the right eye. He still stood rigidly to attention even though blood was starting to roll down his cheek. The Frenchman raised his voice to a shrieking pitch and the guard received blow after blow in the face even before he had time to reply. A few minutes later his lip began to

10 Belsen

quiver and his voice to falter. Then he admitted that he had been sent to Belsen to investigate the possibility of building more gas chambers because inmates were not dying quickly enough of starvation. The French girl and the man then gave evidence that the guard had enjoyed bleeding prisoners every day to see how weak they would get before dying. As this evidence was being given, the Frenchman punched the guard again and again in the face.

It was a horrible scene to witness. The guard had committed the vilest atrocities, but I disliked seeing his face being beaten to pulp. Although it was the usual way to conduct such interrogations, it was sickening to see how the War had enabled us to behave like savages.

None of us spoke much as I drove away from Belsen at great speed. We had seen the living dead, a sight that no one who has not witnessed it can understand. We had been shocked to see how human life could mean so little. Thousands of people were reduced to the level of beasts of the field; thousands more had been ruthlessly massacred. Some 60,000 people crowded into a space about half the size of an aerodrome! The trees that lined the road were no longer beautiful. I imagined dead bodies propped up against every trunk.

Dusk was gathering but Captain Aldershaw was confident that in a few minutes we would be back at Celle. I was not so optimistic. Aldershaw assured us that we couldn't have taken a wrong turning. "Trust the army if you want to get anywhere." Just then, a large sign – DANGER, ROAD UP – prompted him to admit that we might be indeed on the wrong road. Not just that, but that we did not have petrol enough to get back, even going by Belsen. Not that we wanted to do that!

As we were debating what to do, some boys came out of the woods. Belsen had made us nervous. Our hands were on our revolvers. They seemed friendly and, hearing of our predicament, led us for what must have been miles out of their way, and through desolate, swampy land. What an evil, spirit-ridden place

10 Belsen

it felt in that darkness. So nervous were we that throughout our guns were at the ready. In the end we were very grateful to those German boys for taking us to the right main road.

That night I drank far too much whisky and went to bed with my head reeling. Whenever I closed my eyes, I kept remembering the sight of wretched men and women walking about on dead bodies. I slept fitfully and couldn't rid myself of the nightmare scenes and the nauseating smell that seemed to fill my nostrils.

11

Peace

The Soldiers
Now that the battle's over
And the troops have sailed away,
Only sorrow lingers
In hearts which once were gay.

When we who then were heroes
Have faded from all sight,
Our names will be forgotten,
And hopes killed overnight.

The signal brought by the cipher clerk told us that the end of hostilities was to take place officially at 09.00 hours the next morning.

I felt nothing. Statesmen had signed a document, but that did not mean that Europe was at peace. The War had been over for weeks but its evils remained. The armies had stopped fighting, but the disease of war still infected the world.

However, we had to celebrate. Most of the fighter boys at Johnnie Johnson's bash in the officers' mess put on a good show of being very merry although I do wonder if any of us felt particularly cheerful. While we were glad the War was over, we realised that the exciting days of real comradeship were over too. For me personally, peacetime had rather sour beginnings – an augury, perhaps, of what was to come.

Johnnie announced that because the peace agreement would not be signed officially until midday he intended to take his squadron off and shoot up anything he felt worth attacking. I begged him not to. He took no notice and was as good, or as

11 Peace

appalling, as his word. A highly decorated pilot he may have been, but in Brussels he had greatly upset me by persuading my girl friend to leave me for him. I nursed my hurt in private. At Count Werner de Spoelberg's chateau at Wespelaar, he had begun shooting swans on the lake. I stopped him, and he did apologise on that occasion.

Late that night, fires were started all round the aerodrome. It was with difficulty that we prevented the airmen from burning the place down. Usually quite harmless beings, they had apparently gone mad with some form of fire-lust and were now dancing round the flames like wild animals, hurling into the fire anything that would burn.

Next morning, the atmosphere was totally different. Winston Churchill gave a broadcast saying how our great struggle had succeeded. Tears came to my eyes. I thought of the last six years, when comrades had become friends and my very real grief as, one by one, they had died. Young friends were now old in spirit. The battle had been won but we had lost our youth. The fruits of victory surely would be harvested only if we prayed to God to reveal the meaning of justice and enable men to understand what freedom involved.

Orders came through to quit Celle for a base at Lüneburg.

I was de facto in charge of the camp, a position that was about to afford me some glimpses of a world beyond the Air Force.

The whole time I commanded my unit, I never did any work. When a body of men are told what to do, they do it willingly. Technicians and experts see to details. What the leader is expected to do is to give the general directions. I discussed my correspondence with the Adjutant and left it to him to send off the letters. My other officers looked after their own sections.

Every morning I walked round my various buildings and chatted with the men. Occasionally I suggested that the cars were not clean enough, or that the tea for passengers was cold. I never attempted to interfere with any of the sections. I became

11 Peace

convinced that a Cabinet Minister who boasts of working fourteen hours a day must be a fool. It is a waste of time for a man in a responsible position. He should employ men to do routine work and deal only with important problems. Once a decision has been made, the staff must carry it out. I should like to believe that members of the present government belong to respectable clubs and drink port after lunch. They might fall asleep in the afternoon and, on waking up, discover that the world had been working quite happily. All plans today are out of date before they are legalised.

Major Randall of the Intelligence Corps called on me. In civvy street he had been a high-flying Scotland Yard detective; now he was on the trail of prominent Nazis. Casually, he tossed out the information that Heinrich Himmler had been caught that very morning. He observed that Himmler appeared insignificant – harmless, even. It has since become almost a truism that shorn of power, almost every Third Reich bigwig appeared in that light, but at that time it was a revelation. Also 'in the bag' was William Joyce, known as 'Lord Haw Haw', the Nazi stooge who had made propaganda broadcasts to the Allies, which always began with the phrase "Germany calling!" His wife Margaret was with him. Randall wanted me to ship them off to Brussels within hours. It was crucial, he added, that the press be kept well out if it. Hardly had he spoken when an Anson aeroplane taxied up the runway, filled with news reporters.

Mrs Joyce, a slim, dark-haired, attractive lady, was driven up in a jeep with four military SPS men wearing their red caps. Photographers thrust cameras in her face through the windows. Flash bulbs exploded. She blushed, and pleaded with me to remove her from the glare. I felt sorry for her and offered her a cup of tea, then led her to the tent where policemen had orders to stop anyone entering without due clearance.

Though technically I had no right to cross-examine her, I did ask why she and Joyce had stayed in Germany. Without hesitation

11 Peace

she replied, "We believed Hitler was a great man and the Nazi system the best form of government."

"Do you still believe that?"

"Oh no. Everything has collapsed."

"Is that your reason for losing faith in the Nazi government? You must have known about the concentration camps before."

"I knew about them, but I was always told that although life there was hard, there was no torture."

"Even if that were true, isn't it criminal to shut people away from society because they don't accept the doctrines of the state?"

"I know, I know, but I didn't realise that before. Everything has been so awful with the bombardments that I really don't know what to think."

She was in a nervous state. Further questioning would be pointless. I changed the subject and asked her if it was true that she had been an actress before the war. She replied that was not quite the case, but that she used to try to dance. I couldn't help thinking it a pity that she gave up dancing because she fell in love with Joyce. When Cupid aimed his arrow, her life was bound to his. Lovers are blind, but only God can judge our actions.

The following day, I was dismayed to read in the *Daily Mirror* the headline in bold print 'Mrs Joyce Offered Cup of Tea', as though it was a sensation.

William Joyce himself arrived at the aerodrome. He was a mouse of a man – thin, almost bald, wearing a faded blue suit. He had a sinister look, at odds with his overall appearance, the result of a large scar across his right cheek. His voice sounded exactly as it did on the wireless.

I had been told not to ask him about his political opinions or his life in Germany. When he saw me looking at Plato's *The Republic*, in his hand, he said slowly, "I think it's probably a pity I didn't spend more time reading the classics." He added, "… Yes, I think it's a pity that I didn't read Plato before."

As it happens, I have always believed that no one should make

11 Peace

a political speech until they have read *The Republic*, but, salutary tract as it is, I rather doubt if even the wisdom of Plato could have deflected Joyce from his ill-starred course.

Time was up. Via Brussels, England was calling William Joyce.

Day after day, prominent members of the Nazi party were shipped away by air. They all seemed to be quite insignificant little men, clean-shaven with unintelligent eyes. Himmler's two adjutants looked like the ordinary German seen in the streets. Both were wearing rimless spectacles and spoke with quiet voices. Nothing about their manners betrayed their hideous minds. It was difficult to believe that men such as these could have been responsible for organising concentration camps.

Von Ribbentrop was a frail, wizened old man, whose grey hair and wrinkled brow gave him the air somehow of an unsuccessful chemist. He amazed me, arguing that the Conservatives, Baldwin and Chamberlain foremost among them, had urged Hitler to re-arm from the very beginning. This perspective could only gain in the elaboration, and he did not disappoint. The Conservatives, ran his argument, wanted to boost Hitler's war machine, as they wanted Germany to destroy the Russians. In such a context his next allegation added up: Baldwin, no less, was responsible for shipping free steel – note the word 'free' – from England to Germany. The jigsaw was fitting together neatly: when Russia invaded Finland, Churchill had agreed to send allied troops to Germany. Hostilities between Germany and England having suddenly ceased, what else but that England and Germany would unite to finish off the Russians? Here the tale touched a point of history as opposed to – some might say – cloud-cuckoo land: all these machinations helped show why it was that Hitler made no attempt to push home his advantage and invade England after Dunkirk. After all, no useful purpose is served by upsetting your chief ally-to-be!

If these emanations from von Ribbentrop's brain signified what he truly believed about the cosy state in which England's relations with Germany were swaddled, Hitler never did a wiser

11 Peace

thing than when he appointed the man his ambassador to the Court of St James. One might have been forgiven for supposing that von Ribbentrop thought it German policy to help train British Prime Ministers for their job by giving them free run of the Reichstag from boyhood onwards.

And yet, and yet ... Thinking back to my own boyhood experiences at Salem school, had I not myself been struck by the extent of the admiration there for all things English as well as by the apparently paradoxical dislike by young Germans of all things foreign? What of the theories of General von Brauchitsch, the head of the German General Staff? Was he not also – to a much lesser degree, of course, than von Ribbentrop – inclined to read too much into the possibilities of co-operation between Germany and England?

Von Ribbentrop's final remarks to me were, "You made Hitler feel he could fight for you and reunite Europe. You made Hitler feel he could destroy Communism. But you English proved that you are so hypocritical that Europe will never trust you again!"

It was my unpleasant task to oversee the transportation of other leading Nazis. They were not in von Ribbentrop's mould, but if anything their reasoning was more chilling. Their excuse for their atrocities was that everything had been done for the good of the State. This, in their eyes, exonerated them from guilt.

General von Brauchitsch informed me that he had agreed with General Montgomery that if the British took over Berlin and Poland, the German Army would not attack them. The Germans would just keep the Russians at bay. Although Montgomery and General Patton wanted to accept this pact, Roosevelt had forbidden Churchill to let the agreement take place.

Was this sort of thinking typical of the upper echelons of the German General Staff?

Later I heard tell that Montgomery was furious with Churchill. Montgomery's reasoning was that the Americans were determined to destroy our Polish and Czechoslovakian allies by

11 Peace

giving them over to the Russians. The Americans thought they could then control Western Europe.

General von Brauchitsch and fourteen officers of the German General Staff were driven up to the aerodrome in an open 3-ton lorry. They looked like cartoon generals, immaculately dressed in magnificent overcoats and high jackboots. Some wore monocles, some had cigarette-holders, others smoked cigars. They were the cruellest and most calculating-looking men that I ever saw. A party of French prisoners was carried past on stretchers. Their bodies were shrivelled through starvation, their faces disfigured with sores. The generals deliberately turned their backs.

An intelligence officer asked the German officers to look at some of their prisoners. Von Brauchitsch adjusted his monocle and, looking stonily at the officer, said clearly and precisely, "They are not prisoners of the Wehrmacht. They are political prisoners. We are not responsible."

He spoke like a judge who, in his summing up, considers that the last word has been spoken. I detested the frigid, arrogant manner of those officers, yet was forced to respect their upright bearing in defeat. When all hope of victory had vanished, these were the men who kept the German Army fighting on to the end, its morale unbroken by overwhelming air bombardment and military might.

The Danish royal family landed in a Dakota that needed refuelling en route to Copenhagen. My best uniform on, I went to meet the Crown Prince and two Princesses. They were charming, apologising for any problem that the landing might have caused us. Not quite the behaviour of a German Kommandant, at least in my recent experience! They accepted three cups of tea and showed a genuine interest in the displaced persons thronging the aerodrome in their thousands.

Soon after the royal party had flown off, a French lady parachutist turned up. She gave her name as Ginette Julian but later admitted to me that that was a cover. She said that she had been

11 Peace

in SAFA and the French resistance. I was left wondering why she took me into her confidence, and so promptly. She insisted that she was a relation of the Danish royal family, but preferred not to be too specific. She said that a liberation ball was being held in their castle – and she just had to be there. The story seemed farfetched; I had just met the Royal family but I did not make much of the fact that they had kept their plans for this festivity dark from me! What was going on?

As it happened, a few days earlier I had sent men from my squadron to maintain the aerodrome at Kastrup. It was not inconvenient to fly Ginette in my Anson to Denmark and see how my men were making out. I am tempted to say that she was absolutely delicious – not that that affected my decision, of course. As I was inspecting the aerodrome, Ginette phoned the palace. The moment of truth had arrived. To my astonishment, within the hour, a large police car, its driver properly obsequious, arrived to take us to the ball. Ginette was still in battledress! It was like a fairy-tale, finding myself in that castle, with ladies in glamorous gowns and tiaras, waltzing beneath the chandeliers, as if it was all happening in a more gracious age. The royal family greeted us personally. They remembered the three cups of tea! Whether it was gratitude for what the British had done in the War, because of some veiled secret to do with Ginette, or even because of the well-attested qualities of good old English tea, I know not, but they would have none of my returning to the aerodrome that night and insisted on my staying as their guest at the castle. It was all done with such olde worlde courtesy. The next day I flew Ginette back to Lüneburg. Again, this prompted questions. What was in Lüneburg for her?

My AOC, Whitney Straight, had just arrived with Max Aitken, the press baron. Whitney was in rather a bait over my flying off to Denmark without his permission, but was intrigued by Ginette. Over lunch we struck a deal that if I gave him a case of wine, he would forgive my little excursion. The Germans had left

11 Peace

plenty of wine, so I had no problem with my end of the bargain. In fact, I gave him two cases. Ginette, of course, came with us as I drove Whitney and Max Aitken to the aerodrome for a flight to London. On the way Max persuaded her to fly with them to London for a party that they were holding there. I still did not know her real name but she wrote down her address in Paris and seemed genuinely affected at our leave-taking.

It was a big upset for me to find shortly afterwards that I could not fully decipher her handwriting. I wrote, but reply came there none. I spent ages trying to track her down only to discover that 'Ginette Julian' was not a name known to any of the services. Never again did I see the princess who took me to a royal ball – or forgive Max Aitken and Whitney Straight for taking her away from me. War had thrown in my path a beautiful, mysterious spy, one who would break hearts in the furtherance of her own dark ends, only for her to disappear without trace.

Like many, I reflected on what was to be the fate of post-war Germany. The idea of the state as the supreme authority was such a dangerous one. It invariably led to the worst excesses. History furnishes innumerable examples. What was needed now to save the world was belief in God and, above all, an adherence to His precepts. The secular principle had been fully tried, and failed the test.

A Church of England priest with whom I discussed the subject at the time agreed. From his religious standpoint, Germany was not entirely to blame for the War, but after the First War had demoralised her, turning her into a breeding-ground for fanatics of many different types, it was almost a foregone conclusion that any party pandering to them with the objective of rebuilding the country would gain power. With the Nazis ensconced in government, secret police ensured there was no turning back. So far, so uncontroversial, perhaps, but the priest's view, which struck a chord with me, went on further to centre on the responsibility of

11 Peace

a Europe, Britain included, that knew well what befell many Germans professing Christianity. European governments, he stressed, did know about the artists and intellectuals imprisoned for openly expressing their faith, but chose to ignore their fate. Would England seize the chance now of building a new Germany and of leading Europe down a godly path?

My next assignment was to conduct 6,000 Russians from their POW camps to the Russian zone. Before the army interpreter arrived, a Russian colonel, major and captain drove up – a delegation whose importance was mirrored in the formality of their saluting. Speaking in halting German, they informed me that they were there to supervise arrangements for their ex-prisoners of war. Then their eyes lit up at the sight of a bottle of Benedictine. Of course, I offered them a tipple. To my consternation they downed it immediately as if it was vodka. Back to business: in exchange for my providing their ex-prisoners with, of all things, tea – doubtless taken by them as the peculiarly English solution to any problem or crisis – they undertook to superintend all transportation arrangements. They needed me just to contact them when the transport aircraft arrived. I half wondered if the Benedictine had gone to their heads, but put their minds at rest: their quest was at an end. I assured them that I could cope with that task. We did not quaff a toast to our deal with tea! As a token of their thanks, a sumptuous basket of strawberries was sent round later for me.

Two days later, a motley crowd comprised the first load of the Russians to arrive by Dakota. These peasants, as they were described, seemed content at being herded together. On disembarkation, they just lay down on the grass. The Russian colonel informed me that it was unnecessary to segregate the sexes or children in the local barracks for the night. No one cared a tuppenny damn if they all slept in a huddle – or, presumably, what they got up to when left thus to their own vices.

I invited the Russian officers to dinner, and though they were unable to come, the Colonel visited my caravan two days later to

11 Peace

invite me to dine with them. I said that I would be delighted. I arrived punctually. The Colonel – in his shirtsleeves – deigned to appear after half an hour. He was curt.

"I am sorry you cannot dine with me tonight because my General is coming. Come another night."

Nonplussed, I simply said "Thank you," and walked out, wondering if I had offended him in any way. It seemed a strange thing to invite the Commanding Officer of a unit to dinner only to dismiss him in so abrupt a manner. No further invitation was forthcoming, and without informing me, he and his party returned to the Russian zone a few days later. Of a piece with this story, seemingly, were the disturbing stories filtering back about the hostile way the Russians behaved to British POWs liberated by them. Instead of being considered allies, they were treated as if they were the representatives of an enemy state – and, inexcusably, they were deliberately starved.

General Montgomery frequently passed through Lüneburg. I was detailed to look after his aircraft and grew used to his staccato greeting. He would never stop for so much as a cup of tea. He would immediately get into his staff car guarded by military police in jeeps, and set off with outriders. I was told that this motorcade impressed the Germans and made them see we could put on a good show.

Before leaving Lüneburg, I visited the heath where the Germans had surrendered to Monty. Summer sun shone brightly over bracken and trees and lit up the rolling heath where a board marked the site of his caravan. Empty cartridge cases and old German tin hats were amongst the litter in the surrounding trenches, evoking the spectre of recent fighting.

There was a non-fraternisation ban in force but one evening I stopped to talk with a local.

"Why do you English make us farmers stop work at ten o'clock?" he grumbled. "For a good harvest we must work late in the fields, especially when we are short of labour."

11 Peace

The farmer thought the English were mad. How could he grow more food when his working time was restricted?

He spoke of the War. "I'm glad it is over. War is bad. It ruins crops and destroys everything. My son was bombed in Hamburg. He is upstairs in bed with his head badly injured. He has lost a leg and is also deaf ..."

He brushed aside my expression of regret.

"...We expect these things from war. I blame Hitler, not your bombs. All I want is to be able to grow more wheat."

I was glad to have broken the non-fraternisation ban. The weather-beaten old farmer had every reason to be bitter. Despite my being the RAF pilot who might have injured his son, he bore me no malice. Instead, he was kindly and anxious to work harder. He was a man who deserved genuine respect.

Occasionally, in the evenings I would go round to the mess that was run by the French Red Cross and the Belgian Red Cross. They organised the most enjoyable parties. Two old Belgian friends of mind, Count Werner de Spoelberg and Flight-Lieutenant André de Limeletter, flew up one day in a Mosquito and came with me to a dance. André was about to get married and behaved like a little boy. I never saw anyone so completely in love. Werner was the same cheery, amusing person I had known in Brussels. He was always the life and soul of any party with his funny stories. For those few hours I felt that this might have been a party in Belgium; we forgot that the town was full of sullen Germans who had been stunned by the magnitude of defeat.

As the displaced persons shipped back daily to Paris and Brussels decreased in number, I received orders to go to Schleswig and build a permanent staging-post on the aerodrome. Hamburg was only thirty miles from Lüneburg en route to Schleswig. At the wheel of my captured six-seater Mercedes Benz, with three British officers accompanying me as specialist advisers, I ate up the autobahn miles to Hamburg. It was a sight! Virtually nothing

11 Peace

but rubble, bricks and twisted steel girders. The destruction was appalling. I doubted if atom bombs could have created more horror. As far as the eye could see, houses were just piles of broken bricks. The army had been held up in Hamburg because of the difficulties of finding bulldozers enough to clear even the main roads. I slouched down into the back of my car, ashamed to show my wings and decorations. I felt guilty for belonging to a service that had deliberately caused such suffering. To see that scene, to think about the pulverised industries there, it seemed amazing that people were already exercised about the possibility of Germany starting yet another war. Quite aside from the fact that everyone seemed obsessed with the threat posed by the newly dominant Russians.

As we drove towards the town centre, a few buildings were standing and among them was the Atlantic Hotel, so famous before the War. It was undamaged and transformed into an officers' club, complete with orchestra and stylish décor, soft lights and luxurious carpets calculated to dull the impact of the hideous, skeleton buildings in its vicinity. We spent the night there. A sparkling Moselle wine washed down a superb dinner that cost the equivalent of two shillings. The immaculate waiters were only too anxious to please. It was amazing to find that Englishmen were welcome. We were treated like honoured guests rather than conquerors or murderers of women and children. The leader of the orchestra only too willingly played my favourite tunes, including familiar German waltzes. The contrast between a life of leisure and light and pleasure with the sort of existence I had been leading, was sharp indeed. There was a magical world out there ...

The English Army had captured a circus run by Belli, the famous circus family. It promised to round off the evening well. The very idea of the circus brought back memories to me of those trips, long past, with my grandfather... I could recall so well how he would insist on a punctilious correctness in every last detail

11 Peace

before we fellow conspirators on a grand adventure left the security of home in our chauffeur-driven limousine. He would sit back in the car, portentously, puff cigar smoke in my face and unfold for me the drama of business ventures, of the horses he had bought or intended to buy, and a thousand other things too alien and vast for my mind to comprehend at the time. He would frequently make a great show of consulting his immense, golden fob watch to check if the chauffeur had timed our expedition with a sufficient exactitude. And his agitation if any obstacle hindered our progress! It was all brought back to me, once again: the proximity of ferocious animals; the heart-stopping moments while I, with the rest of the audience, was up on the high wire or the trapeze with the artistes, when one hardly dared breathe lest they fell; the galloping horses; lying under an elephant's foot; the head between the lion's jaws, when we all gasped at the daring, oo'ed at the wondrous and laughed at the ridiculous…

As we arrived, the band was playing rousing music and the smell of sawdust, the bright lights and the dancing horses brought back to me the circus evenings of my childhood. It was an outstanding performance, with trapeze artists, elephants, and tumbling dark-skinned Arabians. Magnificently plumed and noble-looking horses trotted around the ring and Harri Belli and his sister made their horses partner each other for the waltz, tango and quickstep. After Belli had taken his bow, he returned leading a chestnut by some long reins. When the band started up, the horse began to dance on its own. As it kept time to the music, it made a double kick in the air with all four feet off the ground.

Afterwards, I found Harri Belli in his caravan. He unbent at my compliments and told me something about his background. When he was four, he had escaped his nanny's watchful eyes and wandered into the Shetland pony tent. Crawling up a wooden stall, he climbed on to Piccolo, the most mischievous of the ponies. Piccolo reared up. Harri grasped his thick mane and hung on. The stable cord snapped and out of the tent the pony

11 Peace

bolted, Harri still mounted. Some circus folk rescued him but only after he was thrown into a stream. When he was seven, he first appeared in the circus dressed as an Indian and did somersaults on the back of a horse, a large chestnut.

When I asked him his nationality, he said he was international. He happened to have born in Germany; the other artistes came from Bulgaria, Morocco, Hungary, France ... One by one they came in. There was Coco, the famous midget clown, and Don José, a star rider at Olympia and now with Belli's circus because his own horses had been bombed. He spoke of the elephants ... When hit, they could cry. If you told a circus girl that you loved her as an elephant loves, you were asking her to marry you. If an elephant loved you, it would go on loving you forever. One elephant cried for three days when a goat, who slept alongside it, died. Then there was Liazeed, the ringmaster, who, with his troupe of leaping Arabians, had performed in America and in England and who had made two films in each country. The best known was *Reaching for the Moon*, starring Douglas Fairbanks. He had appeared at the London Palladium. "Rich or poor, I shall remain a showman until I die," said Liazeed.

It was hard to leave the bright lights of the circus, with those huge tents and their strange, happy people. Amid misery and devastation, our troops had been given a wonderful night out.

12

Germany and my German Friends

We needed a place to billet our men. Schleswig was a town still standing. Small and picturesque, it was in a lakeside setting with old, attractive buildings that had odd woodcarvings, tall roofs, and windows artistically arranged with cardboard designs and pictures. We drove past an old castle, once the home of the Prince of Schleswig-Holstein, where the Army was now quartered. There were several medium-sized middle-class houses that looked suitable. I felt ashamed as an old man and woman humbly showed me round their house. They pleaded with me not to take it because they had nowhere else to live. I promised to try to find another house. Every house had the same pitiful story. There was a family living in every room and none of these poor people had anywhere to go. In the end, I had to decide on the best houses without allowing sentimentality to cloud my judgement.

I told the Major in charge of the town : "The two houses I have chosen will be ideal, but there is a snag. All the people living there have nowhere to go."

He laughed cynically. "Well, I can turn them out into the street."

"No. There are enough people wandering on the roads already. Try to find them temporary accommodation. My unit will probably only stay here for three to six months."

"Quite impossible unless you can give me more time."

"All right, I will not move up here for three weeks. Is that long enough?"

"I dare say I can do something. One of our own units will have cleared out by then."

The Major cut into my thanks and my observations about how it was not these people who had been responsible for the War.

12 Germany and my German Friends

"As far as I'm concerned all Germans are just Huns. They are a wretched sheeplike nation. One minute they spit at you, the next they crawl on their hands and knees. ... Germans have no soul. They are not human beings. ... I shall do my best to find these people a place to sleep – but only because that is part of my work. If you had my job, you would despise all Germans."

It would have been useless to argue with the Major, not the most educated of men in my opinion, but typical in his views.

The next day I visited the Belgian Red Cross Commandante. She was helpful in every way and agreed to formally report that she had sufficient personnel to be shipped from Celle to justify my unit's staying on the airfield for another three weeks. The Army movements officer also agreed that it would be a good idea for us to stay at Celle for another three weeks and promised to get his HQ to make an official request to the RAF to delay our move.

Three days later, I received a signal that the move to Schleswig had been indefinitely postponed. My Group HQ had taken notice of the requests from the Army and the Red Cross. The only people to object were the staff of 83 Group stationed there. The Air Commodore in charge of administration flew into a rage. He demanded to know why a Transport Command unit had not arrived to look after the airfield. To which the answer was that Transport Command served the Army as well as the RAF and that the Army were making more use of the available aircraft at that particular moment. If I had put forward the question of suitable accommodation at Schleswig as an excuse for not moving, I knew where I would be told to go – under canvas again.

There was plenty of time for me to make arrangements to leave Lüneburg. The tents could be dismantled in a few hours and it would take about half a day for the unit to pack up. The men all knew their jobs. The signals officer could easily look after his men and equipment, while the stores and MT personnel were so used to packing up that I had no need to worry about them.

12 Germany and my German Friends

I sat back and waited for the day of our departure from Lüneburg. I had decided to drive ahead in the Mercedes Benz and see that everything was ready for my men. The site that I had selected at Schleswig consisted of several huts built round a square patch of ground. It had once been a vegetable garden, but for several months the ground had been sadly neglected. The huts had been painted but still appeared shoddy and depressing. I decided that we must find some red and blue paint to brighten the outside. This would help to cheer up the men. One of the huts could be a rest and reading room. Another could be used for hobbies, and a corner of this hut would make an ideal photographic department for the many amateurs, who had somewhat conspicuously acquired the most expensive cameras.

The moment my lorries arrived, I realised from the men's faces that they were very unhappy with their sleeping quarters. My officers warned me that there would be a mutiny if nothing was done. I told them that I was certain everyone would be happy in a few days' time. The huts would look different when the beds were inside and pin-up girls had been stuck on the walls. However, I gave the adjutant instructions that red and blue paint had to be found by morning, and that about fifty Germans should be hired to do the painting. Any other practical suggestions were to be carried out.

My intelligence officer informed me that he had personally supervised the job of moving the Germans from the two houses in the town and that he had engaged the domestic staff to run the hostel and officers' mess. I chose two rooms for myself that were pleasantly furnished with soft carpets and oak cupboards. I removed the pictures and replaced them with some of my own. There was a grand piano for the anteroom. With the aid of an old bookshelf we constructed a bar at one corner of the room and were then satisfied that we were comfortably installed.

After arriving at Schleswig one of my first self-appointed tasks was to find a piano-tuner. Our German servants produced one and

12 Germany and my German Friends

I decided to pay the man his wage of 35 marks for a day's work myself. I found a little old man in a black coat and hat, a white collar and a grey tie sitting in the front seat of my lorry. In a gentle voice he apologised for asking for the money, but said that because he was very busy he was unable to call back. He told me he was the only piano-tuner in the district and that he worked from nine in the morning until nine at night. I assured him that that would be all right and held out the 35 marks to him – probably enough to buy some black bread. But he didn't take it and apologised, saying that he was blind and requesting me to put it in his hand. I was stunned by this, and then stayed a little while to hear his story.

For forty years he had practised law until, in 1942, he had been blinded when his town was bombed. He had always loved the piano and found that he could still be of some use. Thinking he had good reason to be bitter, I sympathised with him. However, he told me very graciously that life was not so very hard for him and explained to me how much beauty there still was in the world. As though he guessed my thoughts, he added, "I do not blame the RAF for making me blind. We all suffer from the follies of mankind."

After that I shook his hand. That old man was not resentful, only apologetic that his blindness had caused him to rely more on other people. It was humbling to meet him. He was at peace with the world.

I asked my German staff if they knew the school at Salem. One of the waitresses, who was a baroness, told me that a friend of hers from Salem was living in Schleswig. It was Paul Lindemayer. She told me that he was an officer in the German Navy. I was delighted to have this information and asked her to arrange for him to come and see me as soon as possible. She promised that he would come on the following evening.

Lindemayer arrived to see me at the appointed hour. He was dressed in his naval uniform and looked very smart. He had aged

12 Germany and my German Friends

greatly and was much thinner, yet he was the same charming person I remembered so well.

"Well, Dickie, we meet again. How nice of you to ask to see me." He smiled wistfully. "... Are you allowed to be seen talking with a German officer?"

"My dear Paul, it is delightful to see you again. Come upstairs to my room, and we'll have some tea."

When we were sitting, I offered him a cigarette.

"Dickie, you do not realise what a luxury you are offering me."

"As a matter of fact I do. That reminds me. I have some cigarettes for you." I had gone to my store and found two hundred for him. "Now tell me what you have been doing during the War. In the Navy, I see."

"Yes, I have been in the Navy for six years."

"Tell me, Paul, why did you fight for Germany? You were never a Nazi and you did not believe in Hitler."

"I had no option. I realised before the War began that if Germany lost the War, my family would be destroyed. If she won, we would still be destroyed. I only fought so that Germany might have a chance to survive. I would have tried to fight against the regime if we had won. Despite all its failings, my country is still part of me."

"My dear Paul, we must all try to forget sentimental and patriotic feelings. Countries do not matter. It is the people that matter."

"I wonder. Language is the great barrier between people. Language expresses thought. German words mean more to me than Russian. Or any other language for that matter."

"Yes, there is a great deal of truth in what you say. Still, I believe it is possible to like and understand people even when there is a difference of language. The greatest crime is to believe that any one language is more important than another. No such thing is true. The main thing is not to be influenced by anything other than cold logic and the spiritual interpretation of words.

12 Germany and my German Friends

Alas, the majority of people prefer to live like animals and believe whatever their self-appointed leaders tell them."

Lindemayer did not completely understand me. I offered him another cigarette and asked what he intended to do in the future.

"I really do not know. It is very difficult. One of my lungs has collapsed and the doctor says I shall only survive if I live somewhere near the air of Switzerland. I think I must try to get back to Baden. All my estates have been sequestered and it is difficult to know what to do. I shall try to contact the Markgraf von Baden and try to help with Schloss Salem."

"That is a wonderful idea. It was such an excellent school. I spent such very happy days there."

"You probably heard that the Nazis closed us down in 1939?"

"I'm not surprised. You did not preach the doctrine of National Socialism very effectively."

"We were lucky to remain open so long."

"Tell me, Paul, what do you think about the concentration camps?"

He looked as if I had stabbed him to the heart. Quietly he replied, "It is awful – so awful. I knew that they existed but I never realised what horrors took place there. We officers were once shown around a concentration camp near the Danish border. It was hard work for the inmates, but living conditions were reasonable. Now I know that the SS were simply deceiving us. It has been a great shock to me to discover what those camps were really like."

"I believe you. By the way, how are you going to get to Baden?"

"I am not sure. I must try to find a way."

"I will do what I can to help you. Come round at the same time tomorrow and I will see what I can do. I am sorry to have to ask you to go now, but I have a conference that I must attend. It has been delightful meeting you. Will you come back tomorrow?"

12 Germany and my German Friends

He left the building quickly so as not to be seen by my own officers. Most of them would have been furious to think that I was entertaining a German.

Lindemayer returned the next day, and as before, I hurried him into my room before he was seen. He was most grateful for the tea I gave him and devoured the cakes as if he had not eaten for a long time. To my great surprise he told me that Peter Scharff was living on the island of Sylt. This was wonderful news.

"You must try to find some means of getting in touch with Peter and letting him know that I am down here."

"I will do my best. He would very much like to meet you again."

He paused for a moment, and then continued "… Excuse my asking, but would you like to meet the Princess of Schleswig-Holstein? I know you are interested in painting, and she is quite a good artist."

I thought it a marvellous idea to visit her and see her paintings. Lindemayer told me that she lived in a small cottage in the woods about twelve miles from Schleswig. We decided to go that very afternoon. Although there was a regulation forbidding Germans to be driven about in cars, I decided that I should use my own discretion.

When Lindemayer was seated next to me in the BMW sports car, however, I began to feel self-conscious at having a German officer beside me. I hoped people who saw him would think that he was a British Naval officer. I believe that he also felt uncomfortable and wondered if he ought to behave like a prisoner of war. I tried to put him at ease by discussing the problem of Germany. I asked him how he viewed its future.

"It is going to be very difficult for us. So much has been destroyed. I know nothing of economic affairs, but I think it will be a gigantic task to rebuild. The real trouble is that Germany has given up hope. It no longer believes that it has anything to look forward to. We shall not be allowed to do anything. We have lost

12 Germany and my German Friends

confidence in policies for the future. It is going to be so very difficult. What a pity that the world cannot be organised like Salem. I think everyone who went there was happy."

I knew that he was right.

"Now you know what you have got to do. You have to return to Salem, and continue to spread the good faith amongst the new generation. The school must be started again. I think that if Germans such as yourself really do try to build up a new society, you will succeed in doing something well worth while."

We went on talking and I forgot my nervousness at driving with a German officer. His voice was so pleasantly soft that it was a pleasure to hear him speak. Even so, there was something very tragic in the tone of his voice. He felt guilty about being a German because his nation had committed so many atrocities. He knew that he ought to have opposed the regime instead of fighting for it. He had been born in an age when he was not able to stem the march of events. I did not blame him because he could no more help stop the War than I could. We were both schoolboys when the stage was being set for the bloody engagement. I realised that even if I had detested my own government and it had been foolish enough to be responsible for the War, I would still have fought. In spite of what I had told him about the need to bring down national boundaries, I would always prefer to have Englishmen in power in preference to any foreigners. It was easy to understand why so many Germans had fought hard and well. They were fighting above all for the existence of their own country.

We turned off the main road and drove towards a wood. I was told to drive down a track leading through the wood. Tall trees and their branches cast weird shadows over the car and the blue sky was hidden from sight by thick foliage. The track between the trees became too narrow for the car so we had to stop and get out. I stopped the car and locked the doors. No Germans would touch it, but any Allied troops in the area might be expected to remove a car that had been left in a wood.

12 Germany and my German Friends

The track led us through the trees until we came to a clearing. Three old farm buildings formed a square round a cottage probably built for a gamekeeper. Some dogs barked at us and an old man with a fierce military moustache stopped sweeping the yard. He eyed us suspiciously until he noticed that Lindemayer was a German naval officer. Then he smiled, and touched his head with the gesture of a man who recognises his social superiors. Lindemayer spoke to him and I heard him reply.

"The princess is painting in the cottage."

The cottage had only two rooms and was almost unfurnished. Three faded and rickety chairs occupied the greater part of one room. The walls were covered with oil paintings and photographs of the royal families of Europe. Stacks of watercolours and oil paintings stood beside the walls. The princess greeted us and apologised that she had nothing to offer by way of refreshment. A medium-sized woman with a firm and even dominating manner, she gave me the impression that she was used to having her every wish carried out. Her tightly closed lips suggested a disposition of bitterness. But she took great delight in showing me her pictures.

While we were admiring a landscape of the Baltic coast she said, almost sarcastically, "I cannot understand the politics of England. What are you trying to do? For the first time in history you have allowed the Russians to occupy the Baltic coast. Are you intending them to occupy all Europe?"

She spoke in English with a clear crisp voice. I was taken aback. This was a direct question. I replied with conviction, "We have no intention that any power should occupy all Europe."

She looked steadily at me and almost laughed as she said, "You are foolish. England could not stop the Russians even if she wanted to. You have been stupid about this war. You could have beaten Germany without shattering her. By doing what you have done, you will be unable to support Europe. England, who has always been so clever at playing with the balance of power, has created a situation that she will be unable to control. It is no good

12 Germany and my German Friends

arguing because I know the facts. Our world is finished. All I want now is to paint and smoke. Since I have no tobacco, I have to make my own from these leaves."

She showed me some dried leaves that she had placed in a jar and rolled up in paper. Cigarettes could not be bought in Germany. I hastened to offer her a packet and was amazed at the delight with which she received the twenty Players. They might have been the most precious gift in the world. Before we left, the princess insisted on giving each of us one of her pictures as a souvenir. I promised to send her cigarettes. Mine was a watercolour painting of the surrounding woods. It was alive with colour and yet seemed to reflect the mysterious, almost sinister spirit of German forests. As I gazed at it, I wondered just how much men's characters are affected by their environment. Could the Germans perhaps have produced so many sadistic people because of their mythology of strange spirits lurking in their forests?

A few days after Paul left, I received a letter from Peter Scharff. He told me that he had heard I was in Schleswig and hoped I would see him when he passed through town. I wrote back that I would be more than delighted. He came the following week.

The Nazis had put Peter in prison on the grounds that he had held an exhibition of his paintings in Switzerland without asking permission. He was held for six months, released when the War broke out, and then imprisoned again when he refused to be an artist on the front line. He was very happy to have his freedom again and now spent his time travelling around the countryside and painting.

After we had talked for a while, he told me that der Mangel had been killed in a bombing raid on Goch a few months before the end of the War. I was sad to have lost a friend, someone who had saved my life, and felt even worse when I realised that I could very well have been the bomber pilot whose bombs had killed him.

But I was greatly impressed by the cheerful way Peter spoke of the future. He was full of hope that good things would come out

12 Germany and my German Friends

of the War and that people would learn to live more peacefully and happily together. It was really a pleasure to have met him again and to know that his spirit had not been crushed by his terrible wartime experiences. I was sorry when the time came for him to go. We promised to write to each other and to meet again.

Paul and I set off together for the Russian zone with 2,000 cigarettes that would be useful for bribing the Russians. With these I arranged for the removal of many of the Princess of Schleswig-Holstein's belongings. Accordingly, not long afterwards, a small convoy of lorries from my unit collected paintings and antiques belonging to the Schleswig-Holstein family to be delivered by Paul to a castle of theirs in Bavaria. Never let it be said that the British armed forces have not played their part in the rightful restitution of stolen war property! The Princess gave me a delightful watercolour and signed it for me with a flourish. I treasured that painting. Years later, my mother told me that my sister had taken possession of it. Despite all my protestations I never recovered it, which was deeply upsetting.

13

The Victors and the Vanquished

To a Black-Marketeer
*Doff your hat
with a studied bow
for the man who has fought this war.
Count your gold
with your greasy glee,
that the world
will work as before.
Don't forget
you're the kingpin now;
the soldier
will starve at your door.*

I spent Christmas 1945 at BAFO HQ Bückeburg as a staff officer of Transport Command. Below us was beautiful, rolling woodland. It was a time, if ever there was one, to celebrate. I really felt that we, the victors, should have made an effort to help the Germans enjoy this season of goodwill. However, even my idea of giving the children a party was scoffed at. I was curtly informed that the occupying Army had no intention of throwing a party for the children of the vanquished. Such was the *ex cathedra* pronouncement of officers who disported themselves luxuriously in a constant round of jollities from a castle formerly the property of Prince Schaumburg Lippe, and from a large hotel at Bad Salzuflen. There was little reason to think that the regulars in their cosy billets in the best, and now requisitioned, buildings felt in any way differently. Let the locals in cramped and overcrowded accommodation starve!

13 The Victors and the Vanquished

Come January 1946, I postponed my demobilisation so as to take command of 19 Staging-Post Berlin. I was interested generally in seeing how the victors were divvying up the spoils. And how better to do that than to live like one!

My quarters were in a magnificently appointed castle, formerly the property of Herr Brüning, a cousin of the German ex-Chancellor. I chose a suite of rooms with a view over the lawn and the Wannsee (lake) beyond to the sloping hills and woods of the French sector – and a matchless wine cellar. It took me three weeks to become accustomed to having the choice of seven cars, being invited to house parties or cocktail parties every night, and going to theatres, concerts and art exhibitions free of charge. I obtained a yacht and a motor launch, and was looked after by my own valet.

It did not take me long to get bored with the party circuit, drinking with the same people in one grand setting after another. The artificial lives of the administrators in the four sectors – Russian, American, French and British – seemed much the same. In the English sector the Philharmonic Orchestra played every Sunday; in the Russian sector, the Opera House was full every night. Beyond our eyries, groups of Germans, young and old alike sorted and piled bricks from the ruins. I noticed the scabs on the faces of children.

Officers, including the future Duke of Marlborough from the Life Guards, were stationed in barracks across the road. They preferred coming to the castle to drinking in their own quarters. Jack Cresswell – the adjutant whose job during part of the War had been to protect the young Princesses Elizabeth and Margaret – was a frequent visitor. Distinguished civilian guests included Basil Nield QC, then MP for Chester and later a Court of Appeal judge. Our paths were to intersect later in very different circumstances.

The Germans built shops in the base of skeleton buildings, smearing bright paint on rough wood supports, and using the neat piles of bricks, so that progress was everywhere visible. They bought and sold goods at exorbitant prices. Money bore no relation

13 The Victors and the Vanquished

to the official exchange rate and the black market flourished – it lacked only a tariff detailing values in terms of goods purchasable by quantified numbers of cigarettes! A high percentage of the occupying forces must have been dealing on the black market. How else could men buy porcelain, silver, jewels, cameras, wirelesses, china and glasses? Crate-loads of goods came in via Gatow aerodrome, about eight miles from Berlin, on the edge of the Russian sector where the only noticeable destruction was near the entrance at which the SS had taken its final stand. Russian tanks had blasted only one building into rubbish. Did the Russians have an eye to the use they intended to put that aerodrome in the days following their victory? On one occasion I intercepted 10,000 cigarettes. No one claimed them or was charged with sending such vast quantities.

The months passed slowly.

I enjoyed the concerts and opera but increasingly felt the futility and monotony of my life in Berlin. I wrote to the Air Ministry and asked to be demobilised as soon as possible. They replied that I could not be released until my six months was up. I was disappointed, and decided to devote myself to cleaning up the black market about which I had now gathered considerable information.

I visited the Police Headquarters and told them what I suspected. They promised to investigate. I asked for three houses to be searched, and also a plot of land where I believed food belonging to the services had been hidden before it was sent across the lake in a motorboat to be sold at a nightclub.

The investigations revealed nothing. I was not surprised. My own spy system had reported to me that the occupants of the houses had been warned in advance of when the raid would be made. I tried another line of approach. I ordered all the aircraft arriving at the aerodrome to be searched. During the first week my sergeant confiscated 11,000 cigarettes. Still I noticed the same extensive buying of diamonds, watches, china and cameras. The goods went out under my eyes and I could do nothing about it.

13 The Victors and the Vanquished

I grew furious as I learned more and more about who was behind the organisation. Even though I remembered my old argument that until food arrived for the people, the black market would flourish, I wanted the chief culprits to be caught and exposed. They were too careful. Now they will never be brought to justice, and if I dared mention their names I would face a libel action. The fact remains that at no time while I was in Berlin were any effective steps taken to stop the black market. Indeed, all the homes of the chief officers of the Control Commission were stacked with priceless porcelain and rare pictures. This would not have been possible on a large scale if everyone had been living on their salary.

I was so intrigued by the black market that I made my own investigations. Discreet enquiry led me to the Grünewald district of Berlin. I was told that if I asked for a certain Herr B——, everything could be arranged.

Feeling like a criminal, I was ushered into a large, pleasant house in a graceful tree-lined avenue, the living room of which had comfortable armchairs, a sofa, a Persian carpet, a grand piano, a radiogram and old pictures. I was offered Vat 69 as, through a half-open door, I glimpsed a naval officer descending the stairs while saying his goodbyes. A slim, pleasant, flaxen-haired woman introduced Herr B——, who was short, well dressed, and wore spectacles.

"We are not doing too badly," he said. "But I used to be the *Direktor* of three companies. They have all gone. I have nothing left but this room. That is war!"

As he was speaking, I noticed two fine cameras on the piano. I examined one, a Leica.

"How much is that one?"

"Seventeen thousand marks."

"And what is the price of cigarettes, now?"

"Eight marks each. The price has come down slightly. Do you have some to sell?"

13 The Victors and the Vanquished

"Yes, but not here. Can you dispose of ten thousand?"

"Easily. When can you bring them here?"

"I am not certain. I will let you know."

"Good. I shall have the money here ready."

We talked of Germany, and her many problems. Suddenly the woman said: "When are you going to fight Russia?"

"Not ever, I hope!"

"You English are so strange. Of course you will have to one day. You know how all women were raped when they first came here."

"Yes, I have heard the most appalling stories."

"They are quite true. Little children and old women were the first victims. You think I am making this up? You ask any woman in Berlin."

"I quite understand your reasons for hating them. If we went to war we could easily beat their ragamuffin army, but it is doubtful if England will consider that there are sufficiently good reasons for starting another war. Do you realise that should we fight the Russians, Berlin will be completely destroyed?"

She smiled cynically. "How could life be worse than it is today? Germany has no hope. She may as well be destroyed. What is the point of leaving us to suffer a lingering death?"

Herr B— interrupted. "My sister is rather agitated. She has suffered greatly. I expect things will improve. … English whisky is good."

They were so pleasant and friendly that even if Herr B— was a rogue, I decided not to report them to the police. They were only one of thousands of agents dealing in the black market. If this ugly system was going to be smashed, it would be necessary for the occupying powers to solve, or at least assuage, Germany's economic difficulties.

One morning I heard the depressing news that an airman had reportedly shot a Russian in a boarding house in the British sector. The airman was held under arrest and the police were sent

13 The Victors and the Vanquished

out to investigate. Although the shooting had taken place in our sector, the Russians would not allow our police to lead the investigation. The Russian police took away the body and most of the evidence. The case intrigued me. I hurried down to the house. It was a squalid building in the Augsburger Strasse, near the Kurfürstendam. I knocked at the door. Herr von Marwitz, the proprietor, opened it. I walked through the living room. Bottles lay on the floor. The drab green walls and heavy pictures gave a depressing feel to the room. I walked into another room with bright red wallpaper and a large ugly chandelier in the centre. I nicknamed this the Red Room. It was here that the quarrel had taken place between the Russians and the English. I looked at the bathroom. The bath had been wrenched from the wall and there were bullet-holes near the door and window. Several shots had been fired. It would be difficult to determine who had fired them. This was going to be an interesting case.

The Judge Advocate's department sent Wing Commander Sidney Wilmot to help me organise the Evidential Hearing. Before he arrived I went to see Major Savenko of the Russian legal department, who was conducting his own investigation. Two Russians with fixed bayonets showed me up to Major Savenko's room. The Major was a little man with an unshaven chin, beady black eyes, and a hesitant smile. His long black cigarette-holder seemed strangely out of keeping with his dirty fingernails. We spoke in German. I was surprised that he spoke with a quiet, pleasant voice. His assistant arrived. He was a young Captain dressed in a smart Russian uniform and was obviously a cultured man. I decided that these men would be more helpful if I took them out for a drink. I had come in my big six-seater Porsche car with its black body and white tyres. Large cars impress the Russians. I took my guests to the Embassy Club in the British sector. Here, the heavy gilt walls and chairs created the right atmosphere. The major felt insignificant. The captain was quite at home. After we had enjoyed several drinks I explained that before we held a Court Martial,

13 The Victors and the Vanquished

there would be an Evidential Hearing, at which exhibits would be produced and statements made by all witnesses. The Russians agreed that everything I wanted should be done. They regretted that two of the witnesses had disappeared. One was the young woman who had been sleeping with a Russian officer. The other was a girl who had been in the bedroom when the quarrel began. Both had vanished, and it was considered unlikely that they could be found. I realised that if the accused refused to make a statement at the Evidential Hearing, his defending counsel would probably be able to make a good case for him.

When the Hearing began, I questioned the witnesses and discovered that they were all liars. Every one of them told a different story. Not one was certain at what time the shots had been fired, how they had been fired, or why they had been fired. It appeared that an English Corporal had been sleeping with a German girl. He heard shots and jumped out of bed. A Russian fired at him, so he rushed into another room where he dived under a bed. The bed moved; he discovered that it contained another Russian sleeping with another woman. They left the room and he stayed until the Military Police arrived.

The Russian policeman refused to take an oath when called as a witness. I asked him if he was a Christian.

He laughed and replied, "Russians are not Christians."

Major Savenko explained that he was allowed to take an oath on the honour of the Red Army. His evidence was obviously full of lies, and not of great importance.

Eventually, Sidney Wilmot and I sifted through all the evidence. It was obvious that the accused had fired some shots. Everyone had been very drunk and it was not at all certain what had happened. We asked the accused if he wanted to make a statement. He was about to speak, but after looking at me he changed his mind. I felt this was wise.

After a few weeks, the Judge Advocate's department charged the accused with murder. Basil Nield CMG, KC, MP was

13 The Victors and the Vanquished

appointed defending counsel. I was very pleased because the accused needed the services of the best counsel available. It seemed ironic that I was appointed assistant prosecutor.

When the trial took place all the witnesses except for the two girls were summoned. They all lied as stupidly as before. Major Savenko refused to go into the witness box – he claimed that Moscow would not allow it. It took seven days to hear all of the evidence. The Russian and British experts disagreed with each other. It seemed that the accused would be acquitted.

Basil Nield made a brilliant Churchillian speech. He pointed out that there was evidence to show that the Russian might have fired first, and that the shots fired by the accused could be considered to be the natural act of self-defence. He drew attention to the fact that all the important witnesses for the prosecution were not reliable, and that the only established fact was that everyone involved had been drunk. His eloquent speech held me spellbound. I thought it inevitable that he would become a great politician.

An English jury would probably have acquitted the accused. There seemed to be reasonable grounds for doubt and the accused was entitled to the benefit of this doubt. To my amazement, the court found the accused not guilty of murder, but guilty of manslaughter. I realised that courts martial are a totally unfair system for trying a man. There is no right of appeal to a higher court. Judgements were left in the hands of those who were often quite inexperienced officers – officers who are supposed to be impartial judges of the accused. It seemed to me high time that the services revised their legal system.

Again and again I was struck by the kindliness of the long-suffering Germans. There was Artur, the perfect gentleman's gentleman, who worked in my castle. Nothing was too much for him. He wore tattered shoes and frayed shirts and, frail as he was, carried heavy cases with apparent ease. He saw his wife, an

13 The Victors and the Vanquished

invalid who lived in the Russian zone, once a fortnight. He and his wife understood each other, he said, and he thanked God for being so good to him. He seemed to have discovered the secret of a contented life.

As for the German artists, they were more loquacious. It was hard to persuade them that we had come as liberators of truth and justice and were not merely rapacious conquerors. To them as to many others, the Allies preferred to play the conqueror while the vast concentration camp that the Allies claimed Germany to be, collapsed around their ears. Artists are among the most important members of the community. They attempt to interpret emotions and feelings; they aim at an understanding of truth. Germany had allowed herself to become enslaved by the doctrine of materialism. The Nazi regime had been a logical extension of that doctrine. Now artists had the chance to lead the way out of this impasse – even if the majority of fellow-Germans seemed unable to appreciate them.

A case in point was Herr Busacker. There was an exhibition of his pictures in a small bookshop. They were full of expression, with bright and vivid colours, blue and red forests and, pointing up the contrast, dark and shadowy landscapes. An all too obvious French influence was at work. Remembering what Peter Scharff told me, it was hard to believe that he had been working while the Nazis were in power. He was small and emaciated with a fierce beard and dark, penetrating eyes. He wore old army trousers, tattered shirts and boots with holes, and squatted in a small house, surrounded by a wall of pictures that contrasted with the old army surplus blankets on his bed, and his one cupboard and chair.

Busacker smiled in apparently childlike satisfaction at my interest, when I tracked him down and offered him tobacco for his pipe. We spent an evening drinking, and singing songs with several of his young artist friends. He played the guitar and sang in a dreamy, bewitching voice. Everybody was cheerful and by the light of two candles the room seemed to have become rich and

13 The Victors and the Vanquished

splendid. I knew that no one in the room could be certain when they would enjoy their next meal. They were determined to be happy that night and let the morrow take care of itself.

Wolfgang Wolf, another artist, painted a room in which everybody who stood around drinking and talking was representative of the professions. There was a soldier, a clergyman, a lawyer and a politician. On the far wall was a picture of Christ being crucified. No one was looking at the cross except a small child in the centre of the room. Wolf had entitled the painting *1945*. It was an allegory of a world that had lost interest in Christianity.

Along a sidestreet down the rubble of the Kurfürstendam was a hut, crudely constructed with odd pieces of wood. Through a tiny window could be glimpsed an old woman hammering stone in a room full of statues and figures. She was dressed in an old army greatcoat, trousers and worn gymshoes, and her pale face and hair were covered with white stone dust. Such a cold and damp room! "A famous sculptress" my guide whispered. At a time when no one would be buying her work, her spirit still shone through.

"I have the opportunity to work. That is all that matters."

The weeks passed quickly. With demobilisation, smaller units were losing their identity and being absorbed into larger units. Meanwhile, some of my men had been sent to service aircraft in Warsaw. The Air Attaché, Group Captain Burt Andrews, suggested I become temporary Air Attaché there. It would enable me to serve in a supervisory capacity as well as see life in Poland and meet some of those who had been among the first to confront the forces of tyranny. It would also allow me to gain some insight into what made the Russians tick.

I arranged a farewell party with Busacker and his friends. He was almost in tears and made me promise to try to return. He clutched my hand.

"You have been a good friend. Whatever else anyone may say or do, I shall always be proud to have met an English gentleman."

13 The Victors and the Vanquished

He would probably die of starvation and there was nothing much that could be done about it. I felt that we would never see each one another again.

The curtain on one part of my life was being brought down.

Poland, that great country that had fought so hard for peace, was now in the grip of the steel hand of a tyrannical form of government from which, unaided, it was unable to escape. Our allies were committing the same atrocities as the Germans.

A Pole told me, "The Germans were bad enough but we would far rather have them than the Russians."

From the plane to Warsaw the signs of recent battles could be seen. Tank tracks were clearly visible and innumerable lines of trenches marked the trail of the Red Army. The site of the former aerodrome was now bombed to rubble. Rough huts had been erected for the airfield commander, a Russian colonel, and the signals staff. Russians were everywhere, patrolling with tommy-guns and refusing to allow anyone to leave the plane until every last formality and identity check had been completed. They clearly considered themselves the masters of Poland.

Those soldiers were not the real rulers. As I waited in a run-down restaurant with sandwiches and vodka for an Air Attaché to brief me, I saw there was already a 'security officer', with a scar on one cheek, his hat tilted in approved American gangster style, on my trail. The Secret Police, a branch of the Russian NKVD, so our diplomat told me, were the ones really in charge. Nobody escaped their scrutiny, ambassadors included.

Warsaw was a scene of complete devastation – concrete buildings reduced to twisted steel frameworks, roads coated in dust from fallen houses. Poles looked even more miserable than Berliners. Rags covered skeletal bodies, and poverty was stamped on their faces. Cheap goods were sold from crudely constructed stalls on the pavements, along which soldiers with tommy-guns patrolled, while Russian soldiers, with dark Mongolian features and fixed bayonets,

13 The Victors and the Vanquished

in fur caps and mud-stained overcoats over tattered uniforms, marched up the centre of the road with insolent step.

The British Embassy occupied the fourth floor of the Hotel Polonia with the Scandinavians above and the Belgians, French and Americans below – a truly diplomatic hotel! The Russians, by contrast, occupied eight houses in a street some distance away. From the outside, ours was a run-of-the-mill hotel, but inside there was a strange atmosphere suggestive of melodrama. Burt Andrews said we should walk up the stairs – with their faded and threadbare carpets, past the corridors lined with mirrors covered in dust – as the lift stopped at every floor while the lift operator had a cigarette or a chat with someone. Stranger and stranger! I had a room in the office of John Russell, the First Secretary, who had rented a small villa outside the town. Accommodation was in short supply and most of those staying at the hotel used offices as bedrooms.

I put in a spot of what, in happier times, might be called sightseeing. The streets seemed to whisper a warning not to be out alone when the light of day fled. There were wooden hovels, with oil lamps hanging outside, which looked as grim as anything in Dickensian slums. Beggars were everywhere, almost like Belsen inmates, on the point of collapse, too weak to move from their pitches, rattling their tin cans at any passer-by. Had anyone decided that I was an undesirable, I would have disappeared. No one in the street would have batted an eyelid.

I went to the old Jewish quarter, the Warsaw Ghetto, that I had been told was reduced to rubble. The streets looked deserted, save for two men, following me, obviously spies, wearing overcoats and brown hats and with nothing very sinister about their appearance. In the debris of fallen houses, there was a life-sized statue of Christ standing apart, weighed down by a heavy cross. The base had been smashed but the figure of Christ and the cross were undamaged and seemed to be crying out a message for the world. Did those who passed remember the teach-

13   The Victors and the Vanquished

ings of Christianity and the message of love that Christ gave to the world? At the iron gates marking the entrance to the ghetto, instead of the usual skeleton houses, there was a huge mound of bricks, mortar, and an occasional twisted steel girder. The surrounding streets were still covered with glass and brick. Down a sidestreet, a small child clambered over a pile of rubbish and was lost to sight in a heap of bricks. The destruction eclipsed anything that I had seen yet. I couldn't stay and witness people living in such conditions.

I turned round and came face to face with the two men who had been following me. They were surprised and ill at ease. I hurried back to the hotel and was mightily relieved at reaching the refuge of the fourth floor. It would not have surprised me to have been told there was a mutilated corpse on the fifth. I felt that I could have disappeared without trace in that city.

Burt Andrews arranged a party of three of the embassy staff and three attractive Polish girls in a restaurant that had been rebuilt on the ground floor of a bombed-out building. When we entered there was a sudden silence as everyone stared at us. The band continued playing, but we were left with a very strange feeling. We could order any dish that struck our fancy – in marked contrast to the streets outside.

The girl next to me warned me not to discuss politics. She called my attention to the man who was sitting at the table opposite us with a notebook and pencil in his hand and no food on his table. He did not seem to mind that we knew of his role. She insisted that if anything interesting were said, she would be called in for interrogation.

"Of course, they have a torture chamber! It would be better if you say nothing. Then I cannot repeat it. Do you understand?"

While we were dancing, she asked why I had come to Warsaw. When I replied that I was on holiday, she gave a cynical laugh. I was not sure whether she was an agent of the secret police or whether she suspected that I was an agent out to entrap *her*. The

13 The Victors and the Vanquished

atmosphere could hardly be called propitious for romance! The patrons of the restaurant seemed ill-kempt – some were even in collarless shirts. When they danced, they were clumsy in the extreme. They ate with an absence of even the most rudimentary of table manners. They were important Communist Party officials. The waitresses, on the other hand, were obviously of noble birth. They wore signet rings, were quite graceful and were charming to the customers. The new regime seemed to have completely overturned the old class structure.

There was rifle fire in the streets at night. Burt Andrews said that the Russians frequently went on 'shooting-up parties' at night. It made it sound rather a lark – which it certainly wasn't. Like all of us, he had become inured to dicing with death. Why had these 'parties' not been reported in English newspapers? Why did Polish newspapers frequently attack England? I asked this of a Pole and he retorted that Poland no longer believed that England was a great power; she allowed anything and everything to be said about her without objecting. The Russian presence and the Communist ideology were threatening and all-pervasive. A poster advertised an exhibition of 'modern Italian art'. The pictures were crude cartoons and propaganda posters for the Italian Communist Party. A pamphlet explained that the Party's aim was to seize the country's government – because the British and the Americans supported the old Fascist regime. Anyone opposing Communism was a Fascist – from which one might gather that the worst Fascist in Europe was none other than Winston Churchill!

There were many such impressions to discuss with our Ambassador when I lunched at his new home. Cavendish Bentinck was a charming if cautious man, but there – in a veritable little England set amid an alien scene, with old family pictures, antique furniture and pile carpets – he lowered his guard enough to tell amusing tales of the difficulties of dealing with that government. Not a task to be envied.

13 The Victors and the Vanquished

Back in Berlin, Air Marshal Sholto Douglas, porky and pompous, was the British Commanding Officer. We pilots nicknamed him Goering because they looked alike and he gave the impression he wanted to be a dictator. An attractive young WAAF officer was always with him. One evening over dinner he asked my opinion of a painting he had acquired. I thought it might be a Rubens. Sholto thought so too and told me it was his personal souvenir of the war. The more truthful answer, in my submission, was that he had taken it from the castle owned by Prince Schaumburg Lippe. The King complained about his commanders who had taken pictures from his cousin's castle.

Douglas was not the only one. Air marshals and generals were organising looting on a grand scale and were making themselves a fortune. One air marshal, later knighted, collected yachts near Schleswig and sent them back to members of the Cabinet. I suspect he also kept a few. Sholto, who was no socialist, was joining the Labour Party. Later, he was elevated to the barony. I often wonder what happened to his Rubens.

14

Demobbed: Matters of Intelligence

1946
Around us lie the scars of war,
Humanity dying by the score,
And yet it seems that all mankind
Accepts the doctrine of the blind.

The lives of men who gave their blood
Are being trampled in the mud
By despots, rogues and advocates
Of petty socialistic states.

In this world so tattered and torn,
Thoughts are created, genius born,
We must raise our heads towards the light,
Or witness humanity's last fight.

Peace Again
It is almost over now.
The last shot will sound
with one deafening roar
and then there will be no more.
Perhaps I shall smile,
laugh, and rush with mad delight
to all and sundry, shouting
We are at peace not fighting.
Yet within, there will be
a certain sadness,
a chill realisation that
comrades who were friends

14 Demobbed: Matters of Intelligence

will drift away
and all which brightened
our hectic lives
will disappear.
Rooms which brought memories
of dead friends
will now be deserted.
Perhaps I shall grieve
but it will only be a sadness
at knowing youth has gone
and we, who were once applauded,
will be left unwanted, deserted,
the broken fragments of a world
which threw us into war.

I reported to the demobilisation centre in England on a perfect spring day when the countryside was quiet and peaceful. My mind wandered back through the last few eventful years of my life. Would there ever be peace for the world? We had fought so hard for victory and peace, but what peace could there be in Europe with Germany devastated or with Russia occupying so many countries? Had we been mistaken to adopt saturation bombing as a military weapon? Suppose the RAF had been equipped with medium bombers, able to work with the Army and cut off enemy lines of communications and supplies. Suppose Transport Command and parachute forces had been used in greater numbers. Perhaps we could have occupied Germany and kept intact its houses and industries. Suppose we had gone on to liberate Poland. Or what if we had told the Russians to return to Russia? Would any amount of conquering or liberation in itself ensure future peace?

It was a shock to be demobbed. The moment I put on civilian clothes, I lost part of my identity. I no longer belonged to the Services, a socially cohesive group that had come to mean so much to me. I felt insignificant and extremely insecure.

14 Demobbed: Matters of Intelligence

I didn't know what I wanted to do with my life. I had never honestly thought that I would survive the War. I had not worked out career options. I had reached an age when people usually see their direction in life to some extent clear, but for me it was trackless. Or perhaps there were too many possible tracks.

London seemed sane and secure after my trip around the Continent. On one occasion I sat back in the Reform Club and offered Basil Nield another glass of vintage port. The tall pillars, red carpet, and oil paintings of famous politicians helped to create the atmosphere of calm. Basil was immaculately dressed in a dark grey suit, stiff white collar, grey spotted tie, and well-polished shoes. His long fingers played with the glass as he chatted with me

"Do you remember our week in Berlin?" I asked.

"Most entertaining. I enjoyed it immensely."

"It was rather tragic about your poor client."

"Yes. I felt sorry for the boy."

"So did I. It is all over now, but I cannot help thinking about the case. It seems to me to sum up the work our administration has done in Germany. We have created a sordid, depressing area in which that shooting affair was the logical outcome. The black market, vice, and corruption are the only return the taxpayer is going to receive from Germany under the Control Commission."

"Maybe, dear boy." Basil was not going to commit himself. He sipped his coffee and said, "What would have happened if Germany had conquered us?"

"We would have been exterminated. It would have been good policy for Germany to exterminate us. We have always been a thorn in the side of any country that attempts to dominate Europe. However, it would be bad policy to exterminate Germany. Apart from any sentimental or religious reasons, we cannot afford to have a devastated area in Europe. We need the help of German scientists, industrialists, technicians, and artists, to help build up Europe. If Germany collapses into complete chaos, the curtain may well fall on European civilisation."

14 Demobbed: Matters of Intelligence

"Maybe you are right, dear boy." Basil sipped his port.

"Come and have dinner with me next week, and we can talk it over."

"Nothing would please me more. I warn you that I have worked out the solution for all the problems of Europe."

"I shall look forward to hearing it."

I smiled. "When all is said and done, nothing will be achieved if man still accepts the doctrine of 'Blood and Honour'! He must remember the message of the Cross."

A waiter was passing, and I ordered two more vintage ports which we enjoyed sipping. My wartime experiences would be with me to the end of my days. My survival against the odds surely must have given me a different perspective than would otherwise have been the case. Those moments of critical decision-taking that I had gone through had been over matters of immediate life and death, not the more long-term questions that usually preoccupy a young man embarking on his career. Could I now buckle down to a job if what was entailed was a series of vistas in different hues of grey as seen from successive rungs of a career ladder? Or should I try to live a life that had been almost miraculously given back to me as if I had been put on Earth for some purpose beyond my own understanding? What of normalcy and what of right-thinking behaviour? These very guarantors of respectability were now bound up in my mind with adventure. To be an officer in the RAF was to be a pillar of society. But also it had meant that grappling with the strange and the unexpected had become a norm.

My mind was in a whirl, but being calm in a maelstrom was what I was used to. If I may be allowed a metaphor, my path on Earth had been signposted in the skies. Then again, all this is perhaps the thinking of an older and wiser age. My first thought at the time was to see Joy. We would be a happily married couple. With Joy beside me, I could start again.

I find it difficult to write about girlfriends. Somehow, the thing isn't quite done, not at least by men of my generation. Not for us

14 Demobbed: Matters of Intelligence

the touchy-feely ways of today, of 'letting it all hang out'. All I want to say here is that I had met Joy in Torquay before the War. Her father was a vicar and her aunt had been a lady-in-waiting to Queen Mary. Joy was very fond of horses; she had a magnificent hunter, which she rode well. I was captivated by her. Take it from me that she was absolutely charming and … But that's enough.

Before I left for my pilot's training, Joy had given me a mascot as a parting gift – a small doll whose name was Annabella. Joy had claimed that the doll would look after me and begged me always to fly with her. Annabella not only accompanied me on every flight but she has been with me ever since. My feelings about Joy may be guessed at from my feelings about Annabella.

Joy greeted me in Torquay like an old friend. Then she told me that she had decided to marry a former parachutist that she had only recently met.

"I do love you, Dickie, but I know you can look after yourself. Nigel would be hopeless on his own. I have to look after him."

There was nothing I could say.

I suppose it was foolish to hope for a bed of roses, even after what I had been through.

Joy asked me later to be godfather to her son. I regret that I only met her and her husband once more, and when I did, I felt that I was an intruder on their family life.

I came home to my family in St Albans. A letter from the Control Commission awaited me offering me the job of an intelligence officer, granting me in addition the honorary rank of lieutenant-colonel. My father was delighted. There was to be security for his son at last.

I would have none of it.

Was this peacetime soldiering, rather than the muck and bullets that I had survived, the way to promotion? I reflected on the intelligence matters with which I had been involved. I had been

14 Demobbed: Matters of Intelligence

disgusted at generals and air marshals looting in Germany and appalled that my investigations had been stopped because they involved members of the Cabinet. If we had not fought for ideals, what had we fought for? Was I to be prohibited by contract or oath from speaking out? Had I accepted this post, my value to this country or Germany would have been at an end.

To put it more bluntly, I wanted to fly, not be earth-bound. I must make a bid for freedom, not bondage. So many thoughts wandered through my mind that it was hard to disentangle them. Perhaps no one could.

I declined the offer. I was turning my back on being part of organised society. I had no security to ensure financial independence. It was to be my lot to 'fly by the seat of my pants'. The gypsy streak, if that was what it was, would lead me to ... well, one destination would be to the gypsies! My destiny was veiled from me at the time.

Whatever the mindset, there is a logic at play. My father offered me an introduction to the Stock Exchange. This I rejected too. I didn't want to join his firm nor devote myself to a financial career. I suffered as a pilot when I saw destruction all around me. Now I wanted to try to do something to enrich the world with some of the dreams I had experienced as a child.

The world of the theatre had always fascinated me. So I applied to study at the Central School of Acting.

To my surprise, I passed the audition and obtained a small grant. Life was beginning all over again. I was still young. It seemed both simple and wonderful that instead of being in uniform, with fighting people, I had to get to grips with the acting world. It was so different; it was balm to the soul. The relaxation exercises, the mime and movement, the lectures on the history of the theatre; the companionship of young students who had not been involved in the War. It was all a delight. The Central School blew away the clouds of war with gusts of fresh air. Instead of the follies of flying, I could be involved with creativity and study how

14 Demobbed: Matters of Intelligence

to use body and voice to interpret fictitious characters. The school was based then at the Albert Hall. Out of class we went to rehearsals there and from the gallery watched conductors interpret inspiring music. The school taught me to become a human being.

Yet there would always be another side to my life.

While training as an actor, I sometimes visited the Reform Club. I kept my two lives separate and never divulged what I was doing to club members who, I felt, would not understand my new thespian life. I met Guy Burgess again.

Burgess, in fact, made a point of conversing with me. It wasn't long before we crossed swords on the subject of Russia. Rumour had it that the Russians intended to invade Yugoslavia. I pointed out that they would not be accepted in Eastern European countries because they were incapable of co-operating with the population. Furthermore, the average Russian soldier was illiterate and mentally ill-equipped to play the necessary diplomatic role. Burgess accused me of talking nonsense – although, as I pointed out, it was I, and not he, who had had close contact with Russians. I made it pretty plain that I thought that he had no idea what he was talking about. Hackles rose. Burgess, playing on his official role as adviser to the British Government, told me that the Government would do as he advised. That at least made for a touch of humour as I then capitulated and agreed that – in that case only – the Russians would go into Yugoslavia. Burgess laughed in agreement.

Burgess added that he had just told Ernest Bevin, the Foreign Secretary, what to do about it all. I said I didn't believe him.

Burgess lost his temper. He swore that he would show me the relevant papers on Yugoslavia that he had been working on. He had previously boasted that he had access to classified papers in the Foreign Secretary's office; now he would prove it. He summoned a taxi to take him to the Foreign Office. When he returned an hour later to the Club, to my amazement he flung obviously classified papers at me. These contained two memos

14 Demobbed: Matters of Intelligence

from Burgess to Bevin with requests for permission to negotiate directly with the Russians. Burgess hoped to persuade the Russians to let the British Government negotiate with Yugoslavia and not to intervene militarily. A handwritten note from Bevin to Burgess advised him, in Britain's best interests, to use his own discretion in dealing with the Russians.

Almost a year later, I was sitting on the balcony on the second floor beneath the dome inside the Reform Club with two High Court judges discussing the book *I Chose Freedom*, which had been published recently in America by a Russian defector. Burgess stopped at our table and saw the book on my lap. Conspicuously drunk, he snatched the book away and began to harangue my companions and me about the iniquity of the Americans and his loathing of the American way of life. He announced that the book was a pack of lies and threw it from the balcony to the ground floor. The two judges laughed off the incident and advised me to pay no attention to Burgess as he drank too much, although everyone knew he was 'a jolly clever chap'. I never believed him to be clever. On the contrary, I thought him vulgar and self-opinionated.

Two weeks later, Burgess was sent to the British Embassy in the United States. I was amazed at this appointment, considering Burgess's hatred of the Americans, surely well known to the Foreign Office. It was no surprise to me when Burgess returned from America a shattered man. By now a confirmed alcoholic, he often arrived at the Reform Club in the morning unshaven and, apart from his Old Etonian tie, dressed like a tramp.

One evening I was sitting with Burgess and Anthony Blunt when Burgess told Blunt, "You have got to help me sell some pictures."

Blunt looked at Guy as if he were mad.

"Bring them round to the Club and I'll see what I can do. ... For God's sake, stop talking about your problems. I'm getting everything organised for you."

14 Demobbed: Matters of Intelligence

I had never known Blunt so agitated and was startled at the way in which he addressed Burgess. They had always talked together in quiet, confidential tones.

Guy became quite pathetic and begged me to go back to his flat with him. I had never been to his place before, but because he was upset, I thought I had better help him home. He took me to a small flat near Bond Street that was quite unremarkable except for an old spinet surrounded by a few nondescript chairs in the living room. I had imagined that he lived somewhere more civilised, yet here he was in a tiny little place of no artistic appeal. It seemed more the home of some struggling clerk than that of a man who boasted of running the affairs of the country.

Once inside, Burgess pushed me on to a chair beside the spinet and almost sat on top of me. He was so drunk that I hardly understood what he was saying. Suddenly he put his hands on my legs and tried to clutch my penis. I was appalled and immediately rose to my feet.

Although I knew Guy was drunk, I warned him, "Don't you dare try to attack me. If I had known you were inclined that way, I would never have come here."

Burgess immediately apologised, but went on to say, "I can seduce any man or woman I like. I have always been able to have an affair with anyone I like."

"In that case you have made a mistake with me. ... And I object to your boasting that you can seduce any man or woman who appeals to you."

Guy rose to his feet, swaying slightly, with tipsy grandeur. He groped for some papers.

"You should be careful what you say! Look at this file of letters from my friends!"

Burgess flourished in front of me some handwritten letters from Anthony Eden, Winston Churchill and Lord Salisbury. He said that he, Guy Burgess, could do what he wanted, and that he could control the destiny of the country.

14 Demobbed: Matters of Intelligence

I was glad to get out of that flat and return to the Reform Club where I was booked in for the night.

The following morning I felt so angry about the previous night's encounter that I went to see Grey, the Club's secretary, a World War I squadron leader. I told him that I objected to a member of the Club making homosexual advances to me and telling me that because of his sexual prowess, he could influence the prime ministers of Britain. I made it plain that unless my objections were investigated I wouldn't return to the Reform Club. In fact, I never did.

I forgot to tell Grey that I had paid Burgess £52.00 for two nondescript pictures that he had asked me to buy. Much to my surprise, Guy delivered them to the Club. They suffered the same fate as the painting by the Princess of Schleswig-Holstein: my sister later removed them from our St Albans home without my permission and I never saw them again.

Nine months after my meeting with Guy, he fled to Russia. I expected that he would return to England because, judging from the letters he had shown me, I was certain he would not have been prosecuted as a spy. Two weeks after he left, he wrote to me saying that he intended to return. I showed this letter to Norman Batchelor, a reporter on the *Evening Standard*. Two days later this news was featured on the front page of the *Sunday Express*. I asked Norman Batchelor to return the letter, but he told me, profusely apologetic, that it had got lost in his newspaper's offices; of course he hoped he could find it for me. I never got that letter back.

Many years later, in 1972, when I was reading hands at Brean Down, I was surprised to receive a letter from the Ministry of Defence asking me to contact a Mr Maloney, who felt that I could be of some use in supplying information about certain undisclosed matters. I was intrigued. I met Maloney, previously a Coldstream Guards officer, for lunch in a pub in Shepherds Bush. He asked me for any information that I could provide on the associates of Guy Burgess. He refused to tell me who had given

14 Demobbed: Matters of Intelligence

him my name, only volunteering that it had come through the Reform Club. I told him that Anthony Blunt was possibly the only person who could inform him about associates of Burgess, as they were close friends.

After lunch Maloney asked me to accompany him to the MOD so that he could record my remarks. He added that it was at Prime Minister Edward Heath's request that these enquiries were being made. He said that although Blunt was a friend of Burgess, the MOD was satisfied that he was not involved with spying in any way. I suggested that instead of asking me, Maloney would do much better to ask the secretary of the Reform Club about Blunt.

I returned to Weston-Super-Mare to find a letter from Maloney addressed from the MOD dated 15 September 1972. In it was a postal order reimbursing me for the underpayment of expenses by one pound. Maloney then suggested that because he was otherwise engaged, one of his colleagues should come down and look at the book of memoirs that I was thinking about writing and which at that stage was in draft form.

Maloney's colleague turned out to be Mrs Stella Rimmington, later head of our security services and the first woman to be accorded that position. We had dinner together, which I was to regret. It did not go well. When I first met her I was furious when she suggested that I could have been a spy. She insisted on seeing my journal, and once I complied, took it with her to London. I appeared to have no choice but to let her, much as it rankled. Eventually I wrote to Maloney asking him to return my papers. He replied that I would have to leave them in their hands for the time being. I was very upset and informed Joe Gallagher, a local press agent, about what had gone on. He in turn told me that both the *Sunday Express* and the *Sunday Telegraph* wanted to print my comments and explain why my drafts had been confiscated. It also transpired that the *Sunday Express* had wanted to write an

14 Demobbed: Matters of Intelligence

article about it all, but that apparently the MOD had advised against it.

Roll the clock forward again to when I was a professional palmist and working at Carnaby Market. I read Mrs Thatcher's admission in the press that Blunt was the fourth spy in the ring of Burgess, Philby and Maclean – and that there had been *no previous investigations*. This was nonsense. As early as in 1970 I had been summoned to the MOD, and it was arguably the case that official interest in this story was such that a Sunday newspaper was gagged from publishing my comments. I phoned the *Times* and told them of these facts, as I knew them. The next day, Tuesday 20 November 1979, the *Times* reported that Squadron Leader Leven had stated that in 1942, many years before Burgess defected, Blunt's association with Guy Burgess was well known. The report failed to mention that Mr Maloney had interviewed me at the MOD in 1972.

I was told then that after three investigations about Blunt by former prime ministers, the MOD was satisfied that he was not involved in spying. It defied belief that Mrs Thatcher could have concluded Blunt was a spy simply from Chapman Pincher's book *Their Trade is Treachery*. The MOD must have told her, as they did me, that they were sure he was not a spy. I now think that the MOD had found itself in an impossible position. Victor Rothschild had engaged Blunt and Burgess to keep contact with the Russians, but Rothschild also apparently wanted Wright and Chapman Pincher to reveal that they were spies, although he was the one who had introduced them to the MOD.

Then there is the case of Philby. Inevitably, he could not stay at the MOD because the Americans were determined to continue their investigations into the spy ring and any forthcoming evidence would have implicated Blunt as well. I am convinced that Blunt was encouraged to stay on at Buckingham Palace as Keeper of the Queen's pictures and that the MOD was doing everything in its power to stop his name being mentioned. This accounts for

14 Demobbed: Matters of Intelligence

Mr Maloney's forbidding me to implicate Blunt with Burgess in my book – at the time Maloney was working at the MOD.

After the news about Blunt had become common knowledge, I went to dinner with Adrian Heath and his wife. She greeted me saying, "Richard, you were right. I remember your telling me about Blunt, and now it has turned out just as you said."

I had told all my friends about Blunt's association with Burgess. In addition, the facts were known both to the Ministry of Defence and the Foreign Office. As soon as Maclean and Burgess left this country, it was known that Blunt was their associate.

This is not a book of political theory but I cannot resist putting to paper my personal views about one aspect that helps explain the above events.

After the war the British Government considered US foreign policy dangerous. According to Burgess, the Russians were rearming because they felt threatened by America, both in the Far East and in Europe; furthermore, Russia might risk going into Europe to stop America building up overwhelming forces against her. I am sure that Bevin asked Burgess to liaise with the Russians to diffuse the situation and stop the intended invasion of Yugoslavia. As Bevin was a very close associate of Burgess, he must have known how sympathetic Guy was to the Russians. When Burgess was in America he stayed with the brother of Air Commodore Whitney Straight who had been at Cambridge with him. Straight wanted political power in America and I have no doubt he reported Burgess's remarks to those in American government, who would have been horrified.

Naturally, the British couldn't support Burgess openly because, apart from anything else, they had tied the pound to the dollar and didn't want to risk any financial complications. I suspect that this was one reason why Burgess and his associates from MI5 were turned into spies. The British Government did not want the Americans to think they had been double-crossed. It

14 Demobbed: Matters of Intelligence

was tragic that Burgess was sent to America when it was common knowledge that he was in contact with the Russians with whom he was negotiating. I am of the opinion that Burgess and Maclean were instructed to leave England and go to Russia so that they could be called spies. It enabled the Foreign Office to stop being embarrassed by the Americans, who knew from Burgess how hypocritically the British had behaved.

After Dunkirk Churchill feared that the Russians might make another deal with Hitler when he invaded Russia. He was therefore keen that the MOD should save and recruit Communist sympathisers who could negotiate with the Russians so that we could build up forces to oppose Germany. Burgess told me that not only had Victor Rothschild – who was closely connected with Government circles – given him a flat, but because of Burgess's Communist connections, Rothschild had also invited him to join the MOD. Apparently Churchill trusted Rothschild to recruit people who could continue negotiations with the Russians.

I have not forgotten the remarks of Sir Basil Embry, the first Commander-in-Chief of NATO, who later asked me to be a NATO intelligence officer. When we lunched together at the Reform Club, he shocked me by saying that he was resigning as Commander-in-Chief and would decline ever to represent this country again. He told me his reasons: the Government had instructed him to liaise with the Russians and supply them with information about our forces so that they would not feel obliged to build up theirs. Then he had suddenly been told to stop doing so. He felt this would only make them re-arm and that the work he had already done at the Government's request would have all been for nought. It was his view that the Government had changed its policy at the request of the Americans. I agreed not to accept a post with Sir Basil because he told me he had no intention of staying with NATO. He added that he would never work in any capacity at all for this country again, and he never did. In the end he left to farm in New Zealand and Australia.

14 Demobbed: Matters of Intelligence

When I was at the Central School, Basil Nield – then a barrister and Conservative MP for Chester and later knighted when a High Court judge – invited me to a debate in the House of Commons. He had arranged a privileged seat for me perhaps because I held a few decorations. The debate was boring and futile. Labour and Conservative representatives alike were dreary and had no idea how to speak in public. It was appalling to think that this was the Government of the country. One could understand why the Romans and Greeks had oratory on the curriculum as training for a public life. The speeches at Westminster were worse in their delivery than in any debate at my preparatory school. Studying voice projection at the Central School of Acting, at the least, should have been an essential part of the training for Westminster if the level of performance I witnessed was anything to go by!

The relief of going onto the terrace overlooking the Thames for a drink with Basil was not long-lived. Quentin Hogg, later Lord Hailsham, joined us. I had a lively recollection of his brusqueness to me years previously in Belgium. He asked me what I had thought about the debate, so I told him.

"I'm sorry to say that I have never heard such unmitigated nonsense spoken in the chamber. To see the Thames flowing by as it has done for centuries compensates for the babble I regret I've had to listen to. It's a pity that people have to utter such nonsense in such distinguished surroundings."

Quentin Hogg was furious.

"You have insulted the House of Commons. I hope I never see you again."

With that, the man stood up and left. Basil merely laughed.

"That is typical Quentin. He's so emotional that you can't talk sense with him. I agree with you, but he thinks that the House of Commons is unique and won't listen to any criticism of it. He believes that he should run the place. We are worried he might become Prime Minister."

14 Demobbed: Matters of Intelligence

Quentin tried, but failed to become Prime Minister and the Tories did their best, or worst, and made him Lord Chancellor. He must have spent his time promoting the more boring and pedantic barristers to become judges!

It was not long before it dawned on me that the army and governments were not the only arenas in which the wrong people seemed to make it to the top.

15

Star of Stage, Screen
... and Orchestra Pit

After Central School, I spread my fledgling acting wings. There was no intervening lull. I was engaged to play in weekly repertory at the Grand Theatre, Luton, under the able management of the actor Malcolm Phillips, a truly gifted man of the theatre. After Luton, I had a role in *Arms and the Man* at Swansea, where I was billed as 'an outstanding actor'. Then came London and the Torch Theatre under Julian Fane. One thing led to another and it was not long before I ran up against the tough reality behind the glitzy facade of the film business.

The routine of the film studios – I was in *Angels One Five* – was a very early start in the morning, hanging about waiting to appear on set, saying a few words, and at the end of it all, nothing but a handsome pay packet. I could hardly see why people bothered. The average film star was a grossly overpaid unmitigated bore with a photogenic face, devoid of any but the rudiments of theatre technique. John Gregson had been an ordinary seaman during the war and did not look like any pilot I ever knew but I suppose he had the type of face that casting directors thought glamorous. Jack Hawkins I did find really charming and sympathetic and he had a great knowledge of the theatre, but I didn't care for Zsa Zsa Gabor, who was extraordinarily rude. When she was on the set, it was almost impossible to get any shot filmed as directed because she seemed incapable of giving a consistent performance. I cared even less for Alec Guiness, who was such an unbearable snob that even though I had actual experience of the role he was playing, which he certainly hadn't got – I had led fighters into Malta! – he talked down to me on the set of *Malta Story*, it being beneath him to pick my brains.

15 Star of Stage, Screen ... and Orchestra Pit

I returned with relief to repertory and a succession of dates that, to the thespian, cannot be recited as one might a railway timetable; each had its own whiff of grease-paint, its own often tawdry but evocative aura: ... the Theatre Royal, Brighton; the Grand Theatre, Blackpool; the King's Theatre, Glasgow; the Empire, Grantham; the Theatre Royal, Huddersfield; the Playhouse, Lowestoft. Wartime friendships sometimes intersected those of the theatre world. Lewis Shaw and Kenneth Seale gave me an entrée to Spotlight. Through Helena Pickard, whose brother Percy had flown with me and who was subsequently killed on the raid on Amiens Jail, I met Noël Coward. The Pickards owned the Café de Paris where Helena invited me to the opening night of Coward's show. He was then a most celebrated actor-writer-director and he performed his first post-war cabaret act at the Café.

Before the show, we met John Barbirolli, conductor of the great Hallé Orchestra. He had been told that I read hands and insisted that I read his palm. Embarrassing for me, but I said what I could.

"I have the impression that although you were a cellist in Vienna, in fact you started your career as conductor of a brass band. You became quite intoxicated with Strauss waltzes and enjoyed dancing round the rostrum every time you conducted them."

Barbirolli beamed like a child.

"You're right. I loved Strauss and I love him now. I did start my career as a brass band conductor in Vienna and I'm amazed that you could tell me so because I've never mentioned this fact before. You are also right in saying that I love to dance round the rostrum to Strauss's waltzes. For me Strauss was the greatest composer and I always feel uplifted when I conduct his waltzes. I'm one of the few conductors who know how to make Strauss give the audience a feeling of magic. You can't conduct him merely by doing the waltz-time beat of one-two-three which English conductors think so important. Instead, with him, you must vary the

186

15 Star of Stage, Screen ... and Orchestra Pit

beat so that you produce that sense of magic Strauss knew so well. Next time I conduct the Hallé Orchestra in London you must come as my guest and watch me waltzing round the rostrum so you can understand what I mean."

After the show Coward joined us and I reminded him that he had auditioned me for one of his new plays and had summoned me to the stalls to talk to him. Coward remembered me and apologised for not pursuing the acquaintance further. Because his manager had never discovered my name or agent, he hadn't known how to contact me. I admitted that this was partly my fault as, after the audition, thinking that the management knew my agent's name, I had dashed off to meet a girlfriend.

Six months later, the Hallé Orchestra was playing at the Festival Hall, and Barbirolli gave me a free box. When the Viennese brass band was playing Strauss's *Roses from the South*, he danced round the rostrum.

Would that peacetime life was made up of more such moments ...

While directing *A Multitude of Sins* by Rodney Ackland, I was invited to Terence Rattigan's flat in the Albany. Rattigan suggested I direct one of his new plays. Before we signed a contract, I met the Lunts, famous American actors who had great technical ability. Rattigan pressed me for criticisms of his play. Reluctantly, I asked if the third act had been written in a different context and if it had been altered at the actors' suggestion.

Alfred Lunt laughed and confirmed that I was correct. He and his wife had rewritten it. To my amazement, some young men sitting near Rattigan sprang to their feet and told me that my comments were insulting! Rattigan laughed it off but I was embarrassed. Two days later, Binkie Beaumont, the West End manager of the omnipotent H. M. Tennants, who concealed a quick mind behind an appearance not unlike that of a Jewish grandmother, telephoned to say that he was very upset to hear about what I had said to Terence Rattigan. I would never perform or direct in any

15 Star of Stage, Screen … and Orchestra Pit

theatre with which he was associated. My West End career lay in ashes on his black list.*

I still had my dreams of the circus.

Near my home in St Albans was a small travelling circus, Ringlands by name. After a performance, I was in a pub and seated near me was a voluptuous lady and another woman with flashing eyes, long, flowing, jet-black hair and wearing pendant earrings and a glittering collection of diamond rings. Ladies of the circus! The elder of this striking pair had earlier served me with tickets from a box office in a converted bus and was the mother of the trapeze artist, the girl with flowing dark hair. Next to me was a thickset ginger-haired man, who ordered three pints and spoke in some rural accent. He looked as though he came from the circus, too, so I started talking to him.

"Terrific show tonight. Pity there weren't more people."

He looked at me carefully. "Are you in the business?"

"Sort of. I'm an actor-producer. I'm thinking of doing a film about the circus."

Claude – that was the man's name – was married to Sister, she of the jet-black hair. He insisted on buying me a drink and he took me over to his ladies with the words, "This is Dick. He's a pro."

The famous Mrs Ginette Fossett chuckled to her daughter.

"I told you so. I knew he was a pro the moment I sold him a ticket."

Sister flashed me a look and agreed that business was not what it used to be.

"What d'you know about circuses?" she asked.

---

* Beloved by many in showbiz as Binkie was, the following conversation with the theatrical and literary agent Eric Glass, who represented Rodney Ackland until their acrimonious falling out, might be seen as instructive:
Binkie: "My secretary who has been with me for 17 years is leaving."
Glass: "But why?"
Binkie: "That's what I asked her. She replied that she doesn't think she likes me!"

15 Star of Stage, Screen ... and Orchestra Pit

"Nothing. I go to a circus whenever I can. I saw your show two seasons ago at Swindon when you had Aga, the star of the elephant film."

"Fancy that! We had a better season then." Old Mrs Fossett half-smiled as she tried to divine my thoughts.

Dennis Fossett, a burly man, joined us. An idea came to me on the spur of the moment. I would write the music and script for a show that I hoped, naively, the Fossetts would finance. I described it in some detail: a stage circus that would be a form of musical comedy, constructed around a slender plot. At the time I did not know it, but circus people hoard their money and do not speculate with strangers. Nevertheless, after playing some popular tunes on the piano, even beginning to compose some, they greeted my enthusiasm with pleasure. I was convinced I would soon be producing a circus.

I was equally certain that I had found a new way of life that would appeal to me.

I told the family of my friendship with Alan Russell, then secretary of the Agents Association in London. The Fossetts knew his name and no doubt this tenuous connection influenced their encouragement of my ideas.

Like me, Alan Russell had been in the RAF, he during the First World War and I in the Second. Operations pilots only survived by taking decisions made in seconds, which tended to make them more excitable than other people. They often suffered delayed shellshock. With this experience in common, Alan had become both a friend and an adviser.

When I called at his offices in Charing Cross Road he warned me:

"The Fossetts are a well-known circus family, but no one can do business with circus people. Forget them, Dickie, and keep to the theatre and films."

I was not to be put off so easily. Alan could never resist a drink and that evening in the pub I persuaded him that a

15 Star of Stage, Screen ... and Orchestra Pit

stage show built round a circus had a strong chance of proving a novel attraction.

On a lovely September afternoon, Alan and I drove down to Aylesbury to find Ringlands Circus. Gaily painted caravans brightened the scene: dogs barked and an elephant wandered loose round the fields eating a few branches it pulled from a tree. We strode towards a large caravan. A face peered from behind one of the curtains to watch us. The English circus comprises one huge family who may well be brothers, sisters, aunts, uncles and cousins with rivalries and jealousies all the greater for that. But circus people do not welcome strangers.

Mrs Fossett opened her caravan door and greeted us warmly, giving us the impression that we were about to be invited to a séance or have our fortunes told. This extraordinary eighty-year-old lady had the gift of reading palms and foreseeing the future. She was a circus queen and her family couldn't take any decisions without her approval. While in theory her son Dennis was running the show, it was she and her daughter, Sister, who had the last word. Claude and Dennis did all the manual work, but were completely dominated by their women: it was the way of the circus world. Dennis joined us for tea and stated bluntly that we shouldn't discuss business with the other artistes who liked nothing better to hype up gossip. He insisted that Alan should see the show. Alan, out of his element in the caravan, was determined to adopt the attitude of the successful and knowledgeable variety agent. Alan and I enjoyed it all, the creaking Big Top, the old seating, the heavy redwood king poles, the overhanging lamps and the rough enthusiastic skill of the artistes and animals; all made for an atmosphere of the traditional circus.

We were hooked.

After Alan and I returned to London, we agreed with the Fossetts that I would either procure some theatres for the winter to tour the circus or I would devise my circus musical. We were all enthusiastic. I had the nucleus of a small business and the oppor-

15 Star of Stage, Screen ... and Orchestra Pit

tunity of becoming an agent. It was a time for action. Thus began the Richard Leven Agency, based in the offices of Guy Charles, an old producer friend. It was here that I devised my new circus stage show. The story was simple. A clown falls in love with a beautiful lady who joins the circus and who eventually abandons him. The subplot involved the lions and was based on characters I had known at Ringlands Circus. The romantic tunes that I composed were like old-fashioned waltzes as well as stirring marches, the *Tritch-Tratch Polka*, ragtime and other circus oldies. It would be a show with a difference.

Well, it was certainly that!

My optimism for my project verged on the foolhardy. To be all but broke and reliant for income on a deal with circus folk probably epitomises that state of affairs.

Alan Russell managed to persuade Moss Empires to let me have the Theatre Royal, Portsmouth, for my Christmas stage production. This was a wonderful opportunity. Christmas productions in large theatres played for over £2,000 a week. My script was ready and I only needed the Fossetts to agree. Dennis was cagey on the phone and asked me to go to Birmingham. From there I was to catch a bus for Northampton but alight at a petrol station that apparently the Fossetts owned. I finally met up with the family and explained our luck. The idea met with interest, but neither commitment nor decision. My direct questions were countered by evasions. Sister and Dennis told me that their mother liked to go into a trance to discover what action the spirits decided she should take. I assured Alan that a decision would be made in a few days. Like me, he doubted Moss Empires would appreciate being kept waiting by mystic forces, bearing in mind that many distinguished producers were only too keen for a Christmas booking at that theatre. Ten days later I was flabbergasted to hear that Dennis thought the theatre too big for his mother and requested instead some small theatres for a stage circus.

15 Star of Stage, Screen ... and Orchestra Pit

When I told Alan he laughed.

"I told you so, Dickie. Circus people are the hardest people in the world to deal with. Only their own people can deal with them."

I asked him if he would book some small theatres.

"No!" he said. "If I do, they'll probably not turn up. I can't ruin my business for them."

In the end I managed to book a small unpromising music hall for the Fossett Stage Circus and the family accepted and signed all the contracts. My problems had just begun!

A week before Christmas when the show was due to open, I arrived in Southend to organise the advance publicity and make all the stage arrangements.

Roberto Germains, ringmaster at Great Yarmouth, was horrified by my contract to take the Fossetts on the stage. He said that the real trouble was likely to be between Dennis, Claude, Sister and the mother who could never make up her mind. He also advised me to go armed with my own collection of music.

I was met with a state of chaotic unpreparedness. The theatre manager was in a panic as to where the animals – and in particular, the elephant – were to be stabled. I was aghast when I saw the tiny stage. It couldn't possibly hold an elephant weighing several tons, added to which I very much doubted if the lion cage could be set up. The orchestra leader wanted to know who was to be the conductor – for there wasn't one! Although the programme hadn't even been set, the manager insisted that his printers must have it that evening or there would be no programme.

My spirits were at low ebb and sinking steadily. I had no idea what to do. In the afternoon, I wandered round the town looking for premises for the largest elephant in England – to people's obvious amazement. With the help of the police, I finally found a barn out of town. When I returned, there was an unknown caravan parked outside the theatre. This turned out to belong to Tom Fossett, an uncle of Dennis and Claude, who had come with his

15 Star of Stage, Screen ... and Orchestra Pit

monkeys, two horses and groom. Arty, another relation, came along too. He painted vivid pictures of lions and elephants, the kind that decorate travelling shows. Tom and his wife gave me a welcome cup of tea and solved my printing worries by working out some sort of running order and naming the various acts. The solution to one of the problems revealed a greater horror. It had been decided that I was expected to be the orchestra conductor as well.

I tramped back through the snow to my lodgings. How I regretted ever getting mixed up with a circus! I phoned Dennis at his pub and asked when he was arriving.

"We've got some trouble with the wagons. We'll get there by Christmas Eve," said this angel of light.

"What on earth am I supposed to do about the music and the programmes?"

"I'll leave it to you, Dick. Do the best you can."

Do the best I could!

I was trying to produce a stage circus with no artistes, no music and no knowledge whatsoever of anything to do with circuses. I felt like taking the next train back to London. But my pride wouldn't let me go and I was determined to see the whole thing through. Tom Fossett had assured me his relations would arrive and he knew them better than me. I spent that evening sorting out music that I used to enjoy. Although I could play the piano I had never examined a complete score before, let alone thought that I should ever conduct an orchestra, although in the back of my mind I had dreamed of conducting. So here was my chance!

The following day I arrived at the theatre with my music sorted and in an order that I hoped would suit the programme. I had no idea of the length of the acts and no better notion of what sort of music would be really suitable. The twelve-piece orchestra was flabbergasted. Its players had never encountered a conductor who didn't even know what his show was about. So, as it was almost Christmas, I laughed it off with them when I explained the position and they agreed to be as helpful as possible. I set the

15 Star of Stage, Screen ... and Orchestra Pit

music on the basis that the tune would change when I thought we had played one for long enough. I told them there was nothing like extemporising. It was what circus life was all about! There were to be strong marches for the lions and waltzes and foxtrots for the horses, a slow waltz for the trapeze and an odd polka between acts.

The orchestra was amazed – perhaps 'delighted' is *le mot juste* – to spend so little time rehearsing. They promised to turn up half an hour before the house was admitted on Boxing Day in case I had any changes to make. As I found it impossible to read the score and conduct at one and the same time, I determined to do the whole thing from memory. I still fondly believe that the orchestra never guessed that I had never conducted before. Had they done so, I doubt whether Fossett's Stage Circus would ever have opened on its winter tour of the Number Three Touring Music Halls.

On Christmas Eve, Salt, the elephant, arrived by train in one of British Railways' special trucks. Very much the worse for wear after her trip, Salt was happy to clamber onto the platform. Tiny, her groom, a tall scarecrow of a chap, wore the dirtiest floppy trilby I have ever seen on anyone. He too had clearly suffered the journey in the elephant truck with distaste, and his only concern was where to stable Salt. I had to accompany them through the streets full of Christmas shoppers who hindered our progress by offering Salt buns and titbits as she ambled along. She was in no hurry and made spasmodic raids on parcels that attracted her. Tiny and I rescued more than one collection of Christmas presents from her insatiable appetite. The fact that I never for one moment doubted my sanity is perhaps a comment on my very lack of it! And things were not about to get any better.

The Fossetts didn't arrive until nine o'clock in the evening, 'due to the snow', an insouciant Dennis told me. I discovered later that they had delayed leaving the farm until the last moment as Mrs Fossett had changed her mind and hadn't really wanted to

15 Star of Stage, Screen ... and Orchestra Pit

set out. Then there were long arguments as to what would happen should they fail to undertake their commitments. We had the devil of a job getting the lion boxes up the ramp and on to the stage. The lions took a dim view of the proceedings as we levered up the boxes while avoiding claws that were obviously meant to deter us. Then Dennis grumbled that the stables I had found were too far away for most of the ponies. We were later able to persuade the manager to let six of them be stabled in the dressing rooms, one of which had already been allotted to the monkeys.

Just when everything was sorted out, 'Captain' Yank Miller dampened any chance that my spirits might start to rise.

The Captain was half blind, more than a bit deaf, and nearly seventy – just the right character for a lion trainer! It appeared that at some time a circus ring mauling had failed to complete a job that was by rights that of Father Time. He told me that he was ending his career, thereby striking the most hopeful note in this sorry saga. He was, however, full of good ideas, was Yank. The circus lioness had recently given birth to two spirited cubs. Yank decided they should return with us to enliven our dismal Southend digs. He carried one while I managed the other. Another couple of days of feline growth and it would have been the other way around! They were larger than household cats and already well endowed as far as Nature's equipment went, claws being no exception. We wore protective gloves, and needed to.

Luckily our landlady was amused to have two baby lionesses in her house. Her black cat did not share her view of the matter! The cat went hysterical. Yank growled at the lions and they growled at him.

Yank loved talking about the circus.

"All owners are rotten. They'll grind you into the mud. You're on the scrap-heap when you're no more use to them. Look at me. I've got nothing but scars and they won't give me compensation. I've come right out of hospital and gone straight back in the ring. If I wasn't there, they wouldn't pay me. I knew a trainer who was

15 Star of Stage, Screen ... and Orchestra Pit

mauled and taken to hospital. The circus moved off the next day and left his wife there with no transport – discarded her. That's circus for you. It's a rotten, dirty life."

There was still a week to go till the circus show began. How many more freaks were going to show up? What was I being softened up for? Yank was a hard, embittered man. His stories were tinged with resentment, filled with the threat, all too frequently realised, of catastrophe. He had a fund of tall stories about the circus. He had been stranded on the road when his tent had been ripped in a storm! He had rescued his lions from fire! Or was it a burning hell? Like Dennis Fossett, he had never been to school and could neither read nor write. When he appeared in the lion cage, he wore a flaming red shirt, riding breeches and boots. Though he had never served as an army officer, his clipped moustache and short cut hair made him look like a cavalry officer. As is the tradition for circus owners and artistes to give themselves titles and a rank that is passed down the generations, Yank was 'entitled' to the rank of Captain.

Away from the lion cage and removed to our digs, Yank was an entirely different person. He addressed the landlady as "Lady" and had difficulty sitting at table using a knife, which he gripped with evident desperation. He lost that military bearing and alertness, which was his in spades when in the ring, and that might have given me grounds to think that in him I had some sort of a prop in an hour of need.

Help, circus-style, was, however, at hand. Dennis Fossett had contracted a strong man called Samson who could lift fourteen men on a plank and do iron-bending and nail-hammering tricks. There was also an Indian, who could do an act on top of a swaying pole. But there was no time to teach it to me! He had missed his chance – before I met the cats! By the time young Bob Fossett arrived in a converted bus that was painted in a giant palette of garish colours, I was past caring. He invited me to a cup of tea. Never had man greater need of the Englishman's medicinal balm!

15 Star of Stage, Screen ... and Orchestra Pit

A rehearsal was the only bridge that could get us safely to the day of the performance, which was Boxing Day. It didn't happen. Rehearsals generally don't happen in the circus. But then a man doesn't generally need a lifeline – it is the event of an emergency that alters the case.

Because the stage wouldn't hold the elephant, she paraded up and down outside the theatre to prove her existence. Dolly Yelding did a pony-riding ballerina act on the tiny stage, which was indeed some feat. Sister's dogs performed with gusto, and the monkeys were particularly popular with the children – although that popularity was at the expense of some unpopularity with the adults, particularly those adults that had any musical sensitivity. Ragtime has never been played slower or quicker, according to the mood of a monkey. Before that, however, Cilla, Dennis's wife, appeared on the slack wire when we in the pit were expecting those monkeys, prompting a quick change of music. It wasn't quite *Happy Birthday* suddenly segueing into *God Save the Queen* – but it felt like it to the hapless conductor.

During a delay, explicable in part by the snoring of an ape, Little Bob and Andy Yelding kept things going by a dance with a balloon that was uproariously funny, if only because clowns appeared and disappeared without warning. I discovered later that this intermission came about because the ponies were having difficulties getting up to the stage from the 'dressing rooms'. Dennis was in an ugly mood, the reason for which grew more understandable as time went by, and carried on and on going by. He didn't enjoy showing his horses off when they finally made it to the ring; they and he got into an awful muddle. The audience responded with shrieks of laughter. Dennis got so furious that he mounted one of his steeds as if to charge at the catcalling mob, only to bring forth a redoubled howling of mirth!

Then Captain Yank Miller, apparently falling prey to a sudden fit of pyromania, tried to set light to a hoop for his cats to

15 Star of Stage, Screen ... and Orchestra Pit

jump through. Clearly, he should have stuck to cigarettes. The fire flared upwards – nearly ending his circus career earlier even than he hoped – much to the alarm of the theatre staff. Determined still to go out on a note of death or glory, he then chased the lions through the fiery hoop with a fury that implied the incident was their fault, which made for a stirring performance. A more fitting finale might have seen the lions returning to the chase or, if not that, at least seen the theatre staff jumping through the hoops – but that would have been to imply that there was order somewhere amid this chaos.

I had other nightmares of my own to contend with in the pit. The musicians had begun to pay less and less attention to me or, indeed – judging by the way they insisted by themselves on playing – to what was happening on stage. The more frantic my gesticulations grew, however, the greater and louder the applause. To that, at least, I managed to put a stop. Perhaps my greatest failure as a conductor came at the very end of the show with the playing of the national anthem. I had thought I knew *God Save the Queen*. I had thought it a tune to be beaten out as a slow march, in four-four time. I have to report that on this occasion it was not played as such. I state that as a fact baldly and without elaboration as to its consequences.

We got through it, somehow. And that was that.

There was only one more thing that could happen now to knock what little wind was left out of my sails. And right on cue, happen it did. Our show was declared by all and sundry to be – a success!

What I learned about the circus after the show was over would have been extremely useful had I but known it before. Unlike variety performers, circus artistes are used to improvising the order of their programme; which act follows which does not worry them in the least. For instance, in a tented circus the clowns are used to appearing at a moment's notice often because bad weather necessitates a changed order of the animals' appear-

15 Star of Stage, Screen ... and Orchestra Pit

ances. The clowns can be relied on to work together until the next act – whatever it is – is ready.

In the evenings for the rest of our short season, the local pub welcomed us all after each performance. Mrs Fossett was always in good humour there, and those pub evenings were full of circus reminiscences. After a few scotches Dolly became talkative and confidential, and Sister and Mrs Fossett told outrageous stories of love affairs. They howled with laughter when I reacted with shocked amazement. Because it was a new world to me, I was never quite sure who they were talking about anyway.

In the pub, the grooms and other artistes kept away from the family. Like any queen, Mrs Fossett, who was the actual owner, summoned to her side those to whom she wanted to talk. Circus artistes might be excellent performers, but if they weren't related to any of the established circus families, they were outsiders and were known as 'joshers'. Being 'circus', on the other hand, meant being related to a family that had been in the business for at least a hundred years; even Billy Smart did not qualify. There was intense rivalry between fairground and circus families and the Smarts came from the fairground. The two backgrounds might be similar, but circus families regard themselves as the aristocrats of the travelling showpeople. This is perhaps natural because the tradition of the circus has a more distinguished history. The fairground has closer associations with the tinker, who is not accepted by the Romanies. Since early times, when the horse show in Italy was the forerunner of the European circus, a circus family has resented comparison with the tinker or the fairground.

16

The Impresario

After Southend I took the circus to seven other music halls, finishing up at Pontypridd in Wales. When that experience was behind me, I planned to continue my stage career as an actor or directing plays in the provinces. I had many friends who were out of work, and I was friendly with Lewis Shaw and Kenneth Seale who did the casting at Spotlight and who often recommended actors I suggested. The big London agents cast the West End shows and were primarily interested in promoting artists who were already well known. For this reason, Spotlight was only able to introduce my recommendations to provincial repertory companies.

So the Richard Leven Agency was used mostly to promote circus artists and also to help my friends in the theatre who had no other possibility of making it to the West End. My premises in Great Newport Street opposite the Arts Theatre Club cost a few pounds a week. The coffee bar opposite my agency where I often took clients became almost an extended part of my office. I often met Clement Freud, then in charge of catering at the Arts Theatre. I had been at Bryanston with his brother, Lucian. I thought him rather conceited. Downstairs, an Anglo-Indian couple ran the Kismet Club for the theatre and film business. All in all, it added up to a good centre for theatrical activity.

Janet Munro, a delightful young actress with whom I had acted, was the club hostess. Her father Alex Munro, a well-known music hall comedian, begged me to give her some acting opportunities. Through my old friend Guy Charles, I managed to get her the lead part in *Pick Up Girl*, currently touring the provinces. This led to another of my contacts casting her for the part on Granada Television. Finally, United Artists offered her a

16 The Impresario

contract for £10,000 to play juvenile leads. From the Kismet Club, within a year, this unknown actress became a nationally-known star.

Janet married twice after this success and she and I stayed friends; every Christmas she sent me a case of wine. It came as a great shock to me when I heard that she had committed suicide. She had become an alcoholic and couldn't cope with the emotional demands of the weak men who continually pestered her.

At about the same time I met Susan Hampshire, aged seventeen. She was not particularly impressive as a person but she undoubtedly had star quality. I got her a small part in an advertising film. At about that time she had a romance with Andrew Ray, a juvenile star who loved driving his sports car. I warned him to be careful when driving because I sensed there was danger in it for him. Soon afterwards he had a crash that nearly killed him, and I felt this might have happened because his romance with Susan was falling apart.

My name was known in the circus world now and more and more circus artistes visited me. My tours of plays were not doing too well but opportunity suddenly knocked when Big Bobby Fossett – who used to do a stilts act – called and begged me to visit Bailley and Bobby Fossett who ran Sir Robert Fossett's circus. He told me that because I had done well with Dennis Fossett and family, their cousins would like me to be their manager and ringmaster.

Ever since childhood I'd thought of the circus as a personal form of magic. The circus world was beyond the real world of political complications, including Hitler and the War. As a pilot I had stayed alive when friends had died. Now I had the chance of finding out how the world of magic worked – and this would then destroy or resurrect my childhood dreams. So I accepted Big Bobby Fossett's invitation to meet the owner of Sir Robert Fossett's circus, then at Northampton.

16 The Impresario

Sleepy, a groom who I had met with Dennis Fossett, came to greet me.

"Mary and Bailley are waiting for you. Mary runs the show you know. We all have to deal with Mary. She's Bailley's half-sister but with this circus she's the boss. Come this way."

Bailley Fossett met me in the largest circus wagon I had ever seen, carpeted luxuriously and ornamented with clusters of china lions and elephants.

Mary told me, "You are one of us. I know from my cousins you can read hands but we don't believe in that business in our shows, although we sometimes do it when we feel like using the gift."

I was offered a contract to be ringmaster and general manager for the season. It was, I was told, unprecedented in that the post had never before been offered to anyone outside the circus. We shook hands on the agreement. The world of childhood magic had suddenly become the world of reality. Now, in 1953, I was to discover the life of the tenting, travelling showman – a world about which no one who has not been accepted as a traveller can truthfully write.

At Moss Bros I purchased a second-hand 'pink' hunting-jacket, a top hat, a deep navy blue jacket with tails and two pairs of white gloves. With the dinner jacket and tails and several white bow ties I could always look immaculate in the part of the traditional ringmaster.

Microphone or not, my voice training would come in handy. ...

"My Lords, Ladies and Gentlemen, I have great pleasure in presenting to you Sir Robert Fossett's circus. We commence our performance this evening with Sir Robert Fossett's unique wild animal act presented to you by the world's most famous wild animal trainer, Captain Bailley Fossett. Allez-oop!"

It was the first week in April and bitterly cold. As we drove to the circus outside Coventry snow covered the earth where the canvas of the Big Top tent also lay, although at least the king-poles had been erected. In the circus world if you erect the main

16 The Impresario

poles you always put up the canvas so that the tent (rather like a church in a village) sheds its aura over the wagons. Canvas laid out on the ground gives the impression of some disaster having happened, and no circus showman can sleep happily with such a sense of bad luck around him. The tent has to be erected within 24 hours. It may stay on the ground on a Sunday but must never be allowed to stay unassembled during the week.

The Fossetts' expectations of people were totally unrealistic. They depended on George Biddell and his family more than on any other people. The Biddells performed several acts in the show including a trapeze act, clowning and trampoline acts. To this family the Fossetts paid a mere £40 a week. A Hungarian girl missed a chair that was balanced on a perch held by two men in her double-somersault act and broke her leg. It took a blazing row to get her just a part of her contracted wages.

Those Fossetts trusted no one unless they had to. They kept their families together like a primitive tribe, the chieftain being the banker. Their interest in outsiders was minimal.

When a Lady Mayoress wanted to come round to the back after a show, it was my job to head her off. But then it was also my job to help take down the Big Top in the early hours of the morning in the drenching rain and get up at five in the morning to prepare to move on, again in the drenching rain. It was my job to cope with everything that Bailley threw at me, often as not to save money.

There was a wanton lack of concern for anything else.

"The brakes aren't very good, so if you get stuck on a hill, put wooden blocks against the bus in front of the tiger trailer. We don't want to lose our tigers," was the sort of remark one could expect.

My respect for the forces of law and order in this country was once again put to the test. I had to visit local police stations to inform them of our arrival – and give them 200 free seats: a bribe by the Fossetts which prevented trouble with the wagons.

When I questioned Mary about this, she said, "The police get what they want from us and we get what we want from them.

16 The Impresario

If they ask you for two hundred seats, let them have them. We don't want any trouble with the police."

Whimsy Walker, the clown cheered me up, telling me he would keep the audience laughing if any of the acts were delayed. He became my best friend on the show and we worked out a series of comedy acts together which never failed to make the audience roar with laughter. Whimsy wore long shoes and walked into the ring with his head poking backwards and forwards above his tall figure. His long boots created an element of fantasy that made even me laugh. On one occasion, entering the ring with him, I rushed through the ring fence, accidentally tripped up and fell face forwards into the sawdust. My top hat careered away from me and I felt I had completely lost my dignity as ringmaster. The audience didn't realise it was an accident and the whole tent dissolved into laughter as I rose to my feet. How close laughter is to tears! It is also why the 'Auguste' clowns tend to involve themselves with slapstick comedy.

By tradition the white clown never falls over and is the Master of Ceremonies. The English have never appreciated the comedy of the white clown because English audiences are amused by slapstick that doesn't appeal to continental audiences. There are so few sophisticated clown acts in England. Whimsy was one of them. His path and mine were to cross under circumstances very different from that of the circus.

Nothing affected me more than the saga of Aga, the elephant.

Like humans, elephants only become adult when they are about eighteen years old. A trainer told me he always got on with his elephant family by stroking their tongues. I used to do this on the show. I found the base of the tongue would come up and, when I stroked it, I felt the elephant was almost talking to me.

One of my jobs was to make sure that the parade of elephants took place without a hitch. The elephants arrived in three

16 The Impresario

elephant trucks which in those days the railways kept for the travelling circus. While nine of the elephants were half-size, one, Aga, was one of the biggest elephants I had ever seen. This fantastic animal was the one used in the film *Elephant Boy*, featuring Sabu. Her keeper was a small Indian called Jacobs who had brought her over from India and had been with her all his life. The two were inseparable and Jacobs always slept in the hay beside the elephant. They were as if they were locked together and, in the show, Jacobs always ended his performance with Aga taking his head in her mouth and carrying him round the ring before they left the tent together. There was a remarkable unity between them that clearly transcended the animal and human world. They were in love with each other and neither could live without the other.

Two days after we opened at Coventry, Bailley told me: "Tomorrow I have to go down to Bournemouth with Jacobs. He is being charged with cruelty."

You could have knocked me down with a feather.

"How did that happen?"

"Last Christmas some woman saw Jacobs hit Aga with a stick and swear at the elephant. So she had him charged with cruelty."

"Doesn't the woman realise that Jacobs can only use a few English swear words and that he and the elephant always sleep together?"

"I wasn't on the show, so I don't know what she was told. You know Jacobs always uses that bit of wood because Aga's almost deaf and she knows which way to go when Jacobs slaps her with the wood. The elephant's hide is so tough you couldn't hurt it with a plank!"

We heard soon afterwards that Bailley and Jacobs had to stay on in Bournemouth for an extra day for the case to be concluded.

That evening no one could take Aga into the ring and when she missed her performance she started screaming. Several of us tried to comfort her, but there was nothing we could do and she howled all that night. The scream of that huge elephant still

16 The Impresario

haunts me, and it went on until Jacobs returned the following evening. It was the first time they had ever been parted and Aga made herself ill. Although she did her act as usual, she never recovered her composure – and if Jacobs wandered even a few feet from her tent she started wailing again. She died at the end of the season when the circus returned to the farm. Jacobs went quite mental after her death; they said that he kept his wagon over the ground in which she was buried and never left again. A few months later he died of a broken heart. The woman who brought the charge of cruelty against him destroyed a great and lovely elephant and its devoted servant.

The episode of Aga and Jacobs upset me profoundly, as it did everyone else in the show. The small elephants were obviously children compared to Aga, who had been so tall and magnificent.

I tented for 14 weeks – a rich experience, for circuses would probably never again be produced in such a primitive way, with no modern aids such as a microphone or electric lighting effects. The Fossett circus kept to the sawdust tradition; it was the horses, ponies, elephants and wild animals that were the true artistes of the circus. Although there were exceptions. Every evening I would raise my arm in a horror that was utterly unfeigned as Marius Biddell appeared to fall off the trapeze above the tiger cage. He was always caught up by his ankles at its base, but there was no safety net. If he hadn't kept the top part of his legs in the corner of the trapeze, he would have fallen to his death. I didn't need to be an actor to communicate my fears to the audience.

The day I was leaving, Bailley came round to my wagon.

"Dickie, I'm sorry that you've decided to go. I know that you've had difficulties with us, but you will come back and work with us again."

I didn't think I would ever accept another engagement with Sir Robert Fossett's circus, but Bailley was right. Twenty years later I became its musical director and played all the circus music I ever wanted to hear.

16 The Impresario

I returned to my family in St Albans and a week later read an advertisement in *The World's Fair*. A fairground show at Margate wanted a 'spieler'. I got the job – although my ambitions aimed higher than the spaceship that it was my job to persuade the public to enter.

At Haysham Head I witnessed a circus performance more magical than I believe any other circus has ever achieved. Dressed like a ringmaster in top hat and pink tails, with legs like those of a ballet dancer, Emily Paulos showed her ponies magnificently. Arab dummies made by the family were fixed on the backs of the ponies. They looked so natural that I almost believed miniature Arabs were riding. Never before or since have I seen ponies so superbly displayed or so magnificently attired. June, Emily's daughter, did a ballerina act on horseback partnered by Bill Thompson. First she danced in the ring and then she mounted her horse and continued to dance like a fairy on its back. She jumped through the raised hoops and was the first and only ballerina on horseback that I have ever seen.

Just as June was a unique ballerina, her mother Emily was the only lady ringmaster in the world. The trapeze act was excellent, and the four-handed riding an incredible act. This began with two riders on two horses, then four would spring on to two horses and this act would end with a finale of four people springing on to the back on one horse. I felt at once that I must try to present this magic to as many people as I could.

We agreed that I would produce my circus show with the Paulos family using their ponies and doing their individual performances. I would create the rest of the show around this act. So I arranged a chimp act with Billy Russell who owned a circus at Great Yarmouth that was idle in the winter months. I persuaded Dokansky, a lion trainer with experience of the fairground, to bring his lions. And so it went on. Life had never been more exhilarating.

My first stage circus at Margate was a fantastic success. We were packed full after the second day and had to turn people

16 The Impresario

away at the box office. For the summer season we went to Birmingham. I was also asked to put on the show at Chessington Zoo. I arranged to put the Paulos family into Chessington for an agreed salary and they stayed there for twenty years. My circus then became the Chessington Zoo Circus.

Meanwhile, I arranged to travel with the stage circus on the music hall circuit for the next two years.

After Margate we went to the Hippodrome, Aldershot, run by my friend Peter Haddon, who had married the daughter of the famous husband and wife acting team, Cecily Courtneidge and Jack Hulbert. We went to London to play at the Chelsea Palace, East Ham and the Metropolitan Music Hall in Edgware Road. I knew that I had created the first and best touring stage circus the music hall had ever witnessed. It gave a meaning and a direction to my life.

Apart from the theatre world, all the owners of English circuses visited me. Aubrey Baring of Barings Bank asked me to lunch and described a film called *Charlie Moon* that he was producing with Max Bygraves. He wanted a small circus and an elephant; this was required to get down on its knees and let Max Bygraves ride it.

I tracked down Dennis Fossett in Devon. Dennis was delighted; not so, Candy the elephant. We both tried to get her to go down on her knees so that we could sit on her, and she screamed. This had not been part of her training. We had two weeks.

The film was shot outside Acton in west London, and began happily enough. Then came the scene when the elephant was to walk down a lane, turn the corner, and stop by the lake where the 'clergyman' would park his bike against the elephant's legs. Candy wandered off when I told her to go. She sauntered down the lane towards the lake on her own. Then she put her trunk in and began to drink. The clergyman turned up and parked his bike beside her. Aubrey Baring was delighted.

16 The Impresario

The next day Max Bygraves was to ride Candy round a field. Both Dennis and I were apprehensive. She got on to her knees and then Max Bygraves climbed on her back. Candy began to scream. When an elephant screams at close quarters, it is impossible to ignore it! Max jumped off in a state of shock. Animals sense if someone is afraid of them and Max had introduced an element of fear.

Then I demonstrated the act with Candy, who didn't make a sound. I suggested we should all go to the pub and do nothing until the afternoon. I gave Max some advice: animals sense fear, but if you give them a feeling of security and confidence, they will stay calm and do their best not to fret. I didn't tell him that she had only been taught to have someone ride her a few days before. Nor did I add that Candy had probably reacted as she had because Max was a stranger. Elephants are very sensitive animals and only feel happy with those they are accustomed to. That afternoon, Max almost sprang on to her back and Candy stood up without making a sound. The two of them then paraded round the lake and the film sequence was shot.

Both Aubrey and the Fossetts were delighted, and I felt truly happy that my family had done all that was required.

Another contract was with Frank Launder, the film producer, who needed a lion act for *Blue Murder at St Trinians*. The lions had to look as if they were entering an arena about to devour someone tied to a pole. After I signed the contract for a considerable fee, I visited Zena Rossaire, who had lions at a circus farm at Billericay, to make the arrangements. I had once helped her and her family when they ran a stage circus. Zena had great charm and dressed delightfully. She looked like an English aristocrat. She was very different from most circus women. We understood each other so well and always seemed able to laugh at the world. I felt that had she not been married, I might well have fallen in love with her.

My agency office in Newport Street was a magnet for a range of glamorous people. Desmond Leslie was making *musique con-*

16 The Impresario

crète, a production of peculiar sounds obtained by mixing various recorded tracks together. I felt this was a gimmick rather than anything of true musical value. Nevertheless, I was inundated with requests from publishers to demonstrate recordings and sign film contracts that wanted background music of the kind that Desmond could produce. He also invited me to stay at Castle Leslie with himself and his father, Sir Shane Leslie, an eccentric Irishman who had written about Irish history and local feuds. The place was a Victorian castle in County Monaghan surrounded by magnificent restful woods and a lake; Winston Churchill had apparently visited as a child.

It was at this castle that I met George Adamski, who with Desmond had co-written *Flying Saucers Have Landed*. When I asked them, they seemed not to want to say anything at all about flying saucers, though – which made me think, rightly or wrongly, that the book had been written primarily for financial considerations.

My life has been an unending series of fascinating and occasionally extraordinary encounters: a kaleidoscope of colours, of meeting people, of disparate ways of living. This self-chosen lifestyle of mine has provided me with experiences I would never have met with in other careers. I consider each and every experience a bonus.

If only others could have seen some of the experiences of life I have been privy to. Surely, if they had, they would have known better the values that make life truly worth living.

I suppose that I should not have been surprised to find that the ethics of the pop scene were as degraded as elsewhere in business …

Artistes almost without number came to my studio believing that they should be recognised as stars. I found it difficult to differentiate between the merits of one band and the next, or to tell if a singer had that unique quality that would make him or

16 The Impresario

her a pop star. I wrote some pop music, collaborating with Ian Grant, formerly a very successful lyric writer. Vera Lynn offered to buy the music of a tune I had composed called *Every Time You Fall in Love*. She changed her mind and I forgot about it until I heard it played under another name two years later. This was typical. Publishers would turn you down, have a few chords changed, and then call it their own composition. This happened many times.

In the late 1950s a group named the Liverpool Syndicate came to my studio. They asked me to help them because they had just returned from Hamburg and had no money to get back to Liverpool. They said that they worked with the Beatles and played at The Cavern in Liverpool. They played with a faster beat than other London groups, but their long, scruffy hair looked ghastly. I persuaded them to have haircuts at my expense, bought them blue polo-neck jumpers, greatly improving their appearance, then arranged for them to stay at the Maurice Hotel in Bayswater and organised venues where they could play several times a week. I asked my friend Peter Jones, who was editor of the *Record Mirror*, to hear some of their recordings. His review was enthusiastic and he too noticed that they had the best sound and fastest beat in London. On the strength of this review, Norrie Paramor of EMI listened to the tapes and said he might consider giving them a contract.

The *Record Mirror* published its review and, a day or so later, one Brian Epstein came into my studio saying that he owned a music shop in Liverpool. He asked me for the address of the Liverpool Syndicate because, he said, he had letters to give them from their parents! I gave him their address and asked him to give them my latest tapes of their music as I was hoping to organise a contract with EMI. Two hours later, the Liverpool Syndicate phoned me to say they were having to return to Liverpool with Epstein: they owed him for the hire-purchase of their guitars and if they failed to come back to Liverpool with him, he would take

16 The Impresario

those guitars away! When I asked for my tapes back, they said that he hadn't given them any tapes!

Whether any members of the group I represented became part of the Beatles, I do not know. But I do know that it was my publicity for the Liverpool sound that attracted both EMI and Decca to take an interest in that different beat. It didn't surprise me that the Liverpool sound became a fantastic success. I had spent money and time in making such recognition possible – and an unknown shopkeeper cashed in on my publicity and made a fortune for himself and the Beatles.

So that was show business. It was iniquitous. It was hard to escape a sense of disillusion about a world of illusion. A world of make-believe that was far from the brutal reality of the world of warfare, which I had also seen at close quarters, was nevertheless one not noted for man's humanity to man. What sort of a country had we fought for? Standards of integrity and loyalty had put me at a disadvantage in dealing with it. Life could be so beautiful if we but gave it a chance. Surely people in authority must realise that society cannot work to everyone's advantage if people behave like my Liverpudlian friends.

17

Stocks, Shares and Paying the Bill

I rushed in, all unknowing, where angels might well fear to tread. I was to discover that the fact that the growth in crime had not been slowed was due, in no small part, to our own police force.

Jack Spot and 'the Dimes' controlled not only most rooms let to French prostitutes in the Soho area, but also Sheila, a girl who was running clip-joints in Macclesfield Street – where my studio was – and Gerrard Street. I was in an area dominated by crooks. The clip-joints were clubs where the hostesses persuaded men to spend their money on drinks under the illusion that the girls would go back to their beds with them. This they never did. They were engaged to ensure that the clients spent money in the club, but when the men expected to meet them outside, the girls never turned up. On the other hand, big nightclubs employed hostesses specifically to have sex with their clients and afterwards to pay a percentage of their takings to the head waiter.

Harry Meadows, a short, ebullient man with thick black hair, an alert air and brimming with bonhomie, ran the Churchill Club in New Bond Street. He enjoyed the reputation of being the man who started the hostess and call-girl racket in the West End. Years later he was charged by the police for an offence to do with procuring girls, but he won his case. The judge appeared to praise him for bringing entertainment to high society.

I knew something of the top nightclubs of those days because I introduced artistes to them. Several out-of-work actresses told me what went on and how sickened they were at the way they were treated. Those who didn't go to bed with clients when asked to do so were sacked on the spot. They were employed as women for sale. Proprietors made a fortune from their earnings. The only nightclub owner who didn't make money in this way was Max

17 Stocks, Shares and Paying the Bill

Smetty, who ran the Blue Angel in Berkeley Street. But he admitted that he had to pay police officers a lot of money to prevent his club being smashed up by crooks. Max allowed only debutantes and the cream of society to come to his club, and he presented the best cabaret artistes. I once booked Hutch, the famous pianist entertainer from America, for him.

When I was running my recording studio, the Kray brothers, the infamous gangland figures, moved into the area. They would drink in the De Hems pub opposite. Sheila told me that she would have to give up her club or the Kray boys would break it apart. Try as she might, she couldn't get police protection.

No good was likely to come of following the example of Brer Rabbit: lying low and saying nuffin'. It might not have been wise, but I tackled Reggie Kray.

These are his words: "You keep out of this and we'll leave you alone. We want the club scene here, and we'll get it."

How far my relationships in that blighted part of London might have fared, I do not know. Fate intervened. But not necessarily on my side, though how true that is not for me to say. Through many a twist and turn, the twilight world from which, by now, I hoped to escape was to catch up with me.

My co-director Desmond Leslie was having marriage problems and told me he wanted to give up the studio and return to Ireland. This was depressing news as we had developed the business together; we had discovered new artistes, and the studio was respected by all the leading music publishers in London. I didn't have enough capital to buy Desmond out, so I reluctantly agreed that another company should take over.

The week that I made this decision, my father was taken unwell. I had gone to see him at St Albans, and while we were watching TV he complained of a bad stomach pain and asked me to get a doctor. His best friend was Dr Perkins, who had practised in Harley Street, and he arranged an examination. An ambulance arrived within the hour and as my father seemed quite cheerful

17 Stocks, Shares and Paying the Bill

when he was taken away, I didn't think there was anything seriously wrong. I imagined he would be X-rayed and given an analgesic to calm the sudden pain.

Three hours after my father left the house the hospital phoned to say that the surgeons had operated on him but he didn't appear to be regaining consciousness. My mother and I went to the hospital immediately and found him laid out on a stretcher, apparently in a coma. We knelt beside him and prayed that he would recover consciousness. Our prayers were not answered, and my dear father died that evening.

Since I have been practising the art of palmistry, a leading surgeon has come to me at least twice a year. He tells me that 70 per cent of operations should never be undertaken, but that surgeons operate because they don't know what else to do. I am certain that my dear father would have lived for many more years if he had not been operated on in such haste. I am equally certain that surgeons are responsible for more premature deaths than they are responsible for prolonging life.

Now that my studio was closing, I wanted to discover more about my father's working life on the Stock Exchange. The partners in my father's firm didn't want me to join them, let alone take over his business, so after meeting Edward Miller, the senior partner of A. Miller and Co., I joined that firm as an attaché (a junior member).

The move from circus to Stock Exchange was smooth. With one exception, all my father's clients adopted me as their broker. It seemed quite natural because this was the way things were done in those days. Clearly, I was also regarded as the sort of man who could be trusted – steady in a crisis, solid, and so forth. My father's old friend Leo d'Erlanger promised me his personal business. (It was the d'Erlangers who conceived the ideas for Channel Tunnel schemes which successive governments turned down. Leo d'Erlanger and Baron Emile

17 Stocks, Shares and Paying the Bill

had financed the de Havillands and the Mosquito aircraft during the War.)

It was exciting being on the floor of the Stock Exchange and watching the changing share prices. My father had introduced me to Durlachers, the biggest jobbers on the market. It became clear that we were not dealing in a free market. Instead, it reacted to the whim of these jobbers who could rig prices independently of the market trend. It seemed to me curious that when my friends knew I was a stockbroker, they seemed to hold me in some esteem, as though I had suddenly become a respectable member of the community. In fact, the market was impossible to predict and the public had no legal rights against the broker's advice when it turned out to be a disaster.

Stockbrokers know that they are essentially confidence tricksters donning a professional air of respectability – perhaps that is the reason for their sober suits and self-regard as the judges of the financial world.

When I became a stockbroker, many friends from my previous careers consulted me. One, Anne, to whom I gave lunch, told me the first horse that she had ever owned was running that afternoon.

"Anne, why are you lunching with me when your first horse is running?"

"My trainer told me the horse had no chance of winning and I'd be wasting my time going down and watching him. Naturally, I prefer to lunch with you who can probably give me some good financial advice."

Irma La Douce, the name of Anne's horse, interested me so much that I asked the head waiter to phone my bookmakers and put £5 on it to win.

"Dickie, you're a fool. My trainer told me there was no chance of our horse's winning and here you are, throwing away five pounds. If I thought it had a chance, I wouldn't be sitting here at lunch with you."

17 Stocks, Shares and Paying the Bill

I laughed. However, before our lunch ended the head waiter approached our table.

"Sir, I must congratulate you. Your horse won at 25 to 1 and we on the staff backed it too, so we are all delighted."

Anne was furious.

While at the Stock Exchange, I served on the committee for the Battle of Britain's twenty-fifth anniversary celebration. I suggested that Vera Lynn, 'the Forces' sweetheart' during the War, should be the cabaret act for us at the Dorchester. The ball was a great success and Vera Lynn gave a magnificent performance. She sang all the old well-loved tunes, and at the end, when the lights were dimmed and only the spotlight remained on her, she walked slowly round the arena singing *We'll Meet Again*, the last song that so many of my pilots would remember. It was the performance of a great star, and Vera sang that number with great sensitivity and feeling.

I felt all my old friends were with me that evening at the Dorchester.

Somehow, throughout all the vicissitudes of my life, and my need to be aware of the present as opposed to the past, I felt marked by a common experience with those who had fought. With those people, I always felt a kinship. They were my unseen safety-net: no one could take my memories from me. My early lifestyle ensured that I would never be seen as just a drifter through life's many different scenes. The RAF had given me a standing, a self-assurance. However people might act towards me, fundamentally they knew what our boys had done to preserve their freedoms, abuse them as they might.

During the winter I would go on a cruise to escape the English weather. On the *Mauretania* I met Richard Baron White, who owned the soft-drinks firm, R. White & Co. I liked him immensely. Accompanying him was his niece Anne Boughton Leigh, whose father had been in the Air Force with me. After the cruise I stayed with Anne at her Elizabethan cottage and she

17 Stocks, Shares and Paying the Bill

showed me her family home. It was actually more like a baronial castle. At the time I felt I was too old for her, but I now regret not asking her to marry me. She was fond of me, and in retrospect I know we had a lot in common.

Richard Baron White visited my firm. He told us in confidence that he owned over 150,000 shares in his family company and wanted to sell the lot and get out of the business. Despite having negotiated with several merchant banks, none had made him a satisfactory offer for all his shares. One morning I met Durlacher's son who told me he would offer 35 shillings a share for the lot. However, the contract had to be confirmed before five o'clock that same day. Richard was delighted when I rang him. He was being offered virtually a quarter of a million pounds for his share-holding for which no merchant bank was prepared to make him an offer. In those days all major dealings were done by word of mouth – "Your word is your bond". Two days later, Durlachers told me that I had sold the largest amount of shares that anyone had done for many years.

A fortnight after contracts had been exchanged, Richard Leigh – a relation of Anne and Baron White – asked me to dine with him and his Danish wife, a countess in her own right. I took them afterwards to the Blue Angel to see the cabaret. When we were about to leave, I asked for the bill before retiring to the gents. But I returned to find my friends no longer at the table because there had been some rumpus.

Max Smetty, the owner, came up me in great distress and said, "That man you brought down here was rude to my waiter and hit him. I've told your friends to get out of the club and I've called the police."

I was horrified and couldn't believe what he said was true. The police car took Richard away, leaving his wife upstairs with me. I went to the West End Central police station to sort the matter out, thinking that it would only take a few minutes. When the countess and I got there, her husband had been put in a cell. We

17 Stocks, Shares and Paying the Bill

were asked to wait, and after a few minutes several Blue Angel waiters arrived. They told me they were sorry but they had to give evidence that my friend had hit one of the staff. The countess was in a state of shock and fury, and I couldn't get her to tell me what had really happened.

Anne suddenly said, "I've left my bag in the Blue Angel. Can you go back and get it for me?"

A man standing near by said, "I'm a police officer. If you've lost your bag, I'll go back and get it."

When I agreed he added, "Give me £10 and I'll bring the bag back here."

I said at once, "If you're a police officer, you have no right to ask for money to find my friend's bag. Let's have a look at your identity card, if you please!"

The man put his hand into his pocket as if to reach for the card – then made a run for the entrance of the police station. I yelled at the uniformed man on the door to stop him. Naturally, I thought he must be an impostor posing as a police officer. The uniformed man just let him go and did nothing! I was absolutely furious and confronted an inspector in the office. I told him I thought that what had just happened was an obvious example of police corruption.

"You have arrested one of my friends, and now you have allowed someone pretending to be a police officer to walk out of this station without doing anything about it. You police are not entitled to ask for money to collect missing property. If you don't do something about this, you are conniving at a very corrupt operation."

"What did you say?" the inspector asked me.

I repeated what I had said: I had witnessed an attempt at bribery by a person purporting to be a police officer, and I wanted something done about it.

The inspector then turned to the sergeant who was standing beside him.

17 Stocks, Shares and Paying the Bill

"Do something about this man. Take him to the cells."

I was at once marched out and thrown into a cell. I spent half an hour there before being taken out again and virtually stripped. The sergeant standing with another uniformed man announced that I was being charged with violent behaviour in a police station. Then I was hustled back into the cell. The sergeant told the big burly man to hold me against the wall while he smashed his fists into my ribs and kicked me in the groin so badly that I folded over and blacked out.

I woke up in hospital. The doctor told me that they were obliged to keep me there overnight because there were some tests they had to carry out on me. I refused to agree to any tests and demanded that my solicitor should be contacted.

At six o'clock the next morning I was driven back to the cell at the West End Central police station, from where I was taken to the magistrates' court locked in a Black Maria, feeling like some sort of caged animal.

My friends had arranged for my solicitor to attend, and I was granted bail at once, despite the charge of violent behaviour against me. Since I had fought for the freedom of England I was convinced there was nothing to worry about, and that with evidence from the Danish countess it was obvious the police would apologise and drop the case.

But no such thing happened. The police did not withdraw the charges, and in due course I appeared at another magistrates' court. Naturally, I had engaged counsel and had arranged for the countess to return to England and give evidence on my behalf. I had also asked the Earl of Bandon, as a pilot and my commanding officer in the RAF, to speak up for my good character. The countess explained what had happened. I gave my evidence. Then I was shocked to hear the police station's senior officer, an inspector, saying he had seen me trying to use my fists in the police station. It was a pack of lies. In any case, the countess endorsed the fact that I had merely been complaining – and had

17 Stocks, Shares and Paying the Bill

raised my voice without becoming physically violent – about someone who was pretending to be a policeman and who had asked for £10 to retrieve her handbag.

Although he believed my statement to be true, my counsel advised me not to say that the police had beaten me up "because the magistrates hate to hear anything about improper police behaviour". It would be wiser for me, soothed my learned friend, to be proved innocent and then make a formal complaint.

So much for the trusty sword of English justice! I was found guilty and fined £10.

I was appalled. The evidence had all been in my favour. It was an outright mockery of justice – justice I personally had fought for. I couldn't believe that such a verdict could be pronounced in an English court. I decided to appeal, and asked an old friend, Christmas Humphries – a barrister and later a judge who was known affectionately as Father Christmas – to represent me. He told me privately that he was horrified by my case and would do his best for me. All the same, I couldn't help feeling when the time came that he didn't really like questioning the police about what had happened. We lost, and my fine was increased to £40.

It didn't stop there, either.

After the court case I was surprised to be phoned up by a Scotland Yard inspector. He asked me to lunch with him, although I had no idea why. He was quite intelligent and unusually charming, and gave me a very good lunch in the City.

"I know you have been badly treated by our officers, but I want you to help us."

I asked him to explain.

"Not all of us are dishonest, and I regret that you have had a bad deal. We know that the West End police have fitted you up, but we want you to help us and give us more details of the man who claimed to be a police officer. Could you identify him again, if we asked you to visit one or two places?"

17 Stocks, Shares and Paying the Bill

"I'm sorry. I have no intention of helping the police because you might again prefer false charges against me. I am sure you know what actually happened at West End Central, and I'm sure that because of it you understand why I have no intention of helping the police either now or in the future. If you at Scotland Yard were aware of the false charge against me, you should have done something before. Don't expect me to trust you now."

He replied, "It's very foolish of you not to co-operate. Think over what I have said and then get in touch with me."

18

Life Becomes Problematical

A short time after my unpleasant experience with West End Central police, my Aunt Mary – who was dying of cancer – asked me to come down to Weston-Super-Mare. She lived in the house that had once belonged to my grandfather. Almost paralysed with pain, she couldn't get out of her chair. She died a fortnight later. Her death caused me the greatest sadness. She had always shown me affection and understanding. I felt I had lost a true friend. She left me all her property in Somerset. It was a family home, which I had adored as a child. I loved the old books, antique furniture and pictures that belonged to another age but adorned this one. Above all, I was so happy to have the old four-poster double bed that I always slept in when visiting her.

After Aunt Mary's death, I stayed at her home trying to make up my mind what to do. I no longer wanted to return to London or the Stock Exchange, or to the West End police. I wanted to retire and look at the sea and the countryside. I adopted a puppy, a collie of sorts, which had been abandoned. She was so small that she could stand on my hand. I called her Bimbo because she was something of a clown. She began to take over my life. I trained her to respond to my whistle and to understand my words. She became very possessive of me, resenting anyone else's intrusion, barking wildly if anyone came near the place.

Two publicans lived near by and they owned a dog named Ziggy, who laid siege to Bimbo and me, night and day. Ziggy would come to the house trying to get in. I got tired of phoning up the owners asking them to look after him. Ziggy's owners told me that they couldn't control him. If I didn't want him, they would have him put down. Bimbo and Ziggy obviously adored each other; the two of them seemed destined to live together, so

18 Life Becomes Problematical

I decided to take over this impossible rogue dog. He was quite untrained and would wander off for days and then reappear without any sense of remorse. It was obvious that he worshipped females. I found him waiting on the doorstep of any local bitch in season. In the end he always returned and Bimbo made him feel decidedly guilty when he rejoined us. She treated him as a naughty boy whom she loved although she did not respect his roaming habits. I spent my days taking them on the sands and for walks in the country. Our time together was quite the happiest of my life and I felt in harmony with nature and the world.

After two years of perfect bliss in Somerset, I decided to convert my house into four flats and build four new flats in the garden. I knew accommodation was needed locally and that it was selfish to live alone with two dogs in a house with four reception rooms and eight bedrooms. I found local architects who worked according to my specifications and I decided to be the chief contractor myself, converting the house into superb flats. The building was unique. The local press praised it as a great attraction for the town.

Three months before this work was completed my London solicitor requested an interview with me. He told me that because of difficulties suffered by the firm he had previously worked for, my family's trust money was in danger of being lost. He advised me to wire the firm to see that both my money and my mother's trust were protected. I did so, but although they assured me that no debts were outstanding, another firm of solicitors claimed that I owed them money. My solicitor explained that this situation had arisen because he had passed on some of my affairs to the second firm of solicitors; they still held my papers and they wanted to make it worth their while. I told them I owed them nothing and that it was monstrous to file a claim against me for a few hundred pounds more than six years after the original claim had been met.

However, even though the statutory period of six years had elapsed, a claim was made against me in the High Court. For

18 Life Becomes Problematical

some reason, my papers could not be found, but I was told that either the Law Society or the Bar Association would have to compensate me when it was decided who had lost the papers.

A fortnight later I was issued with a writ for slander over a telegram allegedly sent by me on matters concerning my family trust. I insisted I had had nothing to do with any such telegram. Shortly afterwards I was sued for libel on account of this telegram, which had been signed by the Post Office in my name. From then on both London solicitors and local ones showed a distinct reluctance to represent me. One London firm said that if I admitted sending the telegram and made an apology it would only cost me £500 and that that would be the end of it.

Needless to say, I refused to apologise for something I had not done. I lost the case. The judge only awarded the plaintiffs £500.

I appealed, but lost.

Before my appeal, I had been issued with a bankruptcy notice by the firm that had obtained a judgement against me when my papers went missing. Sir Lionel Thompson QC told the court that I could pay the few hundred pounds owed, but that it was improper for any such order to be made against me. However, the Registrar dismissed counsel's application and served a bankruptcy notice on me, despite being told that the Law Society and the Bar Association were investigating my position.

After this, I was obliged to attend a public meeting to discuss my assets. The national press said that my personal assets were worth considerably more than the £20,000 that I owed. In fact, I owned eight flats, a cottage and a trust fund of over £10,000 and was in the process of completing four new flats. The Official Receiver took all my property and sold it for a derisory sum without attempting to explore the market. This left me with virtually nothing.

I completely lost faith in British justice. I wanted only to put an end to my life and my struggle, as I saw it, against a hypocritical society.

18 Life Becomes Problematical

I planned my death carefully. First I decided to have a very good meal at the Royal Hotel, Weston-Super-Mare, where the food was the best in Somerset and the service excellent. The manager, Mr Mathews, was a man of great charm. He used to speak to me about my family and in particular would praise my grandfather who had done so much for the town as chairman both of the Urban District Council and of the local magistrates' court. He always made me feel like a prince when I arrived in his dining-room.

After my excellent meal, I returned to my lovely house. As usual my dogs greeted me and I told them that I had found a new home for them where they would be well looked after; to Bimbo I said that if I did not wake up the next morning, she need not worry because I would be waiting for her in heaven. I knew Ziggy would worry neither about heaven nor hell because he could survive no matter what happened, unlike Bimbo who was quite sentimental.

I filled up a glass of wine with a bottle of aspirins, but before drinking it I lay down beside my gas fire in the hope that the gas would render me unconscious. After a short time I felt so terrible that I turned it off and managed to stumble to my four-poster bed. I just managed to drink the contents of the wine glass, despite the unpleasant taste, and in a few seconds I became unconscious.

The next morning I woke to find my housekeeper and the local doctor standing over me. Apparently I had been unconscious for most of the morning. I admitted to my doctor that I had attempted suicide and regretted that I had recovered, but he begged me to allow him to take me to hospital in case I had internal damage. So we drove to Wells Mental Hospital where my doctor told me that I would be looked after because they were used to dealing with people who had suffered like me. I was hardly conscious when I arrived. After two days I recovered sufficiently to realise that I was in the company of many people who were mentally disturbed and who also had failed in their suicide attempts.

Among the patients were some most interesting people, including a teacher and a mathematician, but none of them

18 Life Becomes Problematical

suffered from the feeling of overall disgust for society that had affected me. Though they had suffered acute depression, their faith in society was not shattered.

When the head psychiatrist first interviewed me he remarked at once that we both had the same decorations. He held the Belgian Croix de Guerre from when he had been in the French Resistance during the War. This doctor's attitude seemed to me so arrogant that I felt I didn't want to stay under his charge. He seemed to think he was some sort of divinity and we patients were merely guinea-pigs. So much for *esprit de corps*! After two weeks in Wells Hospital I knew that I would have to discharge myself. It was clear what would happen otherwise: the doctor would destroy my faith in myself. I would indeed become mentally unbalanced if I didn't make the effort to get out of hospital and start life again with my two dogs.

I discharged myself and went back to my home in Somerset. My housekeeper had looked after Bimbo and Ziggy and it was they who restored my faith in life. They greeted me as if I was an angel from heaven and my housekeeper told me that both of them had cried all the time I was away. I hadn't realised how much they both loved and missed me.

My life was beginning to turn full circle. Most of us surely are not set on this Earth to be like the lilies of the field, who toil not. From the very beginning, my life had been one of action filled with new experiences, filled with hope. Life is a gift and it had been given to me to plumb its depths, to fight the good fight – and I certainly considered that I was giving it a fair go. Each of us must try to use the skills we discover within ourselves and endeavour to do that for which we are fitted. Now the voice and words of the submarine commander kept haunting me. Apparently I could read the future in the palm of a man's hand. Was that the course to which my all my struggles, in both war and peace, had led me? Should this be my chosen path through life now that I had left the RAF?

18 Life Becomes Problematical

'To plumb its depths', did I write? To 'fight the good fight'? To 'use my skills'? I felt that the same attitudes that kept me going through the War would serve me well enough when circumstances changed. Purists can say that I should have changed my colours to suit the piping times of peace. Except in times of direst despair, there have always been hopes to keep alive; one of them has been that this story of mine will see the light of day. It is a tale with a moral in a way – at least, I like to think so – and so I do not round off these memoirs at the point at which my war was over

Old habits die hard. After leaving hospital I read that Mary Chipperfield had opened a new circus, the Circus Togni, in Bristol. All the old memories flooded back. I was transported back in time to that exciting yet comfortable period of my life when all was safe. Influenced by nostalgia and needing a career, instead of immediately pursuing palm-reading as a viable occupation, I spoke to my old friend Roberto Germains, who had first introduced me to the Fossetts.

The Fossetts were the top circus agents in London. Mr Fossett told me that Jimmy Chipperfield, Mary's father, wanted him to procure a manager, a position for which he felt I was quite well suited. Jimmy had taken over my job with Sir Robert Fossett's circus and he had made a fortune running safari parks for Lord Bath and other estate owners, both in this country and abroad. Much of what he told me persuaded me to accept the position.

Following this offer, the opportunity arose for me to watch Mary Chipperfield at work producing her first circus. Mary intended to use the Italian name Togni to refer to the circus – a term I personally found disturbing. But foremost among the many reservations I had was the fact that despite a great deal of expenditure, the overall performance had no sense of magic or balance. I felt very disappointed that I was not allowed to improve the show in any way, and decided that the wisest course of action would be to disassociate myself from this venture and return to Weston-Super-Mare to consider my future.

19

The Palmist

At Weston-Super-Mare, I was forced to confront the pressing question of how to earn a living. I went to Brean Down, where the manager of Pontins, apprised of my previous experience – years before I had played for Warner's camp on the Isle of Wight – offered me a job as an organist, providing the musical evening entertainment for the summer season. Playing the sing-along songs enjoyed by holidaymakers was fun.

With the problem of a finding a job taken care of, at least temporarily, I decided that I might try reading people's hands during the day in order to supplement my evening income.

By a lucky chance I discovered that opposite Pontins was a caravan site that was owned by a former House of Commons journalist. Again, a connection from one of my previous lives that, circumstantially, looked set to help me in the present. I asked the journalist if he would consider lending me a caravan on his site in return for reading the hands of his customers. He kindly agreed. He then asked me to read his hand, his wife's hand and those of a few friends. He was so impressed with my predictions and comments during the course of these sessions that he promised to get me a caravan and take care of all of my publicity. Furthermore, he suggested that the caravan could be paid for from my earnings.

I began charging 25 pence a reading and reckoned it a poor day if I didn't have at least twenty clients. There were days when I had more clients than I could cope with. This earned me an average of around £4 a day, which was a considerable sum to me. At this time £25 a week was a reasonable wage.

Every day the caravan and the yard outside bustled with people and it only took eight weeks to pay off the caravan's £200

19 The Palmist

cost. When I finished my period as a palmist at Brean, I calculated that I had read almost 3,000 hands and earned in the region of £1,300. Not only had I paid for, and now owned, my caravan, but was able to buy a car to tow it wherever I wished. This freedom came as a great relief to me. When the opportunity came along to play the organ at the British Legion Club and the Royal Hotel, I began to feel I had truly recovered from the crushing series of events that had resulted in hospitalisation.

Brean was the runway from which my gift of palmistry took off. This was the place that nurtured my skills in an art that became a strong calling for the rest of my life. It seems very odd to me to think that despite all that I had done in the War my appearances on television were the result of my career in palm-reading.

During this part of my life I can honestly say that I met some very interesting people and number their stories among the most fascinating I have heard over the many years.

There was one occasion when a woman asked me if I could read from only one hand because her other arm was paralysed. I looked carefully at her left hand before beginning to read her right palm. It is difficult to explain how I can tell so much from a client's palm, but what I said to her was no effort even though I spoke for some time.

"I can tell you why your other hand is paralysed. Some three years ago you were in Australia living with your husband and three children in a wooden bungalow, miles from the nearest town. Late one evening your husband set fire to the building and then tried to kill you with a knife. As you grappled and you fell to the floor, his knife slipped and your husband lay at your feet with the knife in his stomach. You rushed to get your children outside as the flames consumed the building. You barely managed to do so before you lost consciousness and were taken to the hospital with your children. When you came round you couldn't remember anything and your family decided that because you

19 The Palmist

had lost your memory you were incapable of looking after your children. Although you desperately wanted them back, they were taken away from you. I'm sure that it was this episode that paralysed your arm. Now that I have told you what happened, your memory will return and your arm will be cured."

For a long moment the woman stared at me in silence, then she smiled, her face utterly serene, and said, "You are amazing. Your description of what happened is quite correct, but I couldn't remember any of the details. Do you really think I can get my children back?"

"Yes. I know you can. You have your memory back and with it, your confidence. Soon you will have your children back as well."

And so it turned out. Some months later I was delighted to hear that the family had been reunited.

There is no book on palmistry that can instruct you on how to look at a hand and produce the kind of detail that I was able to detect and relate to that woman. I place little value on the analysis of lines and the comparing of fingers with the widths of the palm. The great secret of reading hands is what takes place between two people when the hand is held: that comes from within. This is a form of communication that often supplies extraordinary knowledge, which has no logical basis. When I look at, and hold, a hand, I am almost always able to form an impression in my mind and then articulate it. I can sense when there has been death, emotional unhappiness, or financial distress. Sometimes I can describe past events in their entirety and sometimes I can accurately predict what the future holds. People are always astonished when I divulge the important occurrences of their past and they are often quite sceptical when I reveal to them what will happen in the future.

When I was at Brean I told a girl that she would marry a Canadian and have two children and that she and her husband would manage a hotel near the sea in Canada. The woman refused

19 The Palmist

to pay me because she didn't believe in marriage and had no intention of having any children. Eight years later she visited me in London. With her were her Canadian husband and two children. The couple now owned a hotel. I was very touched by her efforts to find me and confirm the accuracy of my predictions.

Whimsy Walker, the great clown I had worked with in Sir Robert Fossett's circus, visited me while I was at Pontins camp, accompanied by his wife and son whom I did not know. I persuaded the Pontins manager to employ the family to perform for half an hour a day. For this they received a small fee, food and parking space for their vehicles. When the season ended they moved on. I heard later that Whimsy had died shortly thereafter. For me Whimsy will always live on as the clown who brought me closer than any other to that narrow divide between laughter and tears.

Around this time, I discovered that the local council had passed a resolution to remove me, and my caravan, which had conveniently been deemed a disgrace. Bear in mind that I had previously stood as an Independent candidate on the local council in opposition to the Conservative member. I was shocked that the Weston Council should ban me from operating as a palmist in the seaside town that had developed and flourished largely due to the efforts of my grandfather who, incidentally, had held office as Conservative council chairman for fourteen years. He was also chairman of the local magistrates. For these services he had received the OBE and been recommended for a knighthood. As soon as the resolution was passed, the *Weston Daily Press* and the *News of the World* featured me on their front pages; this story reported disapprovingly of my eviction. They were incensed that a seaside town should publicly ban palmists, a well-known attraction in all major coastal resorts.

To be banned from working in my home-town didn't worry me too much. I could still earn a living most nights by playing the organ in clubs and hotels. Even though it was off-season, the

19 The Palmist

hotels wanted an experienced organist and I had offers to play in Bristol, Bath, Uxbridge and Wells. After Brean it was a relief to take a rest from reading hands, for a little while at least.

Some weeks after I was forced off the square at Weston-Super-Mare, a friend invited me over to Cheddar Gorge where I met a charming man who owned a small café-cum-hotel there. He had read about my plight and received word of my reputation as a palmist and thought it could help his business greatly if I were located near by. So that Easter I accepted his invitation and parked my caravan opposite Gough's cave, the main cave at the top of Cheddar Gorge. There was a certain irony to my situation as this fissure, or gorge, in the Mendip Hills had been a place of sanctuary for thousands of years. The area served as a place of shelter and in prehistoric times humans inhabited the caves. In more recent times – around the eighteenth century, I believe – the Rev. Augustus Toplady composed the hymn *Rock of Ages* while sheltering from a storm here.

From my very first visit I felt that Cheddar was unique among places to which I had travelled. I came to believe that the area functioned as a type of crossroads between humanity's past and future. The place had an aura, a magic about it that left the impression, as with many powerful places, that spirits from another dimension inhabited the region, a presence that was at times almost tangible. The mysteries of space and time and the reality of Earth seemed to converge for me at Cheddar. I would imagine the spirits of the dead and the living roaming on the wind together at night.

Cheddar Gorge did turn out to be quite an eerie place where both the dogs and I were haunted by strange nocturnal sounds. The dogs bristled, but I soon became quite immune to the curious wailing we used to hear in the late hours of the night, possibly caused by wind through some of the smaller caves and apertures. However, siting my caravan here saved me the trouble of getting back to Weston-Super-Mare. Cheddar Gorge held a fasci-

19 The Palmist

nation for me, not just in its geological structure and its atmosphere, which was considerable, but in the remarkable variety of people who journeyed there to see me.

Approaching on the A371, one has no idea of what lies ahead. A quiet drive alongside the Mendips through the village of Cheddar to where the immense gorge cuts into the heart of the hills is impressive. The limestone cliffs tower above to an impressive height, while in the caves themselves crude flint tools have been found that are all of 200,000 years old. Visitors come from all over the world to see these phenomena, and to view the remains of the indigenous fauna of its history: reindeer, wolves, bears and lemmings. There are also remains of Neolithic man to be seen here. Certainly this was a place that attracted tourists – and here was a situation in which I could possibly make a small living.

In a similar situation to Brean Down, there were at least twenty visitors a day to my caravan. I found that I was putting so much into the readings that it was leaving me exhausted. There were times I felt I couldn't continue to give advice.

One day a chauffeur-driven Rolls Royce stopped near by and a gentleman came up to my caravan to consult me. A quick look at his hand told me he was in serious financial trouble. I told him I thought he was in the hotel business, but that some big building project he was involved with threatened to reduce him to the point of bankruptcy. My client confirmed that I was right and asked my advice. I told him to ignore both his accountants and his solicitors and to borrow twice the money he needed. I added that if he took my advice he would soon have a hotel empire at his feet. He took my advice and built a hotel near London Airport in which he later entertained me. He is now a millionaire. He admitted that had he not heeded those offered words of counsel and encouragement, he would have been declared bankrupt and have been finished completely.

On one particular Sunday a young man approached me for a reading. He appeared not to be too serious in his intentions

19 The Palmist

regarding a reading and stated that he thought what I had to say would be a 'good giggle', but he would still pay me. I said little. After he left, his friend came in and said he wanted a 'good giggle' too. Feeling quite angry, I looked at the hand of the second young man who had laughed at me just as his friend had done.

"I want you to promise me you will tell your friend what I say so that you can both have a "good giggle" . On Sunday morning your friend and his girlfriend will go out in his car and will smash into a brick wall. They will both survive, but the girl will seriously damage her left arm, which may never completely recover. Come back on Monday and tell me if I'm right."

The following Monday the young man returned and told me that his friend had indeed been involved in a car accident and his girlfriend's arm had become partially paralysed. He was clearly stunned by what had happened and almost in tears. I told him that eventually the girl would be all right and would, in time, recover the use of her arm. A few months later the young man confirmed that this prediction had also come true.

In the middle of my season at Cheddar Gorge, Axbridge Council passed a resolution disapproving of palmists operating in the Gorge. I suspected that this directive had come from my enemies on the council at Weston-Super-Mare. Since I occupied a private site, the council could do little except express its disapproval. Then through the press I discovered that Axbridge had asked Somerset County Council to approve its decision completely to ban palmists from operating in the area. Two days later I received another warning, this time in person by the council chairman who turned up with a police sergeant and policeman, in an effort to frighten me, I suspect. He told me that if I hadn't left the site by the end of the week I would be in serious trouble. When I protested that I had paid my rent and wanted compensation if I were forced to go, the chairman said that palmists fell under the terms of the Vagrancy Act and therefore had no right of tenancy. I would be forced off if I did not go

19 The Palmist

voluntarily. If on private land, I could be evicted at the behest of the landowner.

I was incensed at such treatment and determined to do something about it. With the help of Joe Gallagher, a friend who was press correspondent for the area and a local lawyer, I managed to establish that any resolution of this nature had to be backed up with a court order. It was through Joe that I was featured in the *Sun* newspaper. The article stated that a palmist had defied an order from Somerset County Council to vacate the premises. After these facts were published and laid out for all to view, the Council took no further action. I stayed on until the end of October, by which time visitors had left the area.

I was continually surprised at the diverse group of people who seemed to have heard of me, and the distances that they often travelled to visit.

On the strength of another article written about my career as a palmist, a number of people now phoned me to have me read their hands. But this increased publicity was a bit much for me in the light of recent events, so I bought another car at Cheddar for £60 and in November towed my caravan back to my mother's house at St Albans. My mother was in poor health and I often felt reluctant to travel to earn a living.

Soon after my return to St Albans, Bailley Fossett, part-owner of Sir Robert Fossett's circus along with his sister, contacted me asking me if I were free to play the organ for them. It appeared that their musicians had left them stranded. Not having had much time in St Albans I was torn between staying with my mother or taking up a position that I could manage well, and at the same time earning a living through the winter months. Bailley was most persuasive and I agreed to take on the offered task: I joined the circus once again.

Finding someone to look after my mother was not easy, but I managed to arrange for a suitable person to come in, and I took

19 The Palmist

my leave, telling her I would only be away for a few weeks. It was perhaps for the best as she had become a bit fed up with my dog Ziggy, who was always up to mischief and had already appeared twice at the local police station in search of eligible police bitches.

Driving off with my dogs I arrived at the prescribed location, a depressing town in the north of England, about a half an hour before the performance was due to begin. The previous night the circus had had to manage, very unsatisfactorily, by playing records. There was no time to study the music that was set to the different acts. Even if there had been, some of the sheet music was almost illegible. I agreed to play on the condition that the artists knew I would improvise. I had to keep time with the horses, and from previous circus experience knew the type of music suitable for elephants and tigers. The continental acts worried me because I had no idea what they were going to do during their acts. I was concerned that the tempo of my music would not marry up with their activities. However, my circus experience stood me in good stead and my first appearance as musical director appeared to be a success.

For subsequent performances I spent time altering the score to reflect my childhood musical memories of the circus and to capture some of that magic I treasured as a child, when I was with my grandfather. Music is the crucial element in any circus for setting the mood and edging emotions in the right direction.

While the circus was in Darlington, I read the hand of Tony Baines who worked for the BBC, and this reading was recorded. The following week the BBC used this recording in a broadcast. When we went up to the Edinburgh Festival, they asked me to make another recording about circus life that included my experience as a clown, ringmaster and musical director. During this interview I emphasised that never again would it be economically viable to produce the great circus shows of the past with all the wild animals, ponies, dogs and aerial acts that were so much a part of any circus. Society could not help the circus

19 The Palmist

people, so their destiny was to be forced off the road. The cost of transportation was becoming prohibitive. The BBC told me afterwards that there had been a great response from the public to my remarks on this half-hour programme.

As the weeks went by I became more and more intoxicated with the circus atmosphere, in which, like the animals, I played my humble part. I enjoyed every fantastic night, each of which was an individual experience, with different audiences reacting uniquely to the artistes.

After I had played for seventeen weeks with the circus, Bailley told me that members of an act who had worked for them for five years had returned from Ireland and that he felt obliged to give them a job. One member also played the organ. So we agreed that when the act arrived I would leave. I told Bailley I should be delighted if they would take over from me because the travelling to and from St Albans was taking it out of me, much as I welcomed the money for doing it. I was still worried about my mother and mortified that I had been unable to visit as often as I wished to.

It is hard for me to express in these lines all that I was feeling. On the one hand I wanted to be with my mother above all else; I felt terrible at being separated from her. I knew that my way of life was a constant worry to her. But it was a comfort to us both to know how much she cared for me.

When the time came to depart I drove up to Hull, then the site of the circus, to read hands. I needed to earn more if I was to help my mother on my return. Hull Fair was the last big market fair and probably the most famous one in the north of England, and I felt that it would offer me the opportunity to build on my savings. I hadn't booked space there, but when I arrived, a showman called Joseph Ling recognised me.

"I know you haven't got a pitch, but you've got one with me," he said.

He refused to accept any money in advance and offered me a place for my caravan near his roundabouts. Just opposite was old

19 The Palmist

Mrs Boswell whose family members were the best-known northern gypsy palmists and showmen around. She sent her granddaughter to me, who was going blind, saying that she felt I could help her. I sensed at once the reason for her affliction: she had had an abortion when she was fifteen years old and hadn't told her family. She was virtually paralysed with fear and the nerves above her eyes had become affected by this constant tension and were causing blindness because they had atrophied. I promised not to tell her grandmother of her unfortunate experience, but I believed I could cure her if I could gain her trust. I needed to try, so I placed my hands on her forehead just above the eyes and prayed aloud to God that the nerves would recover. As I prayed I could feel her relax under my hands and I felt that having her problem shared might help her to recover.

I was delighted when she wrote to me some months later to tell me that she had regained her vision and that she hoped we would meet again. Sadly, we never have.

I realised at this point that I had a gift, such as it is, for healing, since which I have it used to help clients with afflictions that doctors were unable to cure. Palmistry and healing are closely linked, though one has to take care not to mislead anyone.

Once, on a damp, rainy day, I remember dear Mrs Boswell of Fossett's circus speaking to me about palmistry.

"You and I, Richard, have the gift: we don't tell the tale like so many people up this street. ["Telling the tale" is a gypsy expression for 'reading hands'. The gypsies say that if you know what you are doing, then you "have the gift".] Everyone wants their hands read if they can summon up the courage to see us and deal with what we tell them. Everyone wants a pat on the back – but you and I know we can only tell it as it is."

My mother's condition had been on my mind now for some time and having phoned and found the line to be disconnected, I drove my caravan from Hull to her flat at Hall Place

19 The Palmist

Gardens, St Albans. I was shocked to find her house locked up and deserted. The curtains had been taken down and the furniture removed. I knocked on two or three neighbouring doors before I was finally able to speak to someone with information about this disturbing turn of events. This person told me that my sister had removed my mother to a one-room council flat for old people, and more by luck than good fortune, this neighbour had her new address. I also understood that my sister had removed all the antique furniture, books and documents belonging to the family, although she knew that the furniture had been left to me.

My sister and I had disliked each other from early childhood. My father had employed two nurses, one for my sister and one for my brother and me. This I believe created the initial disparity between us. Her dislike of us, because we were boys, was unfortunate and was in part promoted because my father adored and spoiled her.

I found my dear mother in an unpleasant building near to St Stephen's church in St Albans. When I entered the little flat she burst into tears and hugged me. She was in shock and very disorientated, and could hardly speak on seeing me. Eventually she said, "Darling, please take me home. I feel so awful here. I'm a prisoner. Thank God you've arrived."

I tried to reassure her and promised to sort things out, though I was heartbroken to see her in such a state. My mother was on the verge of a mental breakdown and in acute distress, trying to make sense of what had happened. In her own sad state, she seemed less disapproving than had sometimes been the case at what she saw as my inappropriate lifestyle.

Although I knew it was illegal to park my caravan in the road for the night, I had no alternative but to do so. That same evening someone made a terrific din by banging on the outside of my caravan. My dogs started barking at once. I knew I was in trouble from the arrogant way in which this person was hammer-

19 The Palmist

ing on my door. I opened the door to someone who looked like one of those dreadful men I had seen drunk in the gutters of Malta.

Without any sort of introduction he snarled, "Get your bloody self out of here. We don't want any of you f****** gypsies around here."

"How dare you speak to me like that!"

He replied, "You're a f****** gypsy. I'm a respectable man and I won't have you filthy little bastards around me."

The man seemed typical of some of the layabouts under my command during the War, and this made the whole episode seem much the worse in my mind. We had had our share of scroungers but I had never torn them off a strip as I felt like doing now. This so-and-so may have been representative only of a minority but in my book he was a repellent specimen of a certain breed of Englishmen who despite owing their freedom to people who had put their very lives on the line, showed no respect for those who had taken the real risks.

"Get your f****** caravan off here or I'll call the police."

"How dare you talk to me like that! Who the devil d'you think you are? What did *you* do in the War?"

"I was in the RAF," he declared smugly.

That answer could hardly have been better calculated to get my dander up.

"What were you doing in the RAF? Don't tell me you were flying an aircraft?"

"You little bum! I was in the police!" he sneered.

I exploded.

"Really?" I retorted, putting as much sarcasm into my voice as I could muster. "... Then you were another wingless wonder. I'll have you know that you are talking to an ex-wing commander. You are a typical, trashy little man who think you are important but have done nothing to justify your inflated opinion of yourself! Don't *you* threaten *me*!"

19 The Palmist

One says things in the heat of the moment that perhaps are better left unsaid. But why should I have to bite my tongue when this awful man clearly felt under no such constraint? I slammed the door on him. He did not persist in his banging. That was the back of him – but not the end of the episode.

The following morning two police officers arrived and told me I had no right to park my caravan where it was and that I must remove it at once. I explained to them, with much more calmness than on the previous evening, that I had a sick mother to visit – but they could not, or would not, be moved. They threatened to tow the caravan away and gave me two hours to be gone.

I suddenly remembered the gypsy site in Park Street, St Albans. I was fast running out of money and couldn't afford to pay for a site, so hitching the caravan to the car I drove there. A scruffy individual met me. He snarled at me and demanded to know my business. However, as soon as I had established my circus connections and told him about my mother's condition he looked at me in quite a different light.

Then, to my relief, he nodded and said, "You can move in here. You're one of us."

Just as well, as, painful as it is to confess, I was near breaking-point.

Although I had somewhere to live, I still needed to earn a living simply in order to survive. I was in quite a difficult situation – and it *is* difficult if one has nothing to offer except being a palmist and a musician. However, I was used to playing both organ and piano in hotels and pubs.

Having fed my dogs, I set out that evening to make enquiries. After driving to several pubs I was directed to a rather dreary hotel that needed a pianist. In this sort of situation I usually went to the bar and asked if I might play the piano, hoping that if people liked what I played, a fee would be settled on there and then. The woman behind the bar told me that the pianist was ill and that she needed someone for three nights a week. That evening I

19 The Palmist

agreed to play for nothing so she could see if my style would suit her customers. I played, as I always did, a mixture of oldies and musical comedy songs with the odd Strauss waltz thrown in. I made a good impression and was engaged to play for three nights a week.

Two months later, after I had been playing in several other pubs and hotels in the St Albans area, an old family friend who visited my mother regularly confirmed my worst suspicions for me that my mother's health had deteriorated badly and advised looking for a nursing home for her.

The shock she had experienced in being removed from her old home had clearly taken a toll on her well-being. At last I felt in a position to take action on my mother's behalf, to do something for her that I felt she would want me to do, something that the efforts of my sister could do nothing to countervail. I managed to settle on a place for her in what was actually a very pleasant home for elderly people. It took quite some research to find a place where the atmosphere was congenial and lively. At least it was a solution. I felt better about that situation than I had for many a month.

Then, a week before my mother moved, my car disappeared.

I was in utter despair again. I depended on it to help me earn my living. In desperation I reported it to the local police. A charming police inspector was on duty. It was a pleasure to speak to him and his manner went a long way towards dispersing the prejudices that for some time I had harboured. He told me that if I came with him he thought we should find the car. He drove me to another gypsy site outside the town where we found it, broken up into hundreds of component parts, its towbar removed with all the other bits. It was clear that the local gypsies were not seen in a good light by the Council, whatever might be their exonerating features elsewhere. If I had been marked down as a fellow traveller of theirs, perhaps that went some way towards explaining my own problems with authority.

19 The Palmist

"It was obvious that it would be broken up and sold for scrap," the officer said. "If you live on a gypsy site, what do you expect? They are all thieves. The sooner you pull yourself together and lead a respectable life, the better it will be for you. Take some friendly advice. Get out of this area. And don't practise palmistry round here, either. The Council and the Church don't like what you're doing."

There in a nutshell was the problem – so understandable, but only from one particular viewpoint.

This was a most perturbing situation. While I had some idea at this point that my reading hands was resented by many, I found it difficult to understand other people's inability to recognise it as a natural gift. It is a comment again on the degree to which we are hidebound by material things. I was trying to help others in what small way I could and I never charged more than one pound. Reality is often so different from people's perceptions of it.

20

Modus Vivendi

The combined blow of my mother's worsening decline and my own impending destitution forced me to re-evaluate my life once more. My situation had become so dire that when a local butcher, who liked my dogs, gave me bones for them, I tried to scrape off some of the meat for myself, but it was obviously not enough to keep me going. At least my oil stove kept me warm, but it was impossible to extract enough heat from it for cooking.

For two days I had hardly eaten and I was so desperate that I approached the St Albans' Social Security office. At first, a very cold woman brusquely told me that because I was living on an unofficial site and therefore technically not a resident, I was not the type of person they were able to help. When I explained I had nowhere else to go, she suggested that I return the following day, although she doubted if they could help. When I came back the next day, a more sympathetic woman was on duty. She said that in a week's time I could expect a handout – but it would be only at the minimum rate: £7 a week.

Seven pounds was still seven pounds more than I had at that moment. I left the office knowing that somehow I would have to survive with no food and, as far as I could tell, no means of getting help from anyone. Had it not been for my dogs, and the fact my mother needed me, I would have certainly killed myself. It was pretty terrible living in winter in a miserably small leaking caravan that I couldn't afford to heat. Life had become absolute hell.

After four days of starvation and mounting despair I prayed that someone would look after my dogs as I really didn't want to go on living. I nearly made up my mind to throw myself off a bridge because I couldn't afford any more aspirins.

20 *Modus Vivendi*

My mother was due to go into her new home that day, so I walked the five miles down the road to help her. Although I always tried to be cheerful and hide the truth from her, I think she knew I was in desperate trouble. Disorientated as she so often was, she had clearly been thinking about me.

When I arrived she said, "Dick, darling, you should know that the sofa, table and desk belong to you. I can't take them with me, so please take them for yourself. I'm sure you could get some money for them."

After my mother gave me a letter confirming to whoever it might concern that the antique table and desk belonged to me, I took them to a local antiques dealer. The dealer said, "Your table is quite good, but it will take time to sell. But because you are short of money, I'll give you cash."

"How much?" I asked.

He opened his wallet and gave me £200. He was evidently intent on swindling me – the furniture was worth at least five times that much – but I was desperate. No money had come from social security and I couldn't go on any longer, so I accepted £250 for the table and the desk.

When I returned to the gypsy site with £250 in my pocket I felt a different man and asked one of my neighbours if he could help me find a cheap car. I knew that in all likelihood it had been this very man who had organised the theft of my previous car, in which case he was bound to be feeling guilty. Although the gypsies are thieves, their consciences prick them sorely if they steal from an associate.

He said, "I've been looking out for a car for you, and I've got it here – a real bargain. It's a Wolseley, like your old car. Give me seventy quid and it's yours."

The Wolseley I bought from him was in perfect condition. As soon as he put a towbar on it I felt free to start over. It's amazing how different you feel with a full stomach and a few pounds in your pocket.

I was like a person reborn. I suddenly felt I could go on living.

During the War I had met John Grimston, the future Earl Verulam, who lived at Gorehambury, where I had dined. Afterwards I met Marjorie, his wife, and some other members of the family. The fact that I had a few pounds in my pocket gave me the confidence to drive the short distance round to Gorehambury and ask their son Johnny – the current Earl Verulam – if he would give my caravan a stand at their old mill in Fishpool Street. My luck was in, and surprised though they were to see me, they invited me to stay for dinner that evening and also consented to my using their old mill site over Easter.

I was worried about the decrepit-looking state of my caravan. I hoped no one would take much notice, for I couldn't afford to clean it up. However, after the *Herts Advertiser*, on its front page, announced that Earl Verulam had invited me to stay on his land for Easter, I was immediately confronted by a woman from Social Security. She told me very rudely that because I was now working I could expect no more money from them. It was in vain that I told her that I wasn't working until Easter.

So I decided to open my caravan for business early and hope that people would visit me. To my delight people soon began to stop by, and continued to do so until a police inspector called by. He told me that unless I left he would make things very difficult for me; in his opinion the area did not need a palmist. Two days after this I was stopped by the police, who had apparently been looking out for my car. A policeman walked round the back, smashed one of my rear lights and then charged me with having defective lights.

When I complained, he simply said, "Tell that to the magistrates."

Ten minutes after I had driven off, I was stopped again. Another policeman checked the rear lights, and said that further charges would be forthcoming.

20 *Modus Vivendi*

Within another two days, no fewer than seventeen charges concerning my car had been registered under my name. Every time I drove out I was stopped, and on most days there would be a police car parked outside wherever I was, waiting for me to drive off.

I felt my treatment by the St Albans police was so deplorable that I decided to inform the local press. To my surprise I was featured on the front page in the very next edition. The caption read, 'War Hero Hounded by Police'. After this it was obvious to all that the Verulams were not going to be permitted to retain a palmist even on their own private land. I returned to find my caravan towed off its site and left out in the street, where, naturally, a police car sat beside it.

The inspector was waiting for me. He said, "Mr Leven, it would be wise for you to leave this town, or you may find yourself in serious trouble. Will you give me your word that you will get out of Hertfordshire tomorrow?"

"Well, where on earth should I go? I've got nowhere to go to," I replied.

"That's none of my business," he said. "Either you leave this town or you and your dogs will be separated."

In spite of the headlines in the *Herts Advertiser*, I was being threatened. And the threat was succeeding in its purpose.

"Very well. I give you my word that I will leave tomorrow at eleven o'clock."

"Good," he replied. "We'll give you a good escort."

The next day three police cars escorted me along the road north towards Bedford. They disappeared as we crossed the county boundary somewhere just south of Luton. Because I had nowhere in particular to make for, and because I resented being forced in one direction rather than in any other, I at once turned left and found myself on the minor road to Whipsnade Zoo.

It is terrible to drive around with the sole purpose of finding somewhere to stop and pitch your caravan, all the while feeling like a criminal. I am sorry to write these lines but I have to say that my treatment at the hands of the police proved conclusively to me that in England you are relatively safe and secure if you are well off, but without a home you may be regarded as no more than a vagrant, a person for whom the authorities have no sympathy.

I reached Whipsnade and was lucky enough to stop at a pub at which the landlord was acquainted with the circus world and liked palmists. He allowed me to park in his back yard. To my grateful pleasure he also told me of another nearby pub that wanted an organist to play there at weekends.

The tide had turned and I sensed I could get going once more.

On Sunday morning I drove below Dunstable Downs to the area of common land in Whipsnade where there was an ice-cream van and other vans selling coffee and hot dogs. It was just the sort of site for a palmist to attract casual clients.

My first day at Whipsnade was a great success. I had a steady flow of people all afternoon, nearly all of them from London. As usual, they were a diverse collection: unhappily married women who wanted to know what to do about their relationship, unmarried women who wanted to know if they would ever find a man they loved, men who wondered if their business would be a success, and men who wanted to find out if their wives knew they were unfaithful. I read their hands and told them their past problems to prove my authenticity before unfolding what I believed the future would hold for them.

Two weeks after I arrived at Dunstable, I found out that my mother had undergone an operation on her legs. A week later I drove to St Albans to visit her, taking a circuitous route to try to avoid any unnecessary confrontation with the police. When I got to the nursing home, I discovered that my sister had already been there and insisted my mother be moved to a hospital near where she lived in Sudbury, Suffolk. This horrified me, because my mother certainly didn't know anyone in that area. In fact, she had more than once begged me never to allow my sister to take her

20 *Modus Vivendi*

away. I drove all the way over to Sudbury and found my dear mother in tears, in a geriatric ward, pleading with me to take her away from the dreadful place in which she was now confined.

But my sister had notified the nursing home in St Albans that my mother would not be returning. And because I had no money, I could hardly take on my sister's lawyers, who with what seemed rather spiteful satisfaction told me that there was nothing I could do and that they intended to ensure my mother would stay where she was.

Once more I felt as though the world had come to an end and realised how terrible life is when one is destitute.

I knew that I had to get my life back into some sort of order or I would never see my mother again. So I drove to Covent Garden in London, where I knew there was a lunchtime market. The man in charge there agreed to take me on as a palmist if I paid £10 a week in advance to park my caravan. This I did on the spot, and decided to move down to London the following week.

When I arrived with my caravan and Bimbo and Ziggy, who were both in good spirits, I was told I couldn't sleep in my caravan although the dogs would be allowed to stay there. This was a bit of a bombshell. I had no idea what to do. I hadn't enough money to pay a month's rent for a room even if I had even been able to find one. At the end of the first day, one of my clients, a student, told me that he lived in a squat in Islington and that he might be able to help me with accommodation there. I was delighted to be offered a room next to him and his girlfriend. I was even more grateful when they provided me with a mattress, which at that point I regarded as a luxury.

I often had a great many clients in Covent Garden, including artists, writers and MPs. However, I found that the market became deserted after three o'clock, so if I had a bad morning, there was no point in hoping to rectify the situation in the afternoon.

It seems that fate often takes a hand in human affairs. One day a client suggested I move my caravan to Soho market at the end of Gerrard Street, which was especially popular with people in the afternoons and evenings. Although a pitch there would cost £15 a week, it looked a risk worth taking. I was the first palmist in Soho market, and it seemed that word of my presence spread quickly. Within three weeks many old friends I had never expected to see again had found me. There was Michael Mellinger, a fellow student at the Central School, Adrian Heath, the brilliant abstract artist and friend at Bryanston, Guy Charles who helped me promote Janet Munro, and many friends from the RAF. Without my making a single phone call, all these past associates were in touch with me once again.

While I was in Soho market, I made the acquaintance of many Malaysian girls. They were among the most independent-minded women I have ever come across. Almost all of them believed in palmistry, although they were apt to be very analytical. They would always ask me to explain the reasoning behind my predictions. I tried to tell them that any one thing I said shouldn't be seen in isolation but in combination with everything else. I explained that even what I said all together formed only a general guide, and that it was the invisible vibrations from the hands that gave me a photographic impression of the past, present and future.

It was no surprise to me to find that a number of my clients in Soho worked as prostitutes and hostesses in local clubs. La Belle de la Nuit was a strip club near Piccadilly Circus run by Cherie, a very intelligent girl with French connections. She was so impressed by my comments that she allowed me to work in her club in the evenings. All the staff who waited at table were women, as were the bar staff who, behind the bar, went topless. When I read Cherie's hand I told her that before the year was out she would leave the city and lead the life of a country lady. A year later that exact turn of events came to pass. The club then stopped being a place for Birmingham businessmen who were looking for a night out on the town.

All of the hostesses in the club were single mothers, either divorced or separated, who had been forced into their current occupation through necessity. The only way they could make ends meet was to use their charms on men, who were prepared to pay them £100 a night to sleep with them. They knew the men wanted a pleasurable evening and the transaction helped both parties, but they would have been horrified to be described as prostitutes. Whereas a prostitute didn't want any personal involvement with her clients, a hostess was prepared to listen to the problems of her men.

Those clients of mine who were prostitutes were all very romantic girls as well as being great humanitarians. A pressing concern for many of them was whether or not they would one day be happily married.

One West Indian prostitute came to me several times while I was in Soho. She had dreadful wart marks on her legs, which she couldn't get rid of, despite having paid a large amount of money to Harley Street specialists. My gift for healing, I felt, had developed over the years and I was convinced I could cure her of her unsightly problem. I was delighted when I managed to do it within three weeks. She sent me a charming letter of thanks and at Christmas gave me a magnificent – and extremely expensive – sweater.

All of us who rented sites in Soho market run by Westminster Council were periodically threatened with steep increases in rent. The Council then let the market to a company run by two unpleasant men who thereupon let it be known that they intended to put up the rent by even greater margins.

Fortunately, it was coincidentally around that time – Jubilee year – that I transferred to Kensington and agreed with the owners of RAMA market in the High Street to pay them half my earnings if they would arrange a booth for me. I also found a room to let in Kensington Church Street. Once again, it seemed as if my luck had turned.

That summer in Kensington my clients were almost all professional people hailing from all around the world, including New Zealand, Malaysia and the Middle East. I recall a Swiss girl who had come over to England to marry Jonathan Aitken and who wanted me to advise her if the marriage would work. She was enchanting enough to make me regret that I was not a younger man.

Another client, a former US ambassador's granddaughter, was quite a godsend. She and her companions must have been pleased with the reading I gave because they subsequently recommended me to a great number of Americans. Every day I took clients to Jimmy's Wine Bar, a very sociable place in Kensington, run by Jimmy himself, an ex-Coldstream Guards officer. He always cheered me up and his place had a wonderfully warm atmosphere.

At the end of Jubilee year, before people began to spend their money on Christmas presents and business began to die down, Ram, the market owner, said that he wanted to alter my rental agreement and that if I didn't agree I would have to move. He was a ruthless man, evidently only interested in squeezing as much money from people as possible. I decided to leave.

Once again I had to find new premises. This time I was introduced to Jewish people who owned Carnaby Market, just off Regent Street, which used to have a palmist. It was a fair rent at £20 a week so I moved back to the West End.

Meanwhile, because I was so short of money I managed to make only two trips to see my darling mother who was still in the geriatric ward in Sudbury. Although I knew what to expect, it was nevertheless appalling, on those ocasions, to see my mother in such a distressed state. She had become a mere shadow of her former self, taking sedative pills that had clearly befogged her mind. I cannot bear to say any more about that, however.

20 Modus Vivendi

Instinct told me when she was on the verge of death, and I persuaded a friend to drive me to Sudbury. When I arrived, I was greatly relieved to find my mother still alive, although she was indeed dying. She recognised me and I offered silent prayer for her soul. A few hours later she finally lost consciousness. I am sure that she was able to depart in peace with the knowledge that I was there with her at the end.

This was a sad time for me, and not one on which I wish even now to dwell. It was with a heavy heart that I returned to London to resume what had become my livelihood.

At the time Carnaby Market was not very busy and I thought that it would be hard to make ends meet: my expenses were £25 a week for my room and £20 a week for the market. Luckily, I found a restaurant in Kensington run by some Italians and an Iranian in need of a pianist. I played there three nights a week, from 9 p.m. until 3 a.m., although irrespective of the hours I played, they gave me only £10 a night. This was much less than the formal rates demanded by the Musicians' Union – but if I hadn't accepted it, they would have engaged someone else who did.

Shortly thereafter, I found myself in the spotlight for quite a different reason. Golden Square near Carnaby Market was where the offices of many prominent figures of the entertainment world were based. Several people from *Vogue,* including Georgina Howell, the assistant editor, came to me to have their hands read. After I had read her hand, she asked me if I would be prepared to comment on the photographed hands of three well-known people. I had never attempted such a feat before and didn't believe I could make anything of it, but Georgina – charm personified – persuaded me to try. She said I could experiment with a photograph of the hands of one of the girls at *Vogue*.

I looked at the photograph of two hands and for a moment was utterly stumped, unable to find anything at all to say. Then out of the blue, inspiration came to me and I said

20 Modus Vivendi

that I thought the lady had been born in New Zealand and had come to England only a few years before. I felt convinced that she was divorced, but I was certain that before the year was out she would get married and would then settle back in New Zealand.

Georgina was delighted. The lady in question had indeed come from New Zealand – and she was thinking of marrying again and going back there. I was astonished myself because I certainly had not thought that I was capable of making meaningful statements and predictions by looking at photographs.

A week later Georgina invited me to the *Vogue* offices and presented me with three sets of unidentified hands on photos. I made my comments on them into a tape recorder. Afterwards, Georgina told me the hands belonged to Antonia Fraser, Edna O'Brien and Peter Cook. Later my comments were published in *Vogue*, which paid me £100 for my work. Readers apparently thought that I had been pretty accurate, although I must say I don't think I was very kind about Antonia Fraser or Peter Cook. I sensed Antonia was a successful writer with a good knowledge of history, but I also saw a regal attitude and that she enjoyed being the queen of some country house. She had a residence in London. Her fingers looked very determined and I said I thought she was divorced and probably had more than three children. I didn't realise that in fact she had six.

I believe Edna O'Brien was pleased with my pronouncements because, without revealing her identity, she arrived in Carnaby Market and asked me to read her hands.

As I began I said, "Well now, that's extraordinary! Your hands are so like Edna O'Brien's, whose hands I read for *Vogue*."

She then asked me who Edna O'Brien was. I went on reading the hands and became so convinced I was speaking to the author herself that I stopped again and expostulated: "I'm sorry, but your hands are identical to those of Edna O'Brien – and it is nonsense for me to go on talking about *her* if that is not *you*."

And at that point she admitted that she was in fact Edna O'Brien.

I always find it difficult to predict what will happen to people who are in the theatre or who are writers because they find it so hard to get work. I remember how depressed I was as an actor when I was out of work. So I generally try to reassure them that recognition and success will come to them. It is, after all, the role of the palmist to encourage clients as well as to make accurate predictions, so that when they leave they feel more cheerful than when they arrived.

People often think that palmists receive greater numbers of female clients than male, but I found that as many men came to see me as did women. The men were usually of the professional class: lawyers, doctors and psychiatrists. The psychiatrists invariably had such neurotic hands that I frequently wondered how they could possibly help their clients. Before every general election I would get at least ten MPs who wanted to know if they would be re-elected. Apparently, my name was mentioned quite often in the House of Commons. One day a barman, who was employed in the bar at Westminster, visited me. I thought his hand was more humane and wise than that of any MP who came my way.

On another afternoon a very tough-looking but jovial character visited me. A tall and charming Swedish girl accompanied this man. When I looked at the man's hand I told him I thought he was a drummer with a pop group and began to describe some of his past life. He had obviously made a lot of money and I thought he had a studio. He told me that that was so. I warned him that the group's accountant was not to be trusted and that he should do something about it. I told him that I believed he had a boat in Cornwall and that it would be in his interest to spend some time there because I was worried about his health. To my surprise and delight, this drummer – Keith Moon of The Who – paid me £20 although he knew that my standard fee was £5. I also read the hand of the Swedish girl, who I thought was a talented artist.

20 Modus Vivendi

I took Keith's telephone number, so I could remind him to leave London. It was my impression that if he was not careful, he might very well overdose on drink or drugs.

Three weeks later I phoned him and told him that I hoped he was going down to Cornwall. He replied that although I had been right about many of the things I had told him, he had decided not to follow this final piece of advice. When I put the phone down, I had a premonition that Keith was destined to die soon and that there was now nothing I could do to save him. It was the same type of premonition that some of us had during the War when we used to 'know' who among the pilots was soon going to be killed. Three days after I phoned Keith, I read in the paper that he had died. Apparently, the Swedish girl told John Blake, a writer on the *Evening Standard*, that I had predicted Keith Moon's death. After this prediction many who were in show business and other similar walks of life came to see me.

I had been in Carnaby Market for two years when one day the management gave everyone downstairs three weeks' notice to leave. We were all shocked, for we had been promised tenancies there for the whole season. But it seemed that they planned to turn the place into a pool hall – for which, we discovered later, Westminster Council had not granted permission. It was mildly gratifying to find out some time after we had left that the Council had taken action and closed the premises down altogether. But in the meantime I still had to find somewhere to work.

Fortunately, I was able to build a small booth next door in Regent Market. The Market was run by a Greek who was only interested in making money and who, because he knew I was desperate for a place, first charged me £35 a week and the next year told me he was going to raise the rent to £50. From June to July, all my regular clients came to see me, but a poor winter followed, during which I struggled to stay afloat and at the end of which I had to acknowledge that the rent was too much for me to afford. It was the same old story. Pay more than I was able to, or leave.

20 *Modus Vivendi*

A Danish client then insisted that I come and read hands in Denmark. You can imagine my delight when she offered to pay for the trip. I accepted with some surprise and a great deal of pleasure. An opportunity to travel was meat and drink to me. While in Denmark, I was featured in two national newspapers that declared that I was the most interesting palmist that had ever visited their country.

By a strange coincidence, a fellow palmist turned out to be a Danish ex-pilot who had flown on seven operations with me on Mitchells. He received a pension of £200 a week for life from his government. Apparently the Belgian and Dutch pilots who flew with me were all given similar pensions by their governments. This Danish pilot was astounded when I told him that the British Government gave nothing either to me or to any of my pilots who suffered shellshock as a result of the War.

Great Britain is the only country that utterly refused to do anything to help its wartime heroes.

I was delighted to have made a profit of over £1,000 from my palmistry in Denmark. When I returned to England, one of my clients offered me the lease of his flat in Goldhurst Terrace, provided I could pay the deposit. The prospect of having somewhere to live was a delight, and this act of kindness did something towards restoring my faith in England. I decided to see clients there, which was more private and relaxing than in my caravan.

A nightclub called Studio La Valbonne in Kingly Street then phoned me to ask if I would attend a party and read hands. Because I knew the area, I was pleased to accept the offer and sat in the foyer reading hands from eleven that night until three in the morning. The club then asked me to become their regular palmist at weekends. I read hands at the club every weekend thereafter, and enjoyed the atmosphere very much – although I found the disco loud and far too distracting.

Appointments at my flat lasted about an hour, but at the club I only spent about ten minutes on a reading for each person. The people who came to my flat invariably wanted me to go into detail about their lives and try to solve worrying problems. I could usually tell whether they were married or divorced or if they had a friend they were attracted to. Often, people were preoccupied by the future and especially whether or not they would stay married.

I was delighted when people whose hands I had read returned to tell me whether my predictions had been correct.

An American psychiatrist told me I had foretold the year of his marriage and that he would write a book. I was very pleased to hear that he did marry when I had predicted and that his book about psychology and palmistry had been printed in America.

Joanne Gautier I first met when I was in Carnaby Market. I told her I thought she was a lady barrister and that in April the following year she would defend a shipping case in France that involved almost £1 million. I told her that I hoped she would visit me again if what I said turned out to be correct. However, she replied that she didn't intend to visit Europe for some time to come. A year later I was delighted when she phoned to tell me that my prediction had been right, and that she wanted to take me out to dinner. Eight years have now passed since I first read Joanne's hands, during which we have met three times and I'm glad to say that all my subsequent predictions about her have come true.

On the strength of my having accurately read his daughter's hands, an MP thereafter came to visit me several times over the years. The last time he came he was certain that on account of his age, he would be replaced in his constituency. I told him he should stand once more as a candidate. He was successfully re-elected to Parliament.

Many of the people who came to me in my professional capacity had personal or financial difficulties, and it was difficult to say anything that would not create more distress. Women used to come to me in despair because they had discovered that their

20 *Modus Vivendi*

husbands were having affairs and they feared their marriages would collapse. Generally, I found that I could tell if there was any future in their relationship; sometimes the husband had only been seduced because he wanted to find out if he was still sexually attractive to other women. I did my best to tell them the truth as I saw it.

My experience in Soho market, where many of my clients were prostitutes and nightclub hostesses, allowed me a great insight into relationships. Those people all told me their clients were married men who were deceiving their wives. I am probably a throwback to a time when olde worlde courtesies and gallantries were the norm – or at least some would like to think they were – but I still cannot understand why happily married men want to boost their egos by going to bed with women with whom they had no personal relationship. Worldly wise I may not be, but are the more worldly ones so wise themselves? Not if the stories I heard are anything to go by!

One day a man arrived at my flat in a very aggressive mood. Before I looked at his hands he announced that he would only pay me if I could tell him what he had been doing during the last few years. There was something about the man that intrigued me even as it worried me, so I told him that if I could see his hands, I would try to tell him.

The moment I glanced at one of them I said, "You have just come out of prison, where you have been for some time."

He laughed and replied, "You're right. But do you know why I was there?"

I told him at once that he had been charged with murder, and I had the impression that when he left me he intended to murder someone else.

Once again he laughed and said, "You're quite right. I'll pay you now and take you out for a drink."

Although I didn't accept any money from him – because I knew he was broke – we did go round to my local pub. I warned him that he would not succeed in murdering the person he wanted to, and said I hoped he would take my advice and try to do something to help society. Again he laughed and said he would consider what I had said. After he left me, I was certain he would get involved with an armed robbery and be arrested again before he committed another murder. However, I don't know what happened, and I never met him again.

Another client was a lovely and very intelligent woman. As I read her hand I started telling her about her past life and present romantic connections.

Suddenly I exclaimed, "Now, there's a surprise! You are the only person whose hands I've read which are similar to John Barbirolli's."

She replied at once that Barbirolli was her uncle. She was amazed that I had mentioned his name. She had greatly loved him and had been very depressed when he died.

In May 1988, an Indian lady came to me. I could tell she was a writer and probably worked for a magazine. After telling her about her parents and childhood, I suddenly told her that I thought there was something wrong with her present marriage. I felt that unless she and her husband left their present living quarters, they might separate. The reason for my prediction was that her husband was anxious about some aspect of their home. The lady in question was Yasmin Alibhai who, after she had visited me, phoned back to tell me her husband had confirmed what I had said. She wanted me to feature in an article she was writing on palmistry and clairvoyance in the magazine *New Society*.

In this article she wrote, "Richard Leven confounds my expectations by stating remarkably accurate facts about my childhood and life."

I am always surprised that I can pick out significant facts about people and delighted when clients visit me by personal recommendation.

One such client was a distinguished singer called Dionne Warwick from California. I predicted at once that she would do

20 *Modus Vivendi*

a show in the West End. She confirmed that this was so and invited me to the London Palladium.

In November 1989 Derek Jameson interviewed me on Sky TV about the War as well as about the theatre and palmistry. The day before the show I had tried to phone Mike Nolan, my navigator, only to hear that he had died of a heart attack. I mentioned on the programme how sad I was that Mike was no longer with us and that I hoped that his soul would be happy in heaven. I content myself in these pages by simply recording the fact.

In 1990, the publisher of Ina Books in Wells, Somerset, wrote to me saying that he had read a copy of my manuscript containing two poems and asked if I could send him some more to read. I wrote a lot of poems during the War, and having thought that I had lost them, was delighted after a vigorous search to find the old file in which I had kept them. I sent it off, and to my amazement was offered a publishing contract that I was delighted to sign. I was just as surprised when in due course the small book of my poems was featured in several papers and had an excellent review in *The Stage*.

Later that year I accepted the request of BSkyB TV to appear on one of their shows and talk about my life and the art of palmistry. My interviewer was the pop singer Boy George. I was much impressed with the way he interviewed me. He was very kind, almost gentle, and was good enough to say that he liked my book of wartime poems.

Epilogue

Earlier in this book I said that I took up palmistry because Commander Dymott of the submarine HMS *Olympus* told me that he doubted I could have survived as a pilot unless I had had a strong psychic gift. Despite books on the subject and my knowledge of the gypsies, I am convinced that fingers and lines are irrelevant to the art of reading hands. I do believe, however, that when you hold a person's hand you receive an impression that transcends any logical definition. It is a strong sense of communication probably belonging to some spiritual realm that is indefinable. It was this that kept me alive during the War. Words, I feel, are inadequate to describe how I can read hands. The gypsies know this, but they also know that everyone likes to hear only positive things about themselves and so they say what they think the client wants to hear in order to make money out of them.

So now I have come to the end of my story. I feel that my life has been rich in events and in encounters with all sorts of people, each of whom has brought me something precious. Even those who thought to do me harm have helped me to gain inner knowledge and to progress along the path which we all must tread – the path of life. As we get older, I think that we discover that events are not random and that there is a hidden thread which connects all of the things that have happened to us. The people whom we have met, we have not met by accident. They were meant to touch our lives at some point, for longer or shorter periods of time. We all write the story of our own lives, though not all of us with paper and ink, as I have done, but on the sands of time. It is our history ... our secret history.

Publisher's note: Obituaries appeared on 23 January 1997 in *The Times* and *The Stage* about Squadron Leader Richard Leven DFC, DFM (b. 3 April 1921 – d. 15 January 1997).

Epilogue

Excuse for Dreaming

*Perhaps, the glory of a dream
Is that it can never be,
For oft the things that I have seen
No man on earth can see.*

*If my dream of things to be
Is what things really are,
I should be foolish not to see
What's seen this very hour.*

*I like to feel there is a life
Far beyond the Earth,
Where I can surely wander
And dreams are given birth.*

Index

Ackland, Rodney (playwright) 82, 107–8, 187
actor, work as 2, 174–5, 185–6, 201
Adamski, George (writer) 211
Aitken, Max, press baron 132–3
Alibhai, Yasmin (journalist) 263
Andrews, Burt 164–6
Angels One Five (movie) 185
Annabella, doll mascot 11, 85, 89, 173
Annique, a Belgian girl 92–3
Anson aircraft 62, 132
Arabian/Arab horses/ponies 139, 208
Ark Royal (aircraft carrier) 45
armistice, signing of the 125
Arnhem 89
art and artists in Germany 24, 151, 161–2
Atcherley, Air Commodore David 80
Atkins, Eric 17n
Auden, W. H. 4
Austria, German invasion of 29

Babbacombe, Devon 4
Bandon, Gp Capt the Earl of 39, 46, 61–2, 222
bankruptcy judgement 227
Barbirolli, John (orchestral conductor) 186–7, 263
Bartley, S/Ldr Tony 117–18
BBC (*Radio Newsreel*) recording 72–3
Beatles, the 212–13
Beaumont, Binkie (impresario) 187–8
Belli, Harri, circus proprietor 138–9
Belli circus family 137
Belsen concentration camp 117–22

bet on a horse 218–19
Beveridge, Lord William 80–1
Bicester aerodrome 8–9
Bimbo and Ziggy (pet dogs) 225–6, 228, 229, 239, 247, 252
black market in post-war Germany 154–7
Blenheim aircraft 1, 8, 10–12, 15, 36, 45, 50, 55, 70
Blue Murder at St Trinians (movie) 210
Blunt, Anthony 59, 176–7, 179, 180–1
Boston aircraft 78
Boulogne mission 10–11
Brauchitsch, General Walther von 130–1
Bremen, raid on 13–16, 34
brother Don 3, 67–9
Brussels 89–91, 96
Bryanston (public) school 3–4, 19–21, 68
Bückeburg, Germany 153
Burgess, Guy 59, 175–9, 180, 181
Burgess, Philby and Maclean 180–2
Burnaston, near Derby 4
Buster *see* Evans, 'Buster'
Bygraves, Max 209–10

Calais, raids on 84–7
Castelanne, Count François de 93
Catania, raid on 46–8
Celle, Germany 112, 114–15, 122–3, 126, 142
Cheddar Gorge 235–7
Chessington Zoo 208–9
childhood 2–4
Chipperfield, Mary and her father Jimmy 230
Churchill, Winston 60, 126, 129, 130, 166, 177, 182

Index

circus, and grandfather 2–3, 137–8
  enthusiasm for 3, 138–9, 188–9, 202, 230, 240
  work in/with 2, 189–99, 201, 202, 203–7, 208–9, 238–40
'circus' operations/missions 10–11, 37, 66
Circus Togni, Bristol 230
clip-joints 215
clown(s) 139, 191, 197, 198, 205, 234, 239
Coade, T. F., headmaster of Bryanston 3–4
concentration camp(s) 17, 30, 118–22, 128, 146
Cook, Peter, humorist 257
Coward, Noël 186, 187
crash-landing near Celle 112–13
Cresswell, Adjutant Jack 154
Croix de Guerre Palme, Belgian 1, 229
Cullen, a doomed friend 39–40

Day-Lewis, Cecil 4
death and dying, thoughts of 10, 83
decorations, medals 1, 36, 56, 75
debt 226–7
'der Mangel' (the Crusher) 21–3, 26–8, 150
DFC 1, 75
DFM 1, 34n, 56
Douglas, Air Marshal Sholto 167
Dunsfold, Surrey 83
Dymott, Captain (of the submarine *Olympus*) 55, 57–8, 229, 265

Earl Verulam (John Grimston) 249
Eden, Anthony 19, 30, 177
Edrich, S/Ldr Bill 34–6
Edwards, Wg/Cdr Hughie 13–16
Eindhoven, Holland 106–9
elephant(s) 3, 139, 193, 205–7, 209–10, 239
  Aga 205–7
  Candy 209–10
  Salt 193
Embry, Air Vice Marshal Basil (later C-in-C of NATO) 78–9, 182
Epstein, Brian 212–13
Evans, 'Buster' 34–5, 38–9, 41, 47, 50–2, 56, 61, 63
Excuse for Dreaming (poem) 266

father 3, 69, 173, 174, 216–17, 242
Fear in Flight (poem) 49
Flak (poem) 7
Flight Flight Flight (poem) 61
Flushing *see* Vlissingen
Fossett, Bailley and Bobby 202–7, 230, 238, 240
Fossett, Mrs Ginette and Dennis 188–9, 190, 191–2, 194–7, 198–9, 202, 209–10
Fossett, Tom 192–3
Fraser, (Lady) Antonia 257
Freud, Clement and Lucian 201
Furious (aircraft carrier) 45

Gabor, Zsa Zsa 185
Gardiner, A. R. L. (writer) 58
Gibraltar, stay in 41–5, 58
'Ginette Julian', mysterious parachutist 131–3
grandfather 2–3
Gregson, John (actor) 185
Grimston, John (Earl Verulam) 249
Guinness, Alec 185

Hahn, Kurt, headmaster of Schloss Salem 4
Hall Place Gardens, St Albans 103, 241
Hampshire, Susan 202
Harris, 'Bomber' 60
Harte, Wg Cdr 'Bunny' 37–8, 45, 48
Hawkins, Jack (actor) 185
healer, abilities/work as 2, 241, 254

Index

Heligoland 13
Henry, Mike 34n
Hicks, Patricia ('sheer delight, made flesh') 81–2
High Ercall, Shropshire 78
Hogg, Quentin (later Lord Hailsham) 92, 183
horse-riding in Germany 115–16
Humphries, Christmas, barrister and judge 223
Hurricane aircraft 45, 78

Isherwood, Christopher 4

Johnson, S/Ldr Johnnie 125–6
Joyce, William ('Lord Haw Haw') and Mrs Joyce 127–9

Kempinski's, Swallow St 81
Kray, Reggie and Ronnie 216

Lansdowne Club, the 37, 81
Leigh, Anne Boughton 219–20
Leigh, Richard and Countess Anne 220–2
Leslie, Desmond, musician and writer 210–11, 216
Libya, raids on 46, 48, 49–51, 55
life as trails in a forest 1
Limeletter, Fl/Lt André 136
Lindemayer, Paul 21, 23, 25, 30–1, 144–51
lions 196–8, 208, 210
Liverpool Syndicate (rock group) 212–13
London Gazette, quotation from 56, 75
looting 110, 167, 173–4
'Lord Haw Haw' *see* Joyce, William
Lucas, Laddie 11n
Lüneburg, Germany 126, 133, 135–6, 142
Lunt, Mr and Mrs Alfred 187
Lynn, Vera ('the Forces' sweetheart') 211–12, 219

Madness (poem) 117
Maginot Line, the 31
Malta, flights to and from 45–8, 49–55
Malta Story (movie) 185
Mangel *see* 'der Mangel'
Manston, Kent 40
Mason, Gully and Anne 36–7
Massingham, Norfolk 9
Maximilian, Prince (of Baden) 19
Mazingarbe, raid on 37–8
Melsbach aerodrome, Belgium 90, 91–2, 105
Miller, 'Captain' Yank, lion tamer/trainer 195–6, 197–8
Mitchell aircraft 1, 63, 78–80, 83, 85–6, 95–6, 103, 260
Mons, Belgium 105–6
Montgomery, General Bernard 130, 135
Moon, Keith, drummer of The Who 258–9
Mosquito aircraft ix, 1, 70–5, 78, 217
Mossie, The (magazine) 17n
mother 3, 69, 217, 238–9, 240, 241–2, 244–5, 247–8, 251–2, 255–6
Munro, Janet (actress) 201–2
music conducting 193–4, 198
music playing 2, 4, 231, 232, 234–5, 238–9, 244–5, 256
My Brother (poem) 67–8
My Friend (poem) 33

Nazi culture 26, 29
Nield, Basil 154, 160, 171–2, 1 82–3
nightclubs 215–16
Nolan, Mike 8–10, 12–16, 35–6, 39, 41, 43–4, 45–6, 50–2, 56, 61, 63–4, 70–1, 73–4, 78, 80, 83–7, 89–90, 96–103, 263–4

Index

O'Brien, Edna   257
Olympus (submarine)   55
Oxford aircraft   10, 78

palmist, work as   2, 180, 186, 231–4, 236–7, 238, 240–1, 251, 252–63
  in Denmark   259–60
palmistry and abilities in   2, 57–8, 232, 233, 246, 253, 265
  blind tests for *Vogue* magazine   256–7
Paramor, Norrie, EMI record producer   212
Paris, liberation of   89
Parsons, Ronald *see* 'Poons'
Pas-de-Calais, raids on   70–5
Paulos, Emily, and daughter June   208–9
Peace Again (poem)   169–70
Pearl Harbor   55, 57
Petley, Wg Cdr   10–11, 13
Philby *see* Burgess, Philby and Maclean
Philip, HRH Prince   19
piano playing   2, 34n, 244–5, 256
Pickard, Capt Percy Charles   70, 75, 186
pilot officer, commission to   55–6
poetry   4, 7, 25, 264
police, relations with   204, 221–4, 244, 245, 249–51
police corruption   216, 221
political philosophy   109–10
'Poons' (Ronald) Parsons   9, 41–3, 53–5, 62
  and art and literature   53–4
Priestley, J. B.   82

Rattigan, Terence   82, 187
recording studio, work in   2
Reform Club, the   58–9, 80–1, 171, 175–8, 182
Rhine aerodrome, the Ruhr   110–12

Ribbentrop, Joachim von   129–30
Rimmington, Stella   179
Ringlands Circus   188, 190–1
ringmaster   3, 139
  female   208
  work as   2, 203, 205
Ritzendorf, Tyrolean village   26–8
Ros, Edmundo   37, 81
Rossaire, Zena, lion trainer   210
Russell, Alan (secretary of the Agents Association)   189–92

St Albans, Hertfordshire   103, 173, 188, 207, 238, 241–5, 247
Salem school *see* Schloss Salem
Savoy Hotel   81
Scharff, Peter   21, 23–5, 26, 147, 150–1, 161
Schleswig, Germany   136, 141–4, 150
Schelswig-Holstein, the Princess of   147, 149–51
Schloss Salem school   4, 19–31, 92, 130, 144, 146, 148
schooling   3–4, 19–31
Sicily, raids on   46, 48
Sigrid (object of youthful adoration)   22, 23, 25, 30
Sinclair, Sir Archibald (Under-Secretary of War)   59–60, 80–1
sister   3, 151, 178, 242, 245, 251–2
slander/libel suit   228
Smetty, Max (of The Blue Angel)   215–16, 220
solo flight, first   4–5
Spitfire aircraft   11n–12, 14, 37–8, 65
Spoelberg, Viscount Werner de   93, 126, 136
squadron leader, promotion to   78
Stephenson, Air Vice Marshal D. F. 'Butcher'   16
Stock Exchange, work at stockbroking   174, 217–19

Index

Straight, Air Commodore Whitney 132–3, 181
strip clubs in London 253–4
Sudbury, Suffolk 252, 255
suicidal thoughts 227–8, 247
suicide attempt 228
Summer (poem) 67
Sunday Express, quotation from 36
Sunday Pictorial, quotation from 99–103
surgeons and unnecessary surgery 217
Sylt (island), raid on 34–6

Tedder, Air Marshal Sir Arthur 79
theatre, work in 2, 174
The Crewroom (poem) 77
The Soldiers (poem) 125
Thornton, Joy 11, 172
To a Black-Marketeer (poem) 153
training instructor, post as 62, 78

V-1s and V-2s 70, 72
Venlo, raid on 95–8
Vlissingen, raid on 64–5
von Ribbentrop *see* Ribbentrop

Wansart, Eric (artist) 93–4
Warsaw, Poland 162, 163–6
Warwick, Dionne 263
Wellbourn, S/Ldr 16
Wespelaar, chateau 93, 126
Weston-Super-Mare, Somerset 225–6, 230–1, 234
West Raynham, Norfolk 61
Whimsy Walker, clown supreme 205, 234
Whipsnade, Bedfordshire 250–1
White, Richard Baron 219–20
Wilmot, Wg Cdr Sidney 158–9

Ziggy (pet dog) *see* Bimbo and Ziggy